Henry Hock Guan Teh

# Principles of the Law of Evidence and Rationality Applied in the Johannine Christology:

## An Argument for the Legal Evidential Apologetics.

# Christliche Philosophie heute – Christian Philosophy Today – Quomodo Philosophia Christianorum Hodie Estimatur

## Volume 18

Vol. 1:    John Warwick Montgomery. Tractatus Logico-Theologicus.

Vol. 2:    John W. Montgomery. Hat die Weltgeschichte einen Sinn? Geschichtsphilosophien auf dem Prüfstand.

Vol. 3:    John W. Montgomery. Jésus: La raison rejoint l'histoire.

Vol. 4:    Horst Waldemar Beck. Marken dieses Äons: Wissenschaftskritische und theologische Diagnosen.

Vol. 5:    Ross Clifford. John Warwick Montgomery's Legal Apologetic: An Apologetic for All Seasons.

Vol. 6:    Thomas K. Johnson. Natural Law Ethics: An Evangelical Proposal.

Vol. 7:    Lydia Jaeger. Wissenschaft ohne Gott? Zum Verhältnis zwischen christlichem Glauben und Wissenschaft.

Vol. 8:    Herman Bavinck. Christliche Weltanschauung. hrsg. von Thomas K. Johnson und Ron Kubsch.

Vol. 9:    John W. Montgomery. La Mort de Dieu: Exposé et critique du plus récent mouvement théologique en Amérique: Réimpression de l'édition 1971.

Vol. 10:   David Andersen. Martin Luther – The Problem of Faith and Reason: A Reexamination in Light of the Epistemological and Christological Issues.

Vol. 11:   Wim Rietkerk. In dubio: Handbuch für Zweifler.

Vol. 12:   Patrick Werder: Wenig niedriger als Gott: Der Mensch als Person von der Antike bis zur Gegenwart.

Vol. 13:   John Warwick Montgomery: Christ As Centre and Circumference: Essays Theological, Cultural and Polemic.

Vol. 14:   Lydia Jaeger. Als Mensch in Gottes Welt: Im Licht der Schöpfung leben.

Vol. 15:   Frederik Herzberg. Theo-Logik: Über den Beitrag des Jansenismus zur formalen Methode in Theologie und Religionsphilosophie.

Vol. 16:   Hanniel Strebel. Eine Theologie des Lernens: Systematisch-theologische Beiträge aus dem Werk von Herman Bavinck.

Vol. 17:   John Warwick Montgomery. Fighting the Good Fight – A Life in Defense of the Faith

Henry Hock Guan Teh

# Principles of the Law of Evidence and Rationality Applied in the Johannine Christology:

# An Argument for the Legal Evidential Apologetics.

Verlag für Kultur und Wissenschaft
Culture and Science Publ.
Dr. Thomas Schirrmacher
Bonn 2015

Bibliographic information published by the Deutsche Nationalbibliothek

The Deutsche Nationalbibliothek lists this publication in the Deutsche Nationalbibliografie; detailed bibliographic data are available in the Internet at http://dnb.d-nb.de

ISSN 1612-1171
ISBN 978-1-49829-156-9

Printed in Germany
coverdesign and manufacturing:
BoD Verlagsservice Beese, Friedensallee 44, 22765 Hamburg
www.rvbeese.de / info@rvbeese.de

Publishing Distribution Center:
IC-Medienhaus
D-71087 Holzgerlingen, Tel. 07031/7414-177 Fax -119
www.icmedienhaus.de
catalog for book stores:
www.vkwonline.de/gesamtprospekt
Private costumers: in any book store or at www.vkwonline.com

# CONTENTS

Foreword, by Craig A. Parton, Esq. .................................................................7

Abstract ...........................................................................................................9

Dedication / Acknowledgment ....................................................................11

Introduction ..................................................................................................15
    Background and Focus of the Study .........................................................17
    Aims and Structure....................................................................................22

Chapter 1: Defending Evidentialism ..........................................................25
    What is Evidentialism?..............................................................................28
    Hyper Evidentialism Not Defended ........................................................31
    But Christian Theistic Evidentialism is Defended ...............................36
    Evidentialism is Apologetics Per Se ........................................................41
    Conclusion..................................................................................................44

Chapter 2: Principles of the Law of Evidence and Legal Apologetics ......47
    What is Law of Evidence and Its Advantages to Apologetics?............48
    Judicial Principles has Its Flexibility ......................................................50
    The Basic Concept of Fact-Finding: Admissibility of Relevant
        Evidence ...............................................................................................60

Chapter 3: The Basic Modern Concept of Judicial Principles of
    Evidence and its Application in Apologetics .........................................65
    Admissibility..............................................................................................66
    Relevancy ...................................................................................................69
    Burden of Proof.........................................................................................74
    The Standard of Proof...............................................................................86
    Hearsay Evidence......................................................................................91
    Other varieties and Classifications of Evidence....................................102
    Testimony Evidence .................................................................................102
    Documentary Evidence ............................................................................103
    Real Evidence............................................................................................109
    Lay Opinion Evidence..............................................................................112
    Expert Opinion Evidence ........................................................................115
    Circumstantial Evidence..........................................................................129

Presumptions..................................................................................139
Conclusion......................................................................................146

**Chapter 4: Legal Apologetic Methodology of the Fourth Gospel .........149**
Evidence of Authorship ................................................................150
Why John?.....................................................................................152
Evidentialism Approach of John...................................................155

**Chapter 5: The Legal Principles of Evidence in the Gospel of John ........161**
John Chapter 1: In the beginning there was the fact in issue ..........161
John's Use of Reason......................................................................164
First Witness: John the Baptist .....................................................168
John Chapter 2...............................................................................171
John Chapter 3...............................................................................172
John Chapter 4...............................................................................175
John Chapter 5...............................................................................177
John Chapter 6...............................................................................184
John Chapter 7...............................................................................186
John Chapter 8...............................................................................188
John Chapter 9...............................................................................191
John Chapter 10.............................................................................193
John Chapter 11.............................................................................194
John Chapter 12.............................................................................195
John Chapter 13.............................................................................197
John Chapters 14 and 15 ...............................................................198
John Chapter 16.............................................................................201
John Chapter 17.............................................................................202
John Chapter 18.............................................................................204
John Chapter 19.............................................................................206
John Chapter 20.............................................................................207
John Chapter 21.............................................................................209

**Conclusion** .....................................................................................213

**Appendices**.....................................................................................223
Table A ..........................................................................................223
List of Cases..................................................................................224
List of Statutes..............................................................................226
Bibliography .................................................................................226

# FOREWORD

## by Craig A. Parton, Esq.

Legally trained professionals have a long tradition of interest in apologetics and in marshaling the facts in support of the Christian faith. It is not accidental that since 1600 A.D. there have been over 120 works of apologetics produced by legal professionals. Malaysian Solicitor Henry Hock Guan Teh's current remarkable contribution, therefore, stands in a long and distinguished literary line that traces through a host of luminaries including Harvard Law School Dean Simon Greenleaf, Hugo Grotius (the so-called "father of international law"), Sir Matthew Hale (Lord High Chancellor under Charles II), Sir Norman Anderson (world authority on Muslim law), Sir William Blackstone (codifier of English common law), Lord Hailsham (former Lord High Chancellor of England), and English Barrister and French advocate John Warwick Montgomery (who has devoted the last six decades and over 60 books to applying legal evidential standards to the central truth claims of Christianity).

Dr. Teh's work, though, breaks new apologetical ground by applying the laws of evidence to the Fourth Gospel in particular, recasting John's stunning "Opening Statement" to read: "In the beginning there was the fact in issue ..." John repeatedly marshals the evidential case for the historicity of Jesus Christ and His death for the sins of the whole world. Henry Teh analyzes each chapter of John with the lawyer's eye for evidence and the application of the canons of evidence. Teh's conclusion is nothing less than that John operates as a legal apologist at every turn, carefully choosing each event to the extent it establishes the central thrust of his argument: namely, that the juror "might believe that Jesus is the Messiah, the Son of God, and that by believing you may have life in His name." (John 20:30-31).

Like a seasoned trial lawyer riveted on a single unifying argument, John the Evangelist readily admits he left out reference to many other miracles done by Jesus and instead focuses his case on the signs which most directly establish Jesus' deity and atoning death for the sins of the world. In the process of being thoroughly Christocentric in focus, John not only acts as a legal and evidential apologist but necessarily as an evangelist going for a verdict, and yet avoiding the errors of the three main (and less than satisfactory) alternative approaches in fashion in contemporary apologetics as noted by Teh:

First, John is hardly "presuppositional" in his approach, choosing not to appeal to "the logical consistency of Christian claims" (a la Greg Bahnsen, John Frame and the Van Tilian Reformed school of apologetics) but to the solid factual and inductive case for placing total trust in the incarnational Christ who saves. Second, John does not engage in "classical apologetics" in his Gospel where one starts with traditional arguments for God's existence and then eventually presents evidence for the incarnation of God in real history and "for our salvation." Operating as a kind of *proto-Lutherie*, John goes to the heart of Christianity's truth claims and centers everything on Christ as the fulfillment of the long awaited promise of the atoning Lamb come to save His people from their sins. Like no other Gospel writer, John presents Christ's three-fold office as prophet, priest and King as in need of the juror's verdict. Third and finally, John is no supporter of fideism or "faith in faith," an experiential euphoria devoid of a gritty, cross-focused factual mooring. The miracle stories and their solid epistemological underpinnings as occurring in real time and space provide the only solid footing for the Christian *gloria*. John's Christ is founded on fact, not on a gnostic or cultic "faith experience."

Henry Teh has done a remarkable job in showing John the Apostle and Evangelist as a defender of the faith foreshadowing the work of Greenleaf, Hailsham, and Montgomery. It is a particular pleasure to have had Dr. Teh participating with us at the 2015 session of the International Academy of Apologetics in Strasbourg, France (www.apologeticsacademy.eu), an institution dedicated to the integration of evidence and legal method in the furthering of the apologetical task. May his hard-hitting volume help bring a generation to the foot of Calvary's cross where *all* those believing (even lawyers) are given, according to the eyewitness Evangelist, "life in His name."

Craig A. Parton, M.A., J.D.
United States Director of the International Academy of Apologetics
(www.apologeticsacademy.eu)
On the Feast of St. John, Apostle and Evangelist
Santa Barbara, California

# ABSTRACT

## Principles of the Law of Evidence and Rationality Applied in the Johannine Christology: An Argument for the Legal Evidential Apologetics.

The focus of this book is an analysis of the apologetic methodology applied by the Apostle John in the fourth Gospel which may coincide with the trial lawyers' application of the principles of the law of evidence accepted as a rational mode of proof. In other words, this legal apologetic model of epistemological emphasis applied by John stresses the importance of evidence and reasons as appealing to the mind to comprehend the truth that Jesus is the Son of God.

Application of apologetics is vital in our Christian growth and the work of evangelism. More so, the application of legal evidential apologetics as reflected in John's ultimate purpose (John 20:30-31) for introducing the Christological narratives in the fourth gospel. It is flexible in the sense it encompasses the emphases of all apologetic schools. Hence, the rigidity of classical apologetics, presuppositional apologetics and fideism should not be over-zealously guarded. If we were to apply the doctrine of sola scriptura and follow the examples of the early fathers, a good example to consider as authority is from the writings of the Apostle John and his logical flow in proving the divinity of Christ.

The research will argue that using reason, evidence and the mind are not wrong in our faith in God. In fact, the use of the 'mind' is compulsory, normal and encouraged in the Bible. The aim of the book is to demonstrate that the Apostle John constantly uses rationality, apologetics and evidence in his writings and he never over-emphasizes the subjectivity of the heart. On the contrary, he is applying the mind to appeal the intellect of the readers, instead of mere faith. Principle of the law of evidence as applied in the courtrooms of common law countries are the legal science for intelligently assessing the rationality and admissibility of evidence for the jury to consider with their mind to make an objective decision. It is of no surprise that these are 'common sense' principles of convincing one's decision-making process.

The Apostle John had consciously and intentionally assessed the logical flow and evidence (but unconsciously applied the principles of the law of evidence) to rationally convince his readers. If this were true, then the Apostle John is truly indeed an evidential apologist and one who loves

God with all his mind. Thus, the relevance is that Christians (especially aspiring apologists) should follow the footsteps of the Apostle John to use our mind and emphasize evidential apologetics (more so legal apologetics), rather than presuppose that all we need is faith without any reason.

*Henry Hock Guan Teh*

# DEDICATION / ACKNOWLEDGMENT

I dedicate this book to my dad, Mr. Charlie Teh Peh Hock and mum, Madam Beh Siew Heang whom had brought me to this world.

I take this opportunity to acknowledge my humble amazement and gratitude to my beloved wife, Dr. Wai-Heng Loke for her profound love, patience, hours of printing the drafts, constructive criticism and encouragement to this work. Outflow from her patience, and at the initiation of this research project, she bought me a new sophisticated laptop in exchange of my extremely slow moving outmoded computer of which I sincerely give her my utmost thanks.

My 13 year old computer savvy daughter, Charity Teh Bei Feng likewise deserves my thanks for some of her editing assistance and pointers on the usage of the laptop to her almost computer illiterate dad.

My immense gratitude to lawyer Vivian Wei-Shu Fu for her willingness to be my proctored examiner for some of the examinations during my stay in Ningbo, Zhejiang Province, China, whilst completing the required course work.

Most important of all, it would be highly remiss on my part if I failed to acknowledge my debt to God for the many 'unanswered' prayers by placing obstacles and restrictions that may distract my focus on completing this book. Without any objective evidence but only subjectively known to me, the Holy Spirit whom I give praise and thanks, had been my invisible academic supervisor, prompting silently with ideas at irregular intervals in times of my humanly mental blocks.

Henry Teh
*Soli Deo Gloria*
16th July 2014.

*"In the beginning was the Evidence,
and the Evidence was with God,
and the Evidence was God."*

The fourth evangelist in his prologue to all lawyers.

# INTRODUCTION

Rational and simple arguments are sometimes found in well-known children stories, especially the ones written by renowned authors. These simple memorable rational advices we read during our younger days are fairly seldom put out of mind, even when we have grown older. One such good example written by C.S. Lewis is worth producing here as an illustration linking towards the prolegomenon of this book. It began with Lucy claiming to have gone through the wardrobe into a new world where she met the Fauns, Dryads, Naiads, Dwarfs and Animals in an enchanted wood. Her two other older siblings had begun to think that Lucy was out of her mind. They decided to acquire the advice from the professor the next morning:

"How do you know", he asked, "that your sister's story is not true?"

"Oh, but -" began Susan, and then stopped. Anyone could see from the old man's face that he was perfectly serious. Then Susan pulled herself together and said, "But Edmund said they had only been pretending."

"That is a point," said the Professor, "which certainly deserves consideration; very careful consideration. For instance – if you will excuse me for asking the question – does your experience lead you to regard your brother or your sister as the more reliable? I mean, which is the more truthful?"

"That's just the funny thing about it, sir," said Peter. "Up till now, I'd have said Lucy every time."

"And what do you think, my dear?" said the Professor, turning to Susan.

"Well," said Susan, "in general, I'd say the same as Peter, but this couldn't be true – all this about the wood and the Faun."

"That is more than I know," said the Professor, "and a charge of lying against someone whom you always found truthful is a very serious thing; a very serious thing indeed."

"We were afraid it mightn't even be lying," said Susan; "we thought there might be something wrong with Lucy."

"Madness, you mean?" said the Professor quite coolly. "Oh, you can make your minds easy about that. One has only to look at her and talk to her to see that she is not mad."

"But then," said Susan, and stopped. She had never dreamed that a grown-up would talk like the Professor and didn't know what to think.

"Logic!" said the Professor half to himself. "Why don't they teach logic at these schools? There are only three possibilities. Either your sister is telling lies, or she is mad, or she is telling the truth. You know she doesn't tell lies and it is obvious that she is not mad. For the moment then and unless any further evidence turn up, we must assume that she is telling the truth."[1]

In this passage, there is a subtle message that can be applied both to theology and epistemology. How do one know that what Lucy is telling is the truth? How do we know that God exists and to what extent our Christian brethren's experience of the divine is veridical? God, similarly through the illustration of the Fauns, Dryads, Naiads, Dwarfs and Animals in the enchanted wood of Narnia, is not tangible entity that can be directly observed or known with our sensory perception in this physical realm. The professor enlighten the children's doubt in Lucy by simple rational deduction from the facts and credibility of Lucy's character.

Like a lawyer, whilst trying to adduce evidences and contend on the credibility of witnesses, he also rationalize to the judge that if there are no existing evidences that can defeat the evidences presented, then his witness has a higher probability in telling the truth. If there are no possibility that the lawyer's witness is telling lies, or she is mad, and unless any further evidence turn up, the jury must assume that she is telling the truth. It would be illogical if the professor had suggested that one should just presuppose the existence of the Fauns, Dryads, Naiads, Dwarfs and Animals in the enchanted wood as a starting point. It would be highly gross negligent to the intellect if the professor had told the children unless they presuppose the existence of the Fauns, Dryads, Naiads, Dwarfs and Animals in the enchanted wood, they cannot and will never able to rationalize, experience or know the ultimate truth of what Lucy had seen and heard.

This book laments together with the professor who cried *"Logic!"* *"Why don't they teach logic at these schools?"* Truly indeed why there is this genus of Christians who blatantly disregard the logic that God had endowed upon mankind, enabling him to access the truth about Him? Isn't it palpable for those Christian theists seeking for the truth and those arriving at whether there is a possibility of Lucy speaking the truth, generally applies the God-given logic in his process of decision-making? For us to think of God, who alone can validate logic, we must first think logically or rationally. In addition to any kind of worthy and relevant evidences, plus the process of exercising logic and reason we come to realize the ex-

---

[1]     C.S. Lewis, *"The Chronicles of Narnia: The Lion, the Witch and the Wardrobe"* (Harper-Collins, 2003) pp. 46- 48.

istence of the God who validates the logical process by which we have arrived at the knowledge of Him.

Obviously, it would be illogical and against the modern principles of the law of evidence for any judge to direct the jury to presuppose the verdict in order that they can understand the evidences and rationality of the case. This may be seen as plainly a breach of natural justice if the court assumes the truth of the allegation in advance without first assessing any reasonable grounds or hear both sides of the arguments.[2] Similarly, it can be illogical to teach that unless men presuppose God, evidences and rationality of the incarnate God can never be apprehended. This is the first concern of the book that should initially be solved/shelved away before we embark into one of the main issues of the research i.e. is the author of the fourth gospel an evidentialist or a presuppositionalist?

## Background and Focus of the Study

Numerous religious thinkers have been for centuries argued that the very precise nature of religion requires that its beliefs rest on faith, not reason. Consequently, it is of no surprise that one of the main prerequisite for any worldview to fall under the definition of 'religion' must involve the exercise of unconditional acceptance on the part of its adherents or devotees, with or without comprehensible reasons. With this notion, laymen is quick to term this unconditional decision to believe as 'faith'. For example, there are some Buddhist thinkers liberally classify Buddhism as a philosophy rather than a religion. According to their argument, Buddhism is a philosophical ideology for man to rationalise its way of life rather than applying mere faith on a divine being. It claims that it

---

[2]  Here, it is not the same as the court applying the presumption of innocence until proven guilty. This criminal presumption imposes a burden of proof on the prosecutor who alleges guilt on the accused. Unless the onus of the prosecutor is discharged or evidences provided beyond a reasonable doubt to justify a guilty verdict, the accused remain innocent as earlier presumed. However, it does not mean that without this presumption (or presupposition) of innocence, the court can never be able to rationalize or comprehend any evidence adduced. This presumption of innocence is a matter of human rights and it insist on a useful starting point based on the maxim 'he who asserts must prove' (*ei incumbit probatio qui dicit, non qui negat*). It is not about epistemology on the clash between faith and reason. This court illustration is to demonstrate the evidential value that leads to justified fairness rather than the irrational presuppositionalism that may be manifestly misinterpreted as bias, unequitable and stark bigotry.

can be rationalised logically by the mind. Buddhism therefore would not be considered a 'religion' under such definition, because it is basically non-theistic and it does not generally involve exercising faith to worship a supernatural entity.[3] Instead of the requirement of faith, Buddhism is logically rational and appeal to the intellect to reason out its propositions and evidences, if any. Along this line, it is argued and criticized by the same Buddhist intellectuals and other non-theist thinkers that Christianity is not rational because they requires 'faith', just like any other religions. With this mind set, that is of no surprise that Christianity are classified as a 'religion' and not a theological propositions which can be objectively assessed that requires the mind to reason.

In a slight different angle, the authors of 'Classical Apologetics'[4] recognise this problem if Christianity is understood through a narrow definition of 'religion' within different religious school of thoughts. They raise their concern that the study of theology (especially Christianity) and the study of religion are not distinguished. Specifically, their main concern is actually on the crisis of secularism influencing the true understanding of a rational Christianity if it is studied through the secular curriculum of 'religious education'. However, the quotation from their book here is equally appropriate to describe the preliminary concern of this book:

> Most of the faculty understood that there is a profound difference between the study of theology and the study of religion. Theology's primary foci are the being and the activity of God. Religion, on the other hand, is a study of human activity, often subsumed under the broader headings of anthropology or sociology. Religion concerns human actions of devotion, liturgical practices, cultic structures, and the like. It focuses on this world, the world of knowable phenomena. Within the philosophical framework of secularism, the study of religion is a possible and legitimate enterprise; the study of the nature of God is not. The secularist regards the study of God as a fool's errand, yielding no viable scientific knowledge.
>
> The study of religious behaviour is a valuable exercise. However, when a Christian institution supplants the study of theology with the study of religion, exclusively, it ceases to be a Christian institution. At some institutions, it is still theology that is studied, albeit under the rubric of religion;

---

[3]  Some argues that Buddhism may not be considered a religion because it does not usually involve belief in supernatural powers. It does not indulge in blind faith over something in the spiritual realm which cannot be perceived with our sensory perception.

[4]  Sproul R.C., J. Gerstner & A. Lindsley. *"Classical Apologetics: A Rational Defense of the Christian Faith and a Critic of Presuppositional Apologetics"* (Grand Rapids: Zondervan, 1984).

the change is merely one of nomenclature. But when the name is changed without an awareness of the significance of this change, the tail is well on the way to wagging the dog."[5]

The initial prolegomenon of this book raises this similar concern that Christianity is classified as any other religion which is based on mere faith and not any rational thinking. Such classification not only source from secularists' narrow definition of religion but unfortunately also contributed by fideistic Christian theologians, including those who approach theological knowledge through revelation presuppositionalism. The presuppositionalists maintain that one cannot get to God or able to comprehend any God knowledge by starting with self. Instead he must begin his thinking with God. In other words, rationality and evidences should be kept down. This unfortunately added to our atheist critics' list of confirmation substantiating Christianity being an irrational faith. Due to this strong emphasis on faith as a starting point and underestimate the value of reason and evidence, they inadvertently portray to the nonbelievers that Christianity like any other religion is illogical and unreasonable. Is this what the Scripture teaches? Did the Bible warn us that human reason, which is a God-given instrument of truth, when applied without first presupposing God's existence can become an instrument leading to error? Are there any examples from the apostles in the New Testament adhere to this methodology of 'faith precedes reason' in evangelism to both the Jews and the Gentiles? Or otherwise?

Whilst we are not bother whether Buddhism is classified as religion or philosophy, we are concern whether Christianity is a religion based on mindless faith or a philosophy full of rational propositions supported by reasons and evidences. Since Christianity has a theistic worldview and requires faith in a divine creator it could vividly be said it is a religion. However, it is not a religion that requires a mindless act of faith. Christianity is not and should not be irrational. God forbid our faith to be mindless or irrational. Otherwise, how could we obey Jesus who reminded us the commandment to love the Lord our God *"with all our heart ... and with all our mind?"*[6] Then, how do we like the Apostle Paul with his mind know Whom he has believed and is convinced that God is able to guard what he has entrusted to Him until that day?[7] Wouldn't it be a paradox when we Christians of this century move away from rational truth whilst the Old

---

5    Ibid., 11-12
6    Mark 12:30; Luke 10:27; Matthew 22:37.
7    2 Timothy 1:12.

Testament prophet of the same God we worship wrote, "*Come now, and let us reason together...*"?[8]

Sometimes we are to be blamed for wrongly emphasizing faith over reason. We inadvertently represent Christianity as a religion of believing something which cannot be seen or rationally explained. We allow our Sunday school definition of '*faith*' to linger into our mind even when it's time for us to leave the infant milk for more solid food. Subsequently, we pass on to our next generation that faith is merely '*believing without seeing*'. Faithful pastors who sincerely preached '*we are saved through faith; and that not of yourselves; not as a result of works ...*' as written in Ephesians 2: 8 & 9 may lead to misinterpretation by their congregations that only faith that saved us, omitting the knowledge that it is actually because of 'the grace of God' we are saved. Faith is only the channel which God is the object of our faith that must be understood and our hearts convicted. Otherwise, I can have faith in anything, including having faith in a disjointed limb of a rabbit's foot in my left pocket. Salvation based on the subjective faith of an individual?

Since according to them, it is only faith that save, then no other physical tangible work or intangible rationalisation can be used as justification to our decision process to believe, *lest we boast*. In the long run, reason is avoided altogether. Fideistic theologians are equally culpable in downplaying the importance of reason. "*For without faith it is impossible to please Him*"[9] is repeatedly and earnestly quoted by them but often omit an understanding of the process towards exercising the true faith that God requires from us. It is utmost unfortunate that due to this abhorrence against reason, Christianity has been misconceived as irrational, requiring unquestionable faith, thus falling under the inadequate definition of '*religion*' of no scientific significance in the real world.

On the other hand, what is faith then? Shouldn't our religious belief rest on faith, rather than reason? Which should be our starting point? If we say religious belief rested entirely on reason i.e. our starting point should be reason, then the unconditional acceptance of religious belief would be unwarranted, leaving no room for the exercise of a decision which is not compelled by any external factor. Then, faith would become meaningless if it cannot be freely exercised. However, if the starting point is faith, we risk our reasoning to become impertinence. Can we have both? If yes, should it be faith or reason that takes ultimate prima-

---

[8]    Isaiah 1:18.
[9]    Hebrews 11:6.

cy? Professor emeritus of philosophy at Purdue University, Dr. William Rowe describes generally what faith is:

> Faith ... is the acceptance of certain statements concerning God and his activities. Sometimes, however, we think of faith not as the acceptance of certain statements as true, but as trust in certain persons or institutions. Thus, we say things like "Have faith in your friends" or "Let's restore faith in our government." But since trusting some person or institution generally involves accepting or believing certain statements about them, faith in someone or something presupposes beliefs that certain statements about them are true. Where such beliefs do not rest on reason, faith in someone or something may presuppose a faith that certain statements are true.[10]

This is precisely the concern if our beliefs do not rest on reason, faith in God may presuppose a faith that certain propositions of Christianity are true. That would in turn raising the alarm that our faith is irrational, but nevertheless we just presuppose that our faith in God is true. To what extent we rely on reason and evidence or just presuppose the truth by just mere faith? These preceding paragraphs serve as a reminder to us the never-ending clashes between faith and reason. It also introduce the concerns on the risk of avoiding the value of evidentialism.

Having said that, the main thesis is not on the disputes between faith and reason but on the value of evidentialism. Of course, one could not escape completely from not criticizing slightly on the circular argument of the presuppositionalists, whilst defending the significance of reason and evidence. There are ample academic papers and books published by talented apologists in regards to evidentialism and presuppositionalism. This book shall not attempt to regurgitate totally their excellent explanations. However, it shall allow their well-researched information influence the main issue of this book. We shall concentrate on the argument which admittedly, I had already presupposed the conclusion: (1) if the Apostle John had set an example in his writing by using reasons and evidence "*so that you may believe that Jesus is Christ, the Son of God; and believing you may have life in His name*",[11] then evidentialism as supported in Scriptures should be the apologetic model in acquiring true knowledge of the truth and should not be totally rejected. (2) One may also observed the modern principles of the law of evidence commonly practised in the western legal

---

[10]   Rowe, William .L. "*Philosophy of Religion: An Introduction*" (Belmont, CA: Wadsworth, 2001), 75.

[11]   John 20:31.

jurisdiction[12] as a legal science in procuring a verdict can be relatively appreciated as similar with the modus operandi of the Apostle John in his writing to persuade others to believe. Through this, it is a support to the continuous research work on the benefits of legal apologetics.[13]

## Aims and Structure

As briefly explained above, the aim of this book is an analysis of the apologetic modus operandi applied by the Apostle John in the fourth Gospel. John's methodology may reflect the criminal trial lawyers' application of the principles of the law of evidence accepted as a rational mode of proof. In other words, one can draw an inference that the apologetic methods the writer of the fourth gospel accord to the legal apologetic model of theological epistemology. Hence, this emphasizes that the Gospel of John, the inspired authority stresses the importance of evidence and reasons as appealing to the mind to comprehend the truth that Jesus is the Son of God.

There are much agreement that application of apologetics is vital in strengthening our Christian faith and as a supportive work in evange-

---

[12]   Especially by countries of the Commonwealth having similar influence from the British Common law.

[13]   For more details of legal apologetics, see Clifford, Ross., *Justification of the Legal Apologetic of John Warwick Montgomery: An Apologetic For All Seasons*, Vol. 3 No. 1, (2002) Global Journal of Classical Theology; Broughton, P. William, *The Historical Development of Legal Apologetics: With An Emphasis on the Resurrection*, (Xulon Press, 2009); Johnson, Philip, *Juridical Apologetics 1600-2000 AD: A Bio-Bibliographical Essay*, Global Journal of Classical Theology, 3(1) (March, 2002); Greenleaf, Simon, *The Testimony of the Evangelists: The Gospel Examined by the Rules of Evidence* (Grand Rapids: Kregel Classics, 1995); Montgomery, John Warwick, *Human Rights and Human Dignity* (Grand Rapids: Zondervan, 1986); Montgomery, John Warwick, 'Neglected Apologetics Styles: The Juridical and the Literary' in Evangelical Apologetics, ed. Bauman, M., Hall, D. & Newman, R., (Camp Hill, PA: Christian Publications, 1996) 119-33; Montgomery, John Warwick, "The Law Above the Law: Why the Law Needs Biblical Foundations / How Legal Thought Support Christian Truth" (Minneapolis: Bethany House, 1975); Montgomery, John Warwick, 'The Jury Returns: A Juridical Defense of Christianity,' in Christian in the Public Square, ed. C.E.B. Cranfield, David Kilgour & John Warwick Montgomery (Edmonton, AB: Canadian Institute for Law, Theology and Public Policy, 1996), 223-250; Ewen, Pamela B., *Faith on Trial: An Attorney Analyzes the Evidence for the Death and Resurrection of Jesus*, (Nashville, Tennessee: Broadman & Holman Publisher, 1999); Clifford, Ross, *Leading Lawyers Look at the Resurrection* (Albatross, 1991); Teh, Henry Hock Guan, 'Legal Apologetics: Principles of Legal Evidence as Applied to the Quest for Religious Truth', Global Journal of Classical Theology: 5(1) (July 2005).

lism. More accurately, the application of evidential apologetics. Evidentialism to a great extent is flexible in the sense it encompasses emphasis of all apologetic schools. Therefore, the rigidity of classical apologetics, presuppositional apologetics and fideism should not be fervently or zealously fortified. The Calvinist presuppositionalists correctly and strongly uphold the principle of sola scriptura which assume Christian truth (including theology and epistemology) are revealed in Scripture, thus set an example for us to follow. Then, it should not be wrong to say evidence and reasoning rationally supports their presupposition that the Scripture must be followed. If we were to apply the doctrine of sola scriptura and follow the examples of the early fathers, a good example to consider as authority is from the fourth gospel and its logical flow of the writer in proving the divinity of Christ, then the presuppositionalists should emulate the evidentialistic stance of the Apostle John.

This research will encourage the appreciation of legal science. It is not going to conclude that legal apologetics is the perfect method but to demonstrate the 'common sense' of our human make-up in assessing the truth. Common sense here does not mean it is in our innate nature but it betokens the normal commonality of investigation. Principle of the law of evidence as applied in the courtrooms of common law countries are the legal science for intelligently investigating whether an act took place or a proposition is real. It is by assessing the rationality and admissibility of evidence for the jury to consider with their mind to make an objective decision. It is of no surprise that these are 'common sense' principle for convincing one's decision-making process.

The Apostle John had consciously and intentionally assessed the logical flow and evidence (but unconsciously applied the modern principles of the law of evidence) to rationally convince his readers. If this were true, then the Apostle John is truly indeed an evidential apologist and one who love God with all his mind. Thus, the relevance is - Christians (especially aspiring apologists) should follow the footsteps of the Apostle John to use our mind and emphasize evidential apologetics (more so legal apologetics), rather than presuppose that all we need is faith without any reason.

We shall defend evidentialism in chapter one. There, we shall distinguish between the rigidity of John Locke and William Clifford's *hyper* evidentialism and the Christian evidentialism. In chapter two, a brief explanation of legal apologetics and how it applied the modern principles of the law of evidence. The various basic judicial principles of evidence and some of its examples used in the task of apologetics are provided in chapter three. This important chapter helps us to get a grasp of what it means by some of the legal terms in evidence. A basic understanding of the terms should be comprehended before we embark into the fourth gospel. In chapter four, a short discussion on why John is chosen for this book. A brief explanation on how John apply legal apologetics in his writings. We shall go through each chapter of John's gospel in the final chapter of this book. As we go through, we shall identify which passage had applied evidentialism, reasoning and the various basic rules of legal evidence. Consequently, whilst we skim through some of the examples of legal apologetics applied by the Apostle John, it will be apparently inevitable that presuppositionalism and reformed epistemological methodology are somewhat criticised.

# CHAPTER I

## Defending Evidentialism

It is humbly hoped that this book can be added to the many scholarly written literatures in support of evidentialism. However, it is not as equal in quality and detailed explanation as written by leading proponents of evidential apologetics such as Bernard Ramm, Clark H. Pinnock, Gary R. Habermas, Joseph Butler, Josh McDowell, John Warwick Montgomery[14], Richard Swinburne, William Paley, Wolfhart Pannenberg and many more. Since the main purpose of this book is on the application of legal apologetics in the fourth gospel, the discourse on evidentialism is limited to the core disagreements (or maybe misunderstanding) between evidentialism and its two widely researched apologetic nemesis i.e. presuppositionalism and reformed epistemology. In defending the value of evidentialism, these two schools of apologetics are briefly criticized together with a brief explanation of why evidentialism should not be looked upon as against the Scriptures.

There is another apologetic school branded in *Five Views*[15] as Cumulative Case Method. Amongst others, two of its leading proponents are Paul D. Feinberg and William J. Abraham[16]. Though it does not says much on historical evidences, Feinberg's cumulative case apologetic "approach could be considered as a sub-species in the camp of evidentialist methodology."[17] In fact, it has a strong flavour of legal apologetics, another sub-species of evidential apologetics. They can be considered as 'triplets in apologetics', the offspring of evidentialism. I will not attempt to dissect these three schools of apologetics to scrutinise their minor differences in this book but consider them as one and be referred as 'evidential apologetics' or just plain 'evidentialism'. However, in some parts of the book,

---

[14]   John Warwick Montgomery's best-known book, *Faith Founded on Fact: Essays in Evidential Apologetics* (Newburgh, Indiana: Trinity Press, 1978) is highly recommended. It well illustrates the methodological perspective of the evidentialist model of apologetics.

[15]   Cowan, Steven (ed.), *Five Views on Apologetics*, (Grand Rapids, Michigan: Zondervan Publishing House, 2000)

[16]   And maybe to some extent, Lee Strobel.

[17]   Gary Habermas' response to Cumulative Case Apologetics in *Five Views on Apologetics*, 184.

when 'legal apologetics'[18] are referred, it is just to emphasize the significance in application of the modern principles of law of evidence in apologetics. Sometimes, these three terms are interchangeably referred. Legal Apologetics will be expounded in greater detail in subsequent chapters.

Although classical apologetics and evidential apologetics have different manner in presenting arguments for theistic proofs, both agreed to a very large extent on the use of reason and evidence. Both have much in common, especially in the evidential task but with some distinction on the use of historical evidences. Generally, classical apologetics 'emphasizes the use of logical criteria (for example, the law of non-contradiction, self-consistency, comprehensiveness, coherence) in determining religious philosophies. These criteria are used to refute the truth claims of non-Christian worldviews and to establish the existence of God through theistic proofs'.[19] This approach can be traced all the way to Thomas Aquinas, a famous thirteenth-century Christian thinker. In our present day, we have leading proponents such as Norman L. Geisler, J. P. Moreland and William Lane Craig.[20] All three can be considered as one of the modern evangelical authorities in classical apologetics, which admittedly their writings provided much insights on reasons to evidentialists. In addition, all serious students of classical method would have read a comprehensive book on classical apologetics[21] very well-written by R.C. Sproul and his friends from the Ligonier Valley Study Center[22]. This book written with a strong critique on Van Til's presuppositionalism.

Like other Christian evidentialists, classical apologists do emphasize the important role of the Holy Spirit as the source of knowledge. Accord-

---

[18] "Legal Apologetics" can also be briefly defined as 'a branch of Christian apologetics that affirms that the available evidence to defend Christianity argues for the veracity of the historical and central claims of Christianity when Western legal standards of weighing evidence are applied.' (From the Glossary of Terms in Broughton, William P., "The Historical Development of Legal Apologetics: With an Emphasis on the Resurrection" (Xulon Press, 2009), 124.

[19] Boa, Kenneth. D. and Robert M. Bowman Jr. "Faith Has Its Reason: An Integrative Approach to Defending Christianity" (Paternoster, 2005), 34.

[20] And maybe to some extent, B.B. Warfield and C.S. Lewis.

[21] R.C. Sproul, John Gerstner & Arthur Lindsley. "Classical Apologetics: A Rational Defense of the Christian Faith and a Critic of Presuppositional Apologetics" (Grand Rapids, Michigan: Zondervan Publishing House, 1984).

[22] Ligonier Ministries is an international Christian discipleship organization founded by theologian Dr. R.C. Sproul in 1971 to equip Christians to articulate what they believe and why they believe it. Its central emphasis is to proclaim God's holiness according to Reformed Theology. Website at: http://www.ligonier.org/

ing to Professor of Philosophy at Talbot School of Theology, Dr. William Lane Craig, classical apologetics is a mixture of natural theology and Christian evidences, but not denying the inner witness of the Holy Spirit:

> The methodological approach ... is that reason in the form of rational arguments and evidence plays an essential role in our showing Christianity to be true, whereas reasons in this form plays a contingent and secondary role in our personally knowing Christianity to be true. The proper ground of our knowing Christianity to be true, is the inner work of the Holy Spirit in our individual selves; and in our showing Christianity to be true, it is his role to open the hearts of unbelievers to assent and respond to the reasons we present ... This approach is comprised of natural theology and Christian evidences.[23]

Specifying natural theology to take precedence over evidences, Professor William Lane Craig explains that this method proceeds in a two-fold manner:

> The methodology of classical apologetics was first to present arguments for theism, which aimed to show that God's existence is at least more probable than not, and then to present Christian evidences, probabilistically construed, for God's revelation in Christ.[24]

Both Classical and Evidential Methods embrace the importance of faith and reason. However, if were to be forced to choose which one should be the starting point, it would be reasons. To avoid any false dilemma, it would be reasons precedes faith. It is not man's wisdom precedes faith in God but reasons as the intellectual gift endowed by God and when sincerely applied with the conviction of the Spirit, it moves us towards faith in action.

These two epistemological schools in defending Christianity rationally can be considered as 'siblings in apologetics', having almost similar mutual repugnant attitude towards their very 'distant cousins in apologetics', namely presuppositionalism and reformed epistemology. They look upon presuppositional method of apologetics as somewhat disoriented in reality in terms of their circular reasoning. With its repulsion of circularity, presuppositionalism is argued to be inevitably heading towards anti-intellectualism and ultimate fideism. Whilst having much respect towards their presuppositional brethren-in-Christ in their faithful

---

[23]   Craig, William Lane, 'Classical Apologetics' in Five Views on Apologetics edited by Cowan, S. B. (Michigan, Grand Rapids: Zondervan, 2000), 28.

[24]   Ibid. 48.

reliance on the Scriptures and the primacy of God as the starting point of all knowledge, classical and evidential apologists look upon its circular argument with a jaundiced eye. Keeping a blind eye to human rationality while emphasizing the sovereignty of God based on their circular reasoning, the presuppositionalists run the risk of being wrongly interpreted as spiritually arrogant and intellectually wanting.

> The question may occur to the reader why presuppositionalists think they reason in a circle when their reasoning is no more circular than any other thinker's. We suspect it is because these men are sincerely devout Christians and presuppositionalism has a pious ring to it. It creates a sort of intellectual halo. Notice for example, this statement from Rushdoony: '*All reasoning is from God to God-given and God-interpreted facts.*' He is talking about moving from God to God. That, of course, makes it sound like a pious, circular movement."[25]

We will sporadically touch on more about presuppositionalism along the way in the next few chapters. At this juncture, it is imperative to have a rough understanding of evidentialism before embarking into the scrutiny whether the author of the fourth gospel can be considered as an evidentialist and the coincidental pre-application of the modern principles of the law of evidence.

## What is Evidentialism?

A very concise, clear and general description of the evidential school of apologetics can be taken from Norman Geisler's Baker Encyclopedia of Christian Apologetics:

> Evidential apologetics stresses the need for evidence in support of the Christian truth claims. The evidence can be rational, historical, archaeological, and even experiential. Since it is so broad, it is understandably overlaps with other types of apologetics. Since evidentialists encompass a large and diverse category, their characteristics will be delineated according to type. Evidentialists often use rational evidence (e.g. proofs of God) in defense of Christianity. As such, they overlap with classical apologetics. However, for an evidentialist this is just one piece of evidence. Also in contrast to classical apologists, evidentialists do not hold that rational evidence is

---

[25]   R.C. Sproul, J. Gerstner, & A. Lindsley, *Classical Apologetics: A Rational Defense of the Christian Faith and a Critic of Presuppositional Apologetics*, (Grand Rapids: Zondervan, 1984), 329.

either necessary (since it is only one piece) or logically prior to the other evidence.

In the use of historical evidence there is again an overlap with evidential and historical apologetics. Evidentialists do not rest their whole case on historical evidence. They are more eclectic, interweaving evidence from various fields. Evidentialists operate as attorneys who combine evidences into an overall brief in defense of their position, trusting that the combined weight will present a persuasive case.

Many evidentialists focus on archaeological evidence in support of the Bible. They stress that both the Old and the New Testaments have been substantiated by thousands of discoveries. This, they believe, gives reason to accept the divine authority of the Scriptures. Other types of apologetics appeal to archaeological evidence, who use the evidence in a different way. Some evidentialists focus to experiential evidence in support of Christianity, most often from changed lives. The testimony of those converted to Christianity is offered as evidence of the truth of Christianity. How else, it is argued, one can explain the dramatic, transforming, enduring, and often radical changes? The conversion of Saul of Tarsus (Acts 9) is a classic case in point.

Prophetic evidence is often offered to substantiate Christianity. It is argued that only divine origin accounts for the numerous, precise biblical predictions that have been fulfilled. For the evidentialists prophetic and other evidences do not comprise a specific step in an overall logical order (as it is in classical apologetics). Rather, it is the sum total of all the interlocking evidences that offer high probability of the truth of Christianity.[26]

The above is so well defined I sometimes suspect whether Dr. Geisler is a 'secret aficionado' of evidential apologetics. Indeed, evidential apologetics overlaps with classical apologetics since rational evidence are often used. However, the evidential apologists take priority in showing the truth of Christianity by demonstrating its factuality. Whereas classical apologetics characteristically concentrate on logic or reasons as the primary criteria of truth. Although not necessary, evidentialism is primarily inductive, rather than deductive, in its logical form.

However, Kenneth Boa and Robert Bowman[27] explains further:

The priority assigned to factual evidence over against rational deduction does not mean that evidentialists are critical of reason or logic. According to Montgomery, "*The law of contradiction and the logical thinking based upon it*

26   Geisler, Norman L., *Baker Encyclopedia of Christian Apologetics* (Grand Rapids: Baker Book, 1999), 41 – 42.
27   *Faith Has Its Reason: An Integrative Approach to Defending Christianity*, 158.

*are not optional. They must be employed for any meaningful thought, theological or otherwise."*[28] However, evidentialists are suspicious of logic employed in a speculative manner, and they emphasize that rational arguments are only as good as the facts with which they work. Logical coherence or consistency is at best a negative test for truth, because it is possible to construct a coherent worldview that is actually false. Montgomery observes that *"the greatest of the world's madmen have held the most consistent delusions,"*[29] and illustrates his concern in an amusing parable about a man who was convinced he was dead.

His concerned wife and friends sent him to the friendly neighborhood psychiatrist. The psychiatrist determined to cure him by convincing him of one fact that contradicted his belief that he was dead. The fact that the psychiatrist settled on was the simple truth that dead men do not bleed, and he put the patient to work reading medical texts, observing autopsies, etc. After weeks of effort, the patient finally said: "All right, all right! You've convinced me. Dead men do not bleed." Whereupon the psychiatrist stuck him in the arm with a needle, and the blood flowed. The man looked with a contorted, ashen face and cried: "Good Lord! Dead men bleed after all!"

The moral of this amusing story Montgomery wants to emphasize is "that if you hold unsound presuppositions with sufficient tenacity, facts will make no difference to you at all."[30]

As far as I am concerned, the Christian evidential apologetic views that *anything* relevant is considered an evidence when it can persuade a particular individual cognitively whether intelligently or emotionally to move a step closer to the belief that God exist or an additional step that may increase his or her reliance in Jesus Christ, whether that person had originally presumed God may exist as a starting point before being convinced by that *anything* or had first deduced that *anything* (some existing facts or reasoning) adequate for that subjective person to comprehend according to the measure of his or her mental capacity is the process of 'evidentialism'. Thus, evidentialist subscribes to anything morally useful that can probably persuade a person's belief that it is probably true, whether the evidence was concluded inductively[31] or deductively[32]. Any

---

28   Montgomery, *"The Death of the 'Death of God,'"* in Suicide of Christian Theology (Minneapolis: Bethany Fellowship, 1970), 125.

29   Montgomery, *Faith Founded on Fact: Essays in Evidential Apologetics* (Nashville: Thomas Nelson, 1978), 233.

30   Montgomery, *"Death of the 'Death of God,'"* 122.

31   Inductive reasoning assembles facts and argues that a particular conclusion offers the best or most probable explanation of the facts. It usually argue from

other apologetic view that dismiss the importance of reason and evidence is either not evidentialism or moving away from evidentialism. Correspondingly, anything that support the importance of reason and evidence is evidentialism or moving towards evidentialism.

This is not a perfect definition of evidentialism, considering there is no agreed-upon body of beliefs on the most correct definition of evidentialism. I subscribe to a more moderate view of evidentialism and therefore it is professed here that evidentialism generally embrace some of the tenets of classical apologetics and even a few acceptable crumbs from the mild form of presuppositionalism. Of course, there is no such thing as justifying one's belief upon zero evidence. There must be sufficient evidence to convince an individual. That sufficiency may vary according to each and every individual. One does not start by pretending to believe in something exist. He may start his search by believing that something *may* possibly exist but not believing something *is* existing.

## Hyper Evidentialism Not Defended

Sad to admit that there are a few *hyper* evidentialists that go to an extreme measure to say that nothing except evidence plays the only role in convincing one's belief, otherwise it is just plain irrational. To some of them, religious experiences utterly have no role at all in justifying one's belief. William Clifford argued that it is irrational to hold any belief unless we have "sufficient evidence" for it. He argued that unless this is the way we govern our beliefs, we will not only end up holding beliefs that might lead to others being harmed, we will also make ourselves into credulous people who hold beliefs indiscriminately and thus irrational. Clifford summarizes his argument by saying, '*it is wrong always, everywhere, and for anyone, to believe anything upon insufficient evidence.*'[33] This approach is also called epistemological evidentialism. There are those

---

premises to a conclusion in which the premises count in favour of, provide evidence for, the conclusion, without entailing it.

[32]  Deductive arguments, such as those favored in classical apologetics, reason from as few facts, or premises, as are needed to a conclusion that is shown to follow from the facts. The problem is they may start from premises which are far from generally accepted.

[33]  Clifford, William Kingdon, "*The Ethics of Belief*" in *Lectures and Essays* (New York: Macmillan, 1901), 163 - 176. Clifford's essay was originally published in his *Lectures and Essays* (London: MacMillan, 1879) and has been reprinted in numerous anthologies, for example in Brody, Baruch A. (ed.), *Readings in the Philosophy of Religion* (Englewood Cliffs, N.J.: Prentice-Hall, 1974), 246.

calling for absolute evidence for the certainty of theistic belief, otherwise the evidence for Christianity is inadequate and thus irrational. Kretzmann[34] has fervently argued it is a canon of rationality that it is irrational to believe anything on the basis of insufficient evidence.[35]

Clifford's stringent requirement has been rigorously criticised as self-defeating. If everything requires proof, then where is the evidence for his claim? What proof does Clifford provide for his belief that it is immoral to believe anything in the absence of evidence? It is the strict adherence to the terms of Clifford's *hyper* evidential maxim that other philosophers warned that it may lead to a chain of requests for further evidence that would terminate only in such presumably unanswerable questions as "What evidence have you for supposing that your sensory apparatus is reliable?", or "Yes, but what consideration can you adduce in support of the hypothesis that the future will resemble the past?", and they have drawn the conclusion that anyone who accepts such propositions as that one's sensory apparatus is reliable or that the future will resemble the past must do so in defiance of the principle.[36] If one attempts to justify his belief in terms of other beliefs or justify his reason/evidence based on other reason/evidence, then this justification spawns an infinite regress or vicious circularity.

Consequently, this method establishes what we might call an epistemology of suspicion: the belief that we should consider all beliefs false unless proven true by sufficient evidence. If strictly applied, it always places the burden of proof on a belief rather than on its denial. If someone believe that the world exists as a reality independent of his senses, isn't he perfectly right to adhere to his belief in the absence of reasons or evidence to the contrary. It is obviously wrong for the epistemological

---

[34]   Kertzmann, Norman, "Evidence Against Anti-Evidentialism", in *Our Knowledge of God; Essays on Natural and Philosophical Theology* edited by K. Clark (Dordrecht: Kluwer Academic Press, 1992), 17-38.

[35]   This view similarly accepted by Anthony Flew in "*The Presumption of Atheism*", *The Canadian Journal of Philosophy* (2/1972) 29-46; Blanshard, B., "*Reason and Belief*" (London: Allen and Unwin, 1977); Mackie, J., *The Miracles of Theism* (New York: Oxford University Press, 1982); O'Hear, A., "*Experience, Explanation and Faith: An Introduction to the Philosophy of Religion*" (London: Routledge & Kegan Paul, 1984) – all regard the evidence provided for theism as inadequate.

[36]   Inwagen, Peter Van. "*It is Wrong, Everywhere, Always, and for Anyone, to Believe Anything upon Insufficient Evidence*" in Faith, Freedom, and Rationality: Philosophy of Religion Today edited by Jeff Jordan & Daniel Howard-Synder (London: Rowman & Littlefield, 1996) pp. 137-53, reprinted in Stump, Eleanor & Michael Murray, (Ed.) *Philosophy of Religion: The Big Questions*, (Oxford: Blackwell, 2003), 274.

evidentialists to continuously demand on the believer to prove, even though he had provided some sufficient evidence. Legal apologists do not object that the burden of proof are sometimes place on the believer, but never to be succumbed by the vicious circularity and the infinite regression entailed by Clifford's maxim.

Kenneth Boa and Robert Bowman attempt to reformulate a milder definition for evidentialism:

> If we were to formulate a maxim for evidentialist apologetics, it would be something like this: it is wrong, everywhere, always, and for anyone, *to tell someone else* to believe something other than on the basis of evidence. In other words, evidentialism in apologetics places a certain burden of proof on the apologist to show non-Christians why it is rational to believe in Christ. At the same time, evidentialists claim that the truth of the Christian message cannot be successfully or properly denied without a fair consideration of the factual basis for the Christian truth claim. Henceforth when we refer to evidentialism, we are referring to the apologetic approach.[37]

Since Christian apologists do argue that people ought to have evidence or reasons for the beliefs they hold in matters of supreme importance, it is fair that the onus is on the one who alleges the truth claim of this important matters. However, it seems that the standard of the Cliffordians are way beyond a shadow of a doubt. In other words, they will never be satisfied until the standard of mathematical certainty is discharged. Even the believer had discharged his burden on a prima facie evidence[38], the Cliffordians still insists that the burden still rest on the believer. Instead of admitting that to cast rational doubts over the prima facie evidence provided by the Christians apologists is their burden of proof, they nevertheless still argue that the overall burden rest on the Christians apologists. Such obstinate evidentialism is impossible and impracticable in the honest search for religious truth.

Unfortunately, it is generally criticized that this type of evidentialism propounded by atheist has been adopted by thinkers on opposite sides of the theistic fence. Ronald Nash roughly analysed that 'theistic evidentialists and their antitheistic counterparts start from the same presupposition, namely that the rationality of religious belief depends upon the discovery of evidence or arguments to support the belief. Theistic and

---

[37]   Boa & Bowman, "*Faith Has Its Reason: An Integrative Approach to Defending Christianity*" (2005) 156.

[38]   We shall explain on the theory on shifting of the burden of proof in chapter 3 on the principles of the law of evidence.

antitheistic evidentialist part company over the question of whether such evidence actually exists; but both agree that evidence is necessary!'[39]

With this *hyper* evidentialism and Clifford's ethics of belief in mind, C. Stephen Evans in his Pocket Dictionary of Apologetics & Philosophy of Religion[40] defines '*evidentialism*' as:

> The view that religious beliefs (as well as other kinds) are only rational if they are based on evidence. Typically, evidentialists will specify some minimum of evidence that is sufficient (such as "evidence that makes a belief more probable than its competitors"). Another popular form of evidentialism is proportional "ethics of belief" that holds that the strength of one's assent to a belief should be proportioned to the strength of the evidence. This kind of ethic of belief can be traced to John Locke. Evidentialism has been strongly challenged by Reformed Epistemology, particularly the work of Alvin Plantinga and Nicholas Wolterstorff.

Indeed, evidentialism has been intensely challenged and usually Locke's epistemology serves as a perfect test for its critics. The reason is because John Locke has been considered as probably the 'most crucial' thinker in terms of his influence on the evidentialist tradition. Some regard him as the quintessential modern evidentialist. Wolterstorff describes 'Lockean evidentialism' as "*the form of evidentialism concerning theistic beliefs that has been most commonly espoused and discussed in the modern Western world. ... It was John Locke who first propounded the thesis with clarity and force*"[41]

> Locke was the first to develop with profundity and defend the thesis that we are all responsible for our believings, and that to do one's duty with respect to one's believings one must, at appropriate junctures and in appropriate ways, listen to the voice of Reason. Reason must be one's guide ... Locke was the great genius behind our modern ways of thinking of rationality and responsibility in beliefs. And Locke's vision became classic: for many, compelling; by some, contested; by no one, ignored. Locke, on this issue, is the father of modernity.[42]

[39]  Nash, R. H. "*Faith & Reason: Searching for Rational Faith*" (Grand Rapids, Michigan: Zondervan, 1988) 71-72.
[40]  Evans, C.S., *Pocket Dictionary of Apologetics & Philosophy of Religion*, (Leicester: IVP, 2002), 41 – 42.
[41]  Wolterstorff, Nicholas. "*Once Again, Evidentialism—This Time Social*", in Practices of Belief edited by Terence Cuneo (Oxford: Oxford University Press, 2010), 267.
[42]  Wolterstorff, Nicholas, '*John Locke and the Ethics of Belief*' (Cambridge: Cambridge University Press, 1996), xiv.

Though not all modern Christian evidentialists entirely adopt Locke's epistemology in totality, presuppositionalists, reformed epistemologist and fideists[43] find it easy to argue against evidentialism in general by criticising the weaker part of Locke's ideology. Likewise, Van Til also launched his critique of evidentialism by zooming in on Locke's epistemology.

Over emphasis on evidence and reason by John Locke (1632-1704) unfortunately lead him to develop an idea of God which eventually exhibited the characteristic of Deism. It is of no wonder traditional theistic evangelicals shun Locke's evidentialism in order to avoid this 'heretical' theology. John Locke's *An Essay Concerning Human Understanding*[44] is considered to have laid the intellectual foundations of Deism. John Locke seems to have argued that it is reason that only can lead men to the knowledge of certain and evident truth, that there is an *eternal, most powerful and most knowing Being*. The attributes of this Being are those which human reason recognizes as appropriate for God.

Upon considering which moral and rational qualities are suited to the deity, Locke thereon argued that *"we enlarge every one of these with our ideas of infinity, and so, putting them together, make our complex idea of God."* This expresses the idea of God is made up of human rational and moral qualities, projected to infinity. This kind of *hyper* evidentialism, glorifying human reason as the ultimate source of theological knowledge should be totally rejected as unbiblical and affront to divine revelation through the

---

43    Such as Ludwig Wittgenstein, D. Z. Phillips, Norman Malcolm and to some extent George Lindbeck who had roughly argued that religion is groundless; it has no justification, and to look for rational justification for religion is erroneous. Arguments from fideism will not be discussed in this book. However, one may refer their works at Wittgenstein, L. *"Philosophical Investigations"*, G.E.M. Anscombe (tr.), (Oxford: Blackwell, 1953); Wittgenstein, L. *"Lectures and Conversations on Aesthetics, Psychology and Religion"* edited by C. Barrett, (Oxford: Blackwell, 1966); Wittgenstein, L. *"On Certainty"*, D. Paul & G.E.M. Anscombe (tr.), (Oxford: Blackwell, 1979); Phillips, D.Z. *"The Concept of Prayer"* (London: Routledge & Kegan Paul, 1966); Phillips, D.Z. *"Faith After Foundationalism"*, (London; New York: Routledge, 1988); Phillips, D.Z. *"Faith, Skepticism and Religious Understanding"* in Contemporary Perspectives on Religious Epistemology edited by Geivett, R. D. & B. Sweetman (Oxford: Oxford University Press, 1992) 81-91; Malcolm, N. *"The Groundlessness of Belief"* in Contemporary Perspectives on Religious Epistemology edited by Geivett, R. D. & B. Sweetman (Oxford: Oxford University Press, 1992) 92-103; or Lindbeck, G., *"The Nature of Doctrine: Religion and Theology in a Postliberal Age"* (Kentucky: Westminster John Knox Press, 1984).

44    Locke, John. *"An Essay Concerning Human Understanding"*. Edited by Alexander Campbell Fraser (New York: Dover, 1959).

workings of the Holy Spirit. However, it does not mean that man's application of reason should be disdained as being autonomous – assuming that he is a law to himself as though "Man is the measure of all things." By using the God-endowed wisdom upon man whom God created to reason does not necessarily imply that creature exalts himself above the Creator. Locke's atheistic evidentialism or enlightenment rationalism is not the type of evidentialism that is defended in this book.

## But Christian Theistic Evidentialism is Defended

Moving away from hyper evidentialism as advocated by the atheists, the Christian theistic evidentialism[45] take exclusive cognisance of the work of the Holy Spirit which is a necessary role in the initiation of faith. It is "when He comes, will convict the world concerning sin and righteousness and judgment" (John 16:8). However, faith never originates in a cognitive vacuum. Human beings have to know about themselves, the environment and the object of worship in the Christian faith, whose death and resurrection make their salvation possible. It is because man's mental faculty are not perfect (but not totally depraved), various evidences and reasoning are needed to act as a guide for man to move beyond themselves from basic truths towards sufficient truth that incite an acceptance of belief.

The whole process from introducing basic evidence to the final conviction are oversees by the Holy Spirit. Throughout this whole process of overseeing, all tools such as evidences and reasons (even sometimes subjective religious experiences) are provided and guided by God for man to use in this physical realm. Truly indeed, Jesus did not leave us without any evidence or guidance. He promised, "But when He, the Spirit of truth, comes, He will guide you into all the truth; for He will not spoke on His own initiative, but whatever He hears, He will speak; and He will disclose to you what is to come." (John 16:13). The apostle John is aware of the evidential value under the guidance of the Holy Spirit. If evidence and rationality are not needed and all apologetic work are to be done by the Holy Spirit alone, there is no need for the apostle John to write the fourth Gospel. He would not need to write about the signs Jesus performed as evidence to convince his readers. Due to the awareness of the value of apologetic evidentialism (as guided by the Holy Spirit), John wrote with evidence "so that

---

45    Note that Boa and Bowman referred the Christian version as 'apologetical evidentialism' in *Faith Has Its Reason* (2005), 156 – "*Apologetical evidentialism does not assume epistemological evidentialism, and most if not all evidentialist apologists would reject Clifford's maxim.*"

*you may believe that Jesus is the Christ, the Son of God; and that believing you may have life in His name.*" (John 20:31).

We will expound the evidential epistemology applied in the Gospel of John in chapter 4 and 5. Like the apostle John, evidentialists stresses all relevant evidences that can assist in the persuasion towards belief in the Christian truth claims.

Besides the apostle John, the Book of Acts records a series of addresses and apologetic approaches adopted by Paul and other prominent early Christians, especially Peter. The examples set out by them are explicitly evidential apologetic in nature. While addressing the gospel, Paul and others directly interacted with the ideas and concerns of a number of major social groups. As the narrative of Acts (and the history of the early church) makes clear, each of these groups came to be represented in the early church. The apologetic approaches illustrated in Acts led to conversions within each of these groups. These early apologetic approaches offer insights into authentically biblical methods of apologetics, as well as strategies for interacting with specific groups that were of major importance to the development of the early church.

The same issues remain as relevant today as they did at the emergence of the Christianity in the 1st century A.D. The strategies used by Peter and Paul in key speeches in Acts depends on the presuppositions or secular philosophy of those they engaged directly i.e. the Jews, the Greeks, and the Romans. In each case the concerns and approaches differ. The starting point, evidence and rationale vary. Yet the same gospel is defended, conveyed, and affirmed, reflecting the apostles' perception of the most appropriate ways to bring the good news of Jesus Christ to these specific groups. Hence, we have biblical authority on the characteristics of what the task of apologetics should be. Instead of restricting evidentialism in seeking the truth like what the presuppositionalist taught, evidentialism is a vital mode of strategy used by the Disciples of Christ. Any evidence can be relevant including rational, historical, archaeological, fulfilled prophecies and even through religious experience. There is no exact precise starting point. One may want to begin from natural law dealing with the existence of God as in John 1:1; or begin by emphasizing a fulfilled prophecy as in John 1:23; or a miracle as direct evidence of divinity as in John 2:11; or a deep philosophical & theological rationality as in the discussion of 'new birth' in John 3: 3-21; or a large number of witnesses' testimonies as in John 3:22-34; or a collection of evidences. The same evidential method should remain as relevant today as they did at the dawn of the Christian era.

Since different people have different levels of intellectual capability; different subjects that most able to convince them; different levels of credulity or scepticisms (or even different presuppositions) any piece of evidence or rational argument can be a starting point. It can be a single piece of evidence or an accumulation of evidences depending on the target audience. Our creative God made everyone unique with their own sets of psychological influence. Our creative God created different languages and allowed groups of people to form different social structures, and hence had for thousands of years gradually transformed their cultural, religious worldview and sensitivity to persuasion. With various social background, temperaments, peer pressure, exposure to critical thinking and varying shades of intellectual indifference means an eclectic evidence and various process of reasoning are required. What an ingenious God we have that creatively made our intellectual and epistemological environment so colorful! I am sure our presuppositionalist friends would agree that it is right to presuppose that our God is creative. Creativity entails creative rationality. Man are not identical robots with the same 'mechanical' emotions programmed. We cannot presuppose only one solution to solve the epistemological problem of all man. Otherwise, we might be listening to the same old dull romantic story in a wedding party how that bride is convinced that her groom loves her. Similarly, nobody come to experience the love of God the same way.

God's wisdom and creativity display a rich variety by shining in different ways in the different people who are joined to Christ. No two are exactly alike, and no two come to Christ in exactly the same way. Hence, it is neither always the same starting point nor the same presentation of evidence. God in his wisdom knows exactly how to win over each of his chosen ones. We only obey by using what reasons and evidence we chose best and comfortable with. One person may come to Christ after a dreadful crisis that makes him search for God. Another is quietly and gradually drawn to Christ by the kindness of a Christian friend. Another comes to Christ through the daily instruction and example of Christian parents. Some comes to Christ by hearing a gospel broadcast. Many comes to Christ through a combination of many influences. In each case, God's wisdom shines through in doing exactly what it takes to win the mind and heart of each person for whom Christ died. God arranges all the events in a person's life, and his Holy Spirit works inside the person, to bring about the effect God intends. One single way are not presupposed. Evidence and influences comes in several forms. One of Jesus' last commission in Matthew 28:19 -20 is not phrased in this way: "Go ye therefore and make disciples with presupposition, thereon baptizing them with natural theology in the name of evidence, logic and reason, teaching them to observe methodically all that I commanded you."

Fortunately, with great encouragement Jesus declared rightfully, "*All authority has been given to Me in heaven and on earth.*" (Matthew 28:18). All authority implies everything on earth and heaven is in His control including every area of science, physics, cosmology, natural theology, philosophy, politics, psychology, history, nature and epistemology – the tools of knowledge or the principles of evidence. Whichever area and whatever priority one places his epistemology, Christ has the authority over it and able to exploit it to be used to bring about the divine knowledge to the recipients. The classical apologists may say that theistic arguments necessarily precede Christian evidences. But the evidentialist will reply, "So, what? God is in control." As the saying goes, '*all truths are God's truth*', similarly, all the true epistemologies are God's true theory of knowledge.

Hence, it is understandably that evidentialism encompasses a large and diverse category. Characteristics will be delineated according to type. To say that there is only one epistemology applied to all man for the search of truth is to say that God is not creative. To say there is only a strict method to adhere with and the only legitimate move i.e. 'first to present arguments for theism ... and then to present Christian evidences for God's revelation in Christ' is to say Christ is not in control of the method of priority. That is to imply not all authority is given to Him. Here is where evidentialists shake hands with presuppositionalists, in dispute with the classical apologists.

Evidentialists may choose whether to start with theistic arguments or supplies historical evidences, depending on their target audience. The use of historical evidence there is again an overlap with evidential and historical apologetics. Evidentialists do not rest their whole case on one single historical evidence. There is a more wide-ranging use of evidence, interweaving evidence from various fields. Like a lawyer in a trial, evidentialists combine evidences into an overall brief in defense of their position, trusting that the combined weight will present a persuasive case. Every relevant and area of evidence are useful and its significance should not arbitrarily be reduced. As we broaden our horizon on the creativity and the bounteous evidence of God, like all trial lawyers, Christian apologists should be reminded the legal maxim – '*Facultas probationum non est angustanda*' i.e. the faculty of proofs is not to be narrowed.

As a reminder, Christian evidentialists may also recognize the importance of religious experience as evidence. Christian faith is not merely an intellectual acceptance of facts about Christ, but is a personal experience of a relationship with Christ. Although it has lower probative value from an objective perspective, this subjective evidence can also be considered as a contributing evidence. The testimony of those converted to Christianity, their changed lives or their inner sense of spiritual prompting can be offered as evidence of the truth of Christianity. The credibility of the witness is another matter. His subjective testimony must be corroborated by objective evidence to elevate its probative value. On a word of caution, evidentialists generally hold that the Christian's experience is not self-validating. Robert Sabath, in a paper entitled "*LSD and Religious Truth*," makes the point with astounding cogency:

> It cannot be emphasized too strongly that every psychological by-product of Christianity can be reproduced by LSD and by almost every other religion, including a sense of meaning in life, integration of personality, increased sensitivity to others, greater self-acceptance, psychological relief from anxiety and guilt feelings, tranquility and inner harmony. The religious experience with all its emotional and behavior concomitants is not unique to Christianity. The most one can infer from it is that man is so constituted that he can have this experience ... [46]
>
> Both Christian experience and the LSD experience are alike in their inability to move from psychological language to God-language. The mere fact that a psychological event has taken place in one's brain cannot establish the truth of any metaphysical assertion. No psychological datum necessarily leads to a metaphysical discovery. The assertion "God exists" does not follow from the assertion "I had an experience of God" simply because experiences admit to radically different interpretations. If God exists—the kind of personal creator God most Christians and theists talk about—he must exist independent of my subjective experience of him; his existence must therefore be validated by a criterion other than my own private experience. The uniqueness of Christianity is that there is such a criterion in the personal invasion of God himself into the public world of our objective experience. Christian existential experience is rooted in objective, external works of God himself, fleshing out his life in space and time in the person of Jesus Christ and showing himself to be God by his resurrection from the dead.[47]

The subjective experience of faith is for the Christian evidentialists a response to the objective revelation of God in his historical acts of redemp-

---

[46]  Sabath, Robert A. "*LSD and Religious Truth*" in Christianity for the Tough-Minded edited by John Warwick Montgomery, J.W. (Edmonton: Canadian Institute for Law, Theology and Public Policy Inc., 2001), 198.

[47]  Ibid., 199.

tion through Jesus Christ. For that individual, his personal experience may be a higher degree of reason constituting as an evidence sufficient to substantiate his own personal decision. However, his personal experience may only have a lower degree of persuasive authority in the evaluation of any other external person. Further corroborative evidences are required to raise the probability that leads to conviction. Similar as the jury in a court trial, legal apologists would consider the credibility of that individual, the consistency and similarity of other individuals' experience together with any other objective experience or real evidence which can be assessed by third party. This is to increase the believability on the truth claim of the witness's experience.

As mentioned, no single or a group of evidences do comprise a specific step in an overall logical order. Rather, any evidence or rational argument can be the sum total of all the interlocking evidences that offer high probability of the truth of Christianity. Evidentialists are honest to admit that there is no evidence that can produce 100% certainty as in mathematical certainty. Evidence can strengthen one's belief. Any vacuum for doubt is filled with the specific gift of the Holy Spirit we call it "faith". In other words, "faith" is a gift but one need to make a decision with the free-will that God has given them. Evidence do not convict a person. Evidence are used as a basis for person to decide to open his heart to be convicted by the Holy Spirit. The person who suppresses the truth intentionally close his eye to the apparent evidence. He shut his mental faculty to rationalise the simple reasons. By closing his eye and shutting his mind, he has willingly bolted his heart leaving no room for conviction.

## Evidentialism is Apologetics Per Se

Christian evidentialism is intrinsically apologetics. Let us take cognizance that Christian apologetics is of central importance to modern evangelicalism witnessing. It is an integral part of that program of evangelism. One of the major tasks of evangelicals is to proclaim the gospel effectively and faithfully. To take seriously the Great Commission to "*make disciples of all the nations*" (Matthew 28:19) is to commit oneself to all that he or she can humanly do to ensure that the gospel is preached clearly and cogently.[48] Some argue that apologetics is a kind of pre-evangelism, some-

---

[48]   McGrath, Alister E. 'Evangelical Apologetics', *Bibliotheca Sacra* 155 (January-March 1998), 3-10 at p. 4.

thing that lays the groundwork for evangelism at a later stage. McGrath illustratively and logically explains:

> If evangelism is defined as "inviting someone to become a Christian," then apologetics is clearing the ground for that invitation, so that it is more likely to receive a positive response. Evangelism may be likened to offering someone bread, and apologetics may be thought of as persuading people that bread is available and that it is good to eat. Apologetics stresses the reasonableness and attractiveness of the Christian faith; evangelism makes the offer of that faith ... Apologetics is nonconfrontational; it is not threatening. But evangelism is confrontational, for it asks individuals to consider whether they are ready to take the step of faith—a step for which apologetics has prepared the way.[49]

However, the task of evangelism is *making disciples ... and teaching them to observe* as understood by us in Matthew 28:19 - 20. This also means taking the trouble to clarify central Christian ideas to people who may recognize the words but not the reality they represent words such as "grace" and "redemption" often come easily from the lips of Christian workers. Equally important, it includes effectively explaining and justifying the great themes of the gospel to our unchurched friends. So, if evangelism is a process of explaining, disciplining and teaching *them to observe all things* (v. 20) that Jesus commanded, from unbelief to conviction, from conviction to belief; and from belief to commitment – then apologetics is also a process – a continuous integral task in the work of evangelism and discipleship – in defending the tenets of the Christian faith, with appropriate explanation, reasoning and if necessary, evidence.

Taking evangelism aside, apologetics is by virtue defined as the task of defending the claims of Christianity. All students of apologetics knows that "apologetics" is a branch of theology by which the word itself derived from the Greek word 'apologia' (ἀπολογία) found in 1 Peter 3:15, which means 'defend' or 'a reason for doing or believing something'. The Greek term is a combination of two words, *apo* (ἀπο) and *logia* (λογία) similarly to logos, for 'logic' or 'word'. It is a vivid commandment from the Scripture that we should always be ready to make a defense (apologia) everyone who ask to give an account for the hope that is in us (1 Peter 3:15). The hope that is in us encompasses all the things we believe in Christ. The command that we must always be ready means we shall al-

---

49    Ibid., 5 & 6.

ways be prepared as though we are defending in a court of law.[50] This invites a reference to be equipped with evidence and proper explanation to give an account of our Christian faith. 'Everyone' includes the believers who want to know more of our hope in the many doctrines we adhere to as Christians and to the non-believers who may be seeking for the truth or challenging our hope. So, the task of apologetics requires the espousal of reason and evidence during evangelism and discipleship. One wonders why some cannot comprehend this very basic theory of epistemology – evidentialism is part and parcel of bringing the knowledge of Jesus, the God incarnate and the claims of Christianity whilst fulfilling the work of apologetics as commanded in 1 Peter 3:15.

There is no perfect way in practising apologetics during evangelism. However, there are erroneous apologetics methods that almost instantaneously drive non-believers away at first acquaintance. It expect others to presuppose the truth as they presupposes it. They expect the atheists to presuppose that the theists is right and the atheistic view is wrong, before facts are deduced. Thus, instead evangelism is to draw others nearer to the truth claim of Christianity, its presuppositional apologists are viewed as religious bigots or even self-righteous at the first instance of Christian witness. This is risky way of apologetics which should be totally avoided.

Evidentialism is neither perfect nor the only methodology. It embraces even the classical apologetics' strength of natural theology. They do appreciate philosophical pragmatism and that sometimes the 'moral force' exerted by God to gravity in the sense that both were forces about which humans knew little but which pervaded their lives.[51] These psychological consequences can be a contributing circumstantial evidence for the theistic evidentialists. When they evangelise, they do not ask others to presuppose their claims are right, but do take note of the psychological make-up of an individual person. Sometimes, these individuals do not need any rational cogency and the pragmatic truth of the Higher Power was incontrovertible. Faith worked, that which was useful and "works" was true, and the fact that faith worked was evidence that it tapped into something truly extant.[52] Yet, evidentialist whilst they also

---

50   'Apologia' is the word originally used in the Greek court system referring to a defendant's reply to the accusation of the prosecution.

51   Anonymous in California, "Not My Weak Will But A Greater Power," The Grapevine (February 1968), 14-17.

52   Muravchik, Stephanie. "American Protestantism in the Age of Psychology" (New York: Cambridge University Press, 2011) 131.

apply the way that is savvy to postmodern realities, they do so without capitulating to postmodern philosophies.[53] Evangelism must not only appeal to the postmodernist heart, but also appeal to the mind, avoiding subjectivism to be exploited by other mystical religions.

Yet rightly concluded, Edward John Carnell wrote:

> "... since apologetics is an art and not a science, there is no 'official' way to go about defending the Christian faith. The defense must answer the spirit of the times."[54]

Truly, Christian evidentialism is eclectic, practical and open-mindedness. It embraces all relevant evidence and consideration during evangelism, giving the best effect. In summary, when one is defending something or a claim, he or she will certainly set out the grounds to establish the truth of that claim. These grounds can be provided in a form of proofs, rational argument or sensory perception – which we call it evidence that can convince. The fact apologetics is a task to defend by using evidences, we can conclude the task of apologetics is evidential. The terms and the function of these two may synonymously correspond to each other i.e. Christian apologetics is evidentialism and evidentialism is Christian apologetics. Anything that is not applying the function of evidence is not Christian apologetics.

## Conclusion

The above describes the position of Christian evidentialism, a milder version from the atheistic evidentialism. Agreeing with classical apologists, the apologetical evidentialism in this book characterized the witness of the Holy Spirit as self-authenticating. Such religious experience is veridical and the person who experience it does not need supplementary arguments or evidence in order for him to know. However, only a few has that privilege of such inner experience. Man is inquisitive by nature and he requires some sort of rationalisation either base on reasons or evidence to decide a particular truth claim. This is where it depart from presuppositionalist and reformed epistemologist in terms of religious belief. We shall conclude this chapter in defending evidentialism as fundamen-

[53]   Groothuis, Douglas. "*Truth Decay: Defending Christianity Against the Challenges of Postmodernism*" (Leicester: Inter-Varsity Press, 2000) 140.

[54]   Carnell, E.J. "*Christian Commitment: An Apologetic*" (New York: MacMillan, 1957), p. vii quoted in Groothuis, D., *Truth Decay: Defending Christianity Against the Challenges of Postmodernism*, 139.

tal tool for the task of apologetics and evangelism. However, we shall continue to point out sporadically some of the inconsistencies of these two apologetics schools as we go along analysing legal apologetics and the narratives in the Gospel of John.

# CHAPTER 2

## Principles of the Law of Evidence and Legal Apologetics

This is a transitional chapter moving from understanding the value of apologetic evidentialism to its specific branch we called it 'legal apologetics'. In order to appreciate legal apologetics, this chapter steer you through a brief comprehension of the basic principles of the law of evidence as practised in most western legal jurisdiction. We will also discuss the similar concerns of the legal system and legal apologetics. We will appreciate why the law of evidence are applied by legal apologists as a flexible principle rather than as a rigid rule of evidence. In the next chapter, we'll see how this legal science of evidence can be applied in apologetics as one viable theory of knowledge and source of religious epistemology to defend our Christian faith. Thereon in the last two chapters, we will see how the apostle John had intentionally utilised the value of evidence and rationality to bring about belief in the Son of God but unconsciously applied a modern legal method. Thus, this widely accepted principles of the law of evidence as employed by the judges to assess the admissibility of evidences tendered during a court trial corresponds the systematic introduction of evidences and arguments in the fourth Gospel. This serve as an appropriate practical biblical example for the right methodology of apologetics.

Christian evidentialists agree it is imperative to engage methods modeled on those of disciplines other than Christian theology or apologetics, so that non-Christians can also understand and appreciate the validity of the arguments. As John Warwick Montgomery puts it plainly, "*It is time that Christian apologetics came to realize that a string of individually weak arguments for the gospel does not comprise one strong arguments for it. Objective empirical evidence for Jesus Christ and his message is the only truly valid Christian apologetic possible, for it alone is subject to the canons of evidence employed in other fields of endeavor.*"[55]

Indeed the objective empirical ground for accepting the Christian gospel should be equally understood by the non-Christians and one may

---

[55] Montgomery, John Warwick. "*How Muslims Do Apologetics: The Apologetic Approach of Muhammad Ali and Its Implications for Christian Apologetics,*" in Faith Founded on Fact, (Newburgh, Indiana, Trinity Press, 1978) 98.

need a firm but easily understood evidences to be convinced. Instead of Christian theological jargons, a more universally accepted principles for finding truth should be applied. Like the ones we read in the newspaper or the criminal series we watch on TV, the jargons and principles of legal evidence may be more tolerable and understood by the common people. Paranormal activities or mystical experiences are neither objective empirical arguments nor strong probative force which are usually not subject to the canons of evidence as employed in the court of law. Subjective in nature, they are risky evidence similar to those advocated by the fideistic apologists. Principles of the law of evidence ensures a highly probable mode of objective inquiry of empirical evidences. It demands a verdict which can be comprehended by most reasonable persons, rather than subjective religious testimony which can only be appreciated by the individual testifier himself.

Since the writer of this book is trained under the English legal system and as the Commonwealth (including United States of America) legal jurisdiction originated from the British common law, most (if not all) the statutory provisions and case laws are mostly quoted from the UK law[56]. The aim of chapters two and three are to provide a systematic, though not comprehensive as needed by trial lawyers, but a concise analysis of how facts are proved in criminal trials. That does not in any way diminish its value to professional lawyers whose interest are also in apologetics, but emphasizes the importance of the subject-matter to those 'laymen' seeking to grasp the nitty-gritty of the legal principles of evidence. That includes those potential apologists whose inclination is leaning towards evidentialism, in particular legal apologetics. We shall begin with the definition and the overall task of the legal principles of evidence.

## What is Law of Evidence and Its Advantages to Apologetics?

Criminal law reformer, writer and judge, Sir James Fitzjames Stephen (1829 – 1894)[57] is no stranger to many serious law students of evidence. Though written in the 19th century, his concern of the usage of the word 'evidence' expressed in the Indian Evidence Act 1872 is worth quoting here:

---

[56]  Unless otherwise stated.
[57]  Sir JF Stephen was the leading codifier of criminal law and drafted the Indian Evidence Act 1872. He was appointed judge of the Queen's Bench Division in 1879.

The ambiguity of the word 'evidence' is the cause of great deal of obscurity ... In scientific inquiries, and for popular and general purposes, it is no doubt convenient to have one word which includes:
(1) the testimony on which a given fact is believed
(2) the facts so believed, and
(3) the arguments founded upon them.
For instance, in the title of *Paley's Evidences of Christianity*, the word is used in this sense. The nature of the work was not such as to give much importance to the distinction which the word overlooks. So, in scientific inquiries, it is seldom necessary ... to lay stress upon the difference between the testimony on which a fact is believed, and the fact itself. In judicial inquiries, however, the distinction is most important, and the neglect to observe it has thrown the whole subject into confusion by causing English lawyers to overlook the leading distinction which ought to form the principle on which the whole law should be classified. I mean the distinction between the relevancy of facts and the mode of proving relevant facts.

The use of the one name 'evidence' for the fact to be proved, and the means by which it is to be proved, has given a double meaning to every phrase in the which the word occurs. Thus, for instance, the phrase 'primary evidence' sometimes means a relevant fact, and sometimes the original of the document as opposed to a copy. 'Circumstantial evidence' is opposed to 'direct evidence'. But 'circumstantial evidence' usually means a fact, from which some other fact is inferred whereas 'direct evidence' means testimony given by a man as to what he has himself perceived by his own senses. It would thus be correct to say that circumstantial evidence must be proved by direct evidence – a clumsy mode of expression, which is in itself a mark of confusion of thought.[58]

Apologists, especially of the evidentialist school diligently seek convincing evidences sourcing from different spheres and arguments. However, we have to be careful as the word 'evidence' can be used in different ways, purpose, and what 'evidence' refers to will depend on how it is used in any particular context. Presuppositionalists may view evidence as an alternative to the inner conviction of the Holy Spirit and hence the probative value it gives are extremely low. The classical apologist may view any rational argument as an evidence – may refer to a relationship of relevancy between a particular fact of intellectual reasoning and the fact that had ultimately to be proved. Evidentialists may view evidence as a direct data or circumstantial facts that can be inductively or deductively assessed leading to a conclusion. Legal apologists embraced all views but subject to the principles of evidence as adopted by the courts.

---

[58]    Stephen, *Indian Evidence Act 1872*, pp. 6-7.

The word evidence would depends on the law which governs the admissibility of a testimony or a real evidence (e.g. a document, blood stained shroud, tombstone, etc.). Subsequently, assessment of these admissible evidences after being contested by other defeating evidences presented by the opposing party would establish the degree of its reliability and probative value.

What constitute 'evidence' depends on the classification and the admissibility. A satisfactory argument for admissibility which relies on classification requires that the lawyers (and the legal apologists) to make clear what he refers to by his use of a particular classifications, why he says that the disputed item of testimony falls within it and why it follows that the disputed item should be admitted. In practice it will be found that perfectly good arguments for admissibility can be constructed by relying on the function of an item of contested evidence.[59]

This is the evidence based on the legal principles we are talking about and not any mere classification of evidence from other fields. It must entail a strong probative force. It cannot be a mere hunch, conjecture, guesswork, theories, hypothesis, inexpert opinion, speculations, preconceived notion or presupposition and most commonly heard of in the media, unverified rumour. This is the distinction between scientific or other inquiries and judicial inquiries.

Hence, one has to critically identify how he himself or others define and classify 'evidence' and to observe carefully how any term which seems to belong to such a classification is used when it appears in any literature, speech or other evidence text. Particular care should be taken to avoid what may be called the fallacy of justification by labelling. Not all evidences are evidence. Not all definitions or perspectives on a piece of evidence are identically viewed and comprehended by everybody. Definitely not its probative force if the classification of evidence are not generally accepted and agreed upon as the principles of law of evidence.

## Judicial Principles has Its Flexibility

Let us digress slightly before we list down the most common judicial principles of evidence. In the next few paragraphs, we'll discuss briefly on the legal reasoning between rules and principles. It is the principles of evidence that the legal apologists are more concern of rather than the rules of evidence. When a legal apologist refers to the law of evidence, he

---

[59] Allen, Christopher. *"Basic Concepts"* Chapter 1 of Allen, C., Sourcebook on Evidence (London: Routledge Cavendish, 1996), 2 – 3.

is referring to the principles more than the rules. Anyway, most rules legislated by the law makers were to a large extent based on the accepted principles. It is the important features of the principles rather than the strict rules we are adopting. Basically, the rules are rigid but the principles are flexible. Professor Cass Sunstein[60] illustrates:

> "... judges and ... others who design legal requirements, including legislators, administrators, and ordinary citizens – have a complex and ambivalent attitude toward rules. Certainly they do not oppose rules as a general matter. Of course people engaged in legal reasoning (*or truth-seeking*) have no rule against rules. Judges understand that rules help people to plan their affairs (*or help apologists to strategize their methodology*). They understand that rules can constrain official arbitrariness, discrimination, and caprice. But rules may misfire, precisely because they are too rigid and because they are laid down in advance; they can go badly wrong when applied to concrete cases not anticipated when the rule was set down. Does a 60 mile-per-hour speed limit ban an ambulance from rushing to the hospital, or a police officer from driving as fast as he must to apprehend a fleeing suspect? In some cases, the general rule may be far too general to work well; and there may lie, in this example and in this possibility, a pervasive concerns about using rules to order diverse human affairs. Much of legal reasoning reflects this concern."[61]

There should be a balance between strict rules and principles. There are exceptions in most general rules. We are not preaching situational ethics here but to accept the fact there are diverse human affairs. Apologetics covers the area of religious epistemology. Therefore, due to diverse cultures and level of comprehension, one needs to be aware that there is no one absolute method in presenting or persuading the Christian theistic truth. If a Christian apologist adopts the rule set down in advance by the presuppositionalists that one must compulsorily presuppose the existence of God first and approach his target audiences from diverse understanding and epistemological inclination, it can go badly wrong. Principles will guide an apologists to appreciate that there are exceptions. We agree with the presuppositionalists that the minds of man are depraved

---

[60]  Dr. Cass R, Sunstein is Karl N. Llewellyn distinguished Service Professor of Jurisprudence at the University of Chicago. He is one of America's best known commentators on the legal system, often arguing that the courts best enable people to live together, despite their diversity, by resolving particular cases without taking sides in broader more abstract conflicts.

[61]  Sunstein, C. R. "*Legal Reasoning and Political Conflict*" (New York: Oxford University Press, 1996), viii. [Emphasis are mine].

due to original sin but not totally depraved. In fact, there is a diverse degree of depravity, some are influenced by their culture, background, education, upbringing, environment, DNA and many are intentionally self-imposed depravity through their stubbornness in supressing the truth. Each individual has its own cognitive sensitivity.

Even if the Reformed Epistemologist is right in regards to *sensus divinitatis*, the sinful nature and the adverse influence of the world has diluted each person's capacity to immediately infer the existence of God from general revelation. It does not totally diminishes the mind but it leaves different individual with different degrees of insensitivity to the truth of God. This is where the tools of rationality and evidence are able to quicken their mind and thus causes the heart to be more 'sensible' or to a higher level of *sensus divinitatis*. However, agreeing with William Lane Craig, I am quite sceptical that any *sensus divinitatis* exists because there is "no scriptural warrant for such a *sensus divinitatis*, whereas there is a wide biblical support for a *testimonium Spiritu sancti internum*. In the absence of any scriptural support for such an inner instinct, I do not know how one could justify its existence, since the witness and work of the Holy Spirit serve to explain any phenomenon of religious experience that one might think to explain by the *sensus divinitatis*."[62] Taking the analogy from the comparison between legal rules and principles, Reformed Epistemologists seems to place a rigid rule that all man has the basic belief and thus evidence is not a necessary condition. Like believing that other minds exist, there are no exceptions to this absolute rule – in other words there is no need for inquiry to any person of whatever degree of faith or doubt. It is the position of Reformed Epistemology[63] that belief in God, like belief in other person, does not require the support of evidence or argument in

---

[62] William Lane Craig's response to Kelly James Clark's Reformed Epistemology in Cowan, S. B., *Five Views on Apologetics*, (Grand Rapids, Michigan: Zondervan Publishing House, 2000), 285 -286.

[63] This view has been made popular by prominent philosophers, including Alvin Plantinga. He is the first contemporary defender of this apologetic methodology, and his home institution, Calvin College, supported the research of other prominent philosophers in its development, including William Alston, George Mavrodes and Nicholas Wolterstorff. For a more vivid understanding of Reformed Epistemology, see Plantinga, A. and Nicholas Wolterstorff. *"Faith and Rationality: Reason and Belief in God"* (Notre Dame, Indiana: University of Notre Dame Press, 1983).

order to be rational.[64] Reformed Epistemology's warrant of belief gives no room for different degree of cognitive sensitivity and mental capability to comprehend. It is not as flexible as the evidentialist.

William Lane Craig defend the role of argument and evidence, basically because everybody has different level of inquiry and cognitive sensitivity to general revelation, and not everybody has the same basic belief:

> ... One school of thought interprets passages like Romans 1:19-20 to sanction natural theology by teaching that from the created order all persons are responsible for inferring the existence of the divine Creator. But an opposing school of thought regards the created order as the context that serves to ground belief in the Creator as properly basic. I think that the arguments of natural theology are not identical with general revelation; general revelation is the traits of the author reflected in his product, the fingerprints of the potter in the clay, so to speak, whereas the arguments of natural theology are the human products of men's rational reflection upon general revelation. That fact does not, however, settle the question whether the created order serves as the basis for inferring the Creator's existence or constitutes the circumstances in which belief in a Creator is properly basic.
>
> It might be thought that Paul's saying that men are "without excuse" for not believing in God favors the basic belief interpretation, since all men could not be held to be without excuse for failing to hold to an inference, whereas they could be held responsible for a belief that is properly basic for all men. But this is to confuse proper basicality with degree of belief. As Mavrodes reminds us, an inferred proposition can be as deeply and irrefragably believed as a basic belief, and many properly basic beliefs may be lightly and defeasibly held. The defender of natural theology could plausibly maintain that the inference from creation to Creator is so evident at any level of inquiry, from the observations of the primitive savage to the investigations of the scientist, that the nontheist is inexcusable in failing to draw this inference.[65]

In addition, it is clearly evident throughout the New Testament that proving the Christian faith to be true was a frequent endeavour in which both Jesus and the apostles were engaged. If *sensus divinitatis* or the philosophy on basic belief were true, there is no need for Jesus or the apos-

64  Clark, K.J., *"Reformed Epistemology Apologetics"* in 'Five Views on Apologetics,' edited by Steven Cowan (Grand Rapids, Michigan: Zondervan Publishing House, 2000), 267.
65  Craig, William L., *Classical Apologetics* in Steven Cowan (ed.), 'Five Views on Apologetics,' 39.

tles to put any effort in rationalising or providing evidences such as miracles, healing, exorcism, appealing to fulfilled prophecies or resurrection. The apologists' task is to help the seeker in his search for the truth of God. Taking cognisance that man has various capacity to acquire facts and different aptitude in drawing inferences, rules of deduction and induction are developed. Yet the legal system acknowledges the importance of the principles for exceptions to the rigidity of rules. Legal reasoning reflects this concern, so is legal apologetics.

We are living in a real world where there is no one rule to represent a single religious epistemology. Apologetics is very similar with the legal system of truth-seeking in our real imperfect world. Legal institutions consist of many people. Courts are run by imperfect human being. Judges have no scale. Similarly, far from having a scale, the facilitator in the truth-seeking process must operate in the face of a particular kind of social heterogeneity: sharp and often intractable disagreements on matters of basic principles. This is the fact of life and to adopt mysterious, superstitious, non-objective presuppositions do not alleviate the existing explicit religious and philosophical disagreements. Are we moving away from the Scriptures? By all means, no! In the next few chapters, we shall see examples that even the apostles understood this problem and had never discard evidence and rationality completely. None of them applied just one basic rule but in fact relying on flexible principles, depending on who were their target audience. Even their writings has a flavour of evidentialism. Strongly relying on the guidance of the Holy Spirit, the apostles are aware that they are not perfect and neither are their highly diverse audience.

Courts consist of highly diverse people, who have a weak democratic pedigree and limited fact-finding capacity, and who must render many decisions, live together, avoid error to the extent possible, and show respect to each other, to the people who come before them, and to those affected by their decisions. Incomplete theorized agreements are an appropriate response to this situation.[66]

We shall not delve deep into the realm of legal philosophy. However, in general, incomplete theorized agreements plays a pervasive role in law and society. Taking Professor Sunstein's political explanation as an analogy to apologetics, he says that *"it is quite rare for a person or group completely to theorize any subject, that is, to accept both a general theory and a series of steps connecting the theory to concrete conclusions. Thus we often have in law an incomplete theorized agreements on a general principle - incompletely theo-*

---

[66]    Sunstein, C. R., *Legal Reasoning and Political Conflict*, 6.

*rized in the sense that people who accept the principle need not agree on what it entails in particular cases."*[67] Correspondingly, we need not impose a complete theorized methodology, insisting everybody to agree on. However, we strive to have everybody agree on the general accepted principles of acquiring knowledge and yet need not agree on the definite conclusions. An incomplete theorized agreements is much more flexible and friendly as long there is a meeting of the minds, at least a point of contact to start off the search for an answer.

This is the great advantage of the application of judicial principles of evidence in apologetics - its flexibility. It does not mean anything goes or any facts can be admissible. Here it means that legal apologetics, similar to judicial principles of evidence are not rigid in the sense subject to the substantive law. Similar to the judicial principles of evidence, evidential apologetics is a principle-based approach. Classical apologetics method seems to be a ruled-based approach. It has more rigid rules than evidentialism in regards to its steps of proving. Classical apologetics has an artificial rules of procedures which actually are unnecessary to most 'not so philosophically trained' laymen. First, the apologist approaches the person being addressed from first principles, such as the laws of logic or the fact of one's own existence. With this established, then the various theistic arguments for God's existence are given. The third step, building on the first two, is to demonstrate that certain empirical or historical evidences may be proved regarding matters such as the truthfulness of Scripture, miracles, or the resurrection of Christ.[68] This rigid process of proof are only appreciated by the academia of philosophy and not to those who already believe there is a supernatural Being or those who already presupposed that truth is knowable. As for evidentialist, only the fact in issue are utmost important to be substantiated. Just like in a trial, unnecessary areas which are not the fact in issues are not to be proven and even its evidence may seem relevant are not admissible.

Presuppositional apologetics on the other hand has a non-negotiable starting point. They assumes that people have certain presuppositions in which they base their beliefs. Strictly, presuppositionalists are so rigid as though they are under a substantive rule that has no exceptions. They began with a complete theorized agreement – actually an agreement they imposed on others. The presuppositionalists begin by the assumption that there is no possibility of common ground between the believer and

---

[67]   Sunstein, 35.
[68]   House, Wayne H. & Dennis W. Jowers. *"Reasons for Our Hope: An Introduction to Christian Apologetics"* (Nashville, Tennessee: B&H Academic, 2011), 39.

the unbeliever. Even if their target audience agree with them to presuppose an existing God, it does not guarantee it entails belief. Evidentialism has most of the advantages of objectivity and flexibility of the judicial principles, thus allowing us to shift any evidential emphasis as a system of rules to a body of principles.[69] Evidential flexibility is important as long it can play the influential part in persuading the decision maker. JH Wigmore's reasoning is applied here:

> The study of the principles of evidence, for a lawyer, falls into two distinct parts. One is proof in the general sense – the part concerned with the ratiocinative process of contentious persuasion – mind to mind, counsel to judge or juror, each partisan seeking to move the mind of the tribunal. The other part is admissibility – the procedural rules devised by the law, and based on litigious experience and tradition, to guard the tribunal (particularly the jury) against erroneous persuasion. Hitherto, the latter has loomed largest in our formal studies – has in fact, monopolized them; while the former, virtually ignored, has been left to the chances of later acquisition, casual and empiric, in the course of practice.
>
> Here we have been wrong; and in two ways:
>
> For one thing, there is, and there must be, a probative science – the principles of proof – independent of the artificial rules of procedure; hence, it can be and should be studied. This science to be sure, may as yet be imperfectly formulated. But all the more need is there to begin in earnest to investigate and develop it. Furthermore, this process of proof represents the objective in every judicial investigation. The procedural rules for admissibility are merely preliminary aid to the main activity, *viz* the persuasion of the tribunal's mind to a correct conclusion by safe materials. This main process is that for which the jury are there, and on which the counsel's duty is focused.
>
> And, for another thing, the judicial rules of admissibility are destined to lessen in relative importance during the next period of development. Proof will assume the important place; and we must therefore prepare ourselves for this shifting of emphasis.[70]

Following Wigmore's explanation, Christopher Allen summarizes the advantages of a principle-based evidence law:

---

[69]   For a presuppositional response to the advantages of evidences, see Whitcomb Jr., J.C. "Contemporary Apologetics and the Christian Faith, Part IV: The Limitations and Values of Christian Evidences" *Bibliotheca Sacra* 135 (1978), 25 – 33.

[70]   Wigmore, J.H., *The Judicial Principles of Judicial Proof* (1931, 2nd edn.) pp. 3-4 quoted in Allen, Christopher, 'Basic Concepts' Chapter 1 of Allen, C., *Sourcebook on Evidence* (London: Routledge Cavendish, 1996), 6.

> The distinction between a rule-based and a principle-based approach to law is important because it governs the form which arguments about admissibility should take. If a part of evidence law is seen as being rule-based there will be less room for manoeuvre because argument will tend to be founded on the wording of statutes or on decisions in precious cases which may seem as binding. By contrast, where part of evidence law is seen as not being rule-based, but based on principle, there will be more room for manoeuvre in its application ... a good advocate will be able to see which approach is more likely to be useful and to develop an argument accordingly.[71]

True enough, legal apologetics' aim is to identify which is a more useful approach and thereon develop the argument accordingly which fits best for the target audience at the appropriate time with the best possible persuasion. This provides more room for manoeuvre in its application of principles in the task of *apologia*. Without subjecting to any procedures or compulsory deductive methods or presuppositions, evidentialist seeks to demonstrate God's existence, and other claims inductively, and not in any particular order or rational relationship. The evidential apologists have more room for manoeuvre in his application of reasons, evidence or even the Scriptures – flexibly depending on what the concern, issue or question of the potential convert might be.

Indeed, evidential apologetics has all the flexible characteristics of the judicial principles, as oppose to legal rules. A suitable quotation here on the reasoning for having the characteristics of principles rather than legal rules is taken from one of the renowned American legal philosopher, Ronald Dworkin:

> The difference between legal principles and legal rules is a logical distinction. Both sets of standards point to a particular decision about legal obligations in particular circumstances, but they differ in the character of the direction they give. Rules are applicable in an all or nothing fashion. If the facts a rule stipulates are given, then either the rule is valid, in which case the answer it supplies must be accepted or it is not, in which case it contributes nothing to the decision...
>
> This all or nothing is seen mostly plainly if we look at the way rules operate, not in law, but in some enterprise they dominate – a game, for example. In a baseball a rule provides that if a batter has had three strikes, he is out. An official cannot consistently acknowledge that this is an accurate statement of a baseball rule, and decide that a batter who has had three strikes is not out...

---

[71]    Allen, C., *Basic Concepts*, 6.

If we take baseball rules as a model, we find that the rules of law, like the rule that a will is invalid unless signed by three witnesses, fit the model well. If the requirement of three witnesses is a valid legal rule, then it cannot be that a will has been signed by only two witnesses and is valid. The rule might have exceptions, but if it does it is inaccurate and incomplete to state the rule so simply, without enumerating the exceptions. In theory, at least, the exceptions could all be listed, and the more of them that are, the more complete is the statement of the rule.

But this is not the way ... principles ... operate. Even those which look most like rules do not set out legal consequences that follows automatically when the conditions provided are met.

... when we say that a particular principle is a principle of our law, is that the principle is one which officials must take into account, if it is relevant, as a consideration inclining in one direction or another ...

Principles have a dimension that rules do not – the dimension of weight or importance. When principles intersect ... one who must resolve the conflict has to take into account the relative weight of each. This cannot be, of course, an exact measurement, and the judgment that a particular principle or policy is more important than another will often be a controversial one. Nevertheless, it is an integral part of the concept of a principle that it has this dimension, that it makes sense to ask how important or how weighty it is.

Rules do not have this dimension. We can speak of rules as being *functionally* important or unimportant (the baseball rule that three strikes are out is more important than the rule that runners may advance on a bulk, because the game would be much more changed with the first rule altered than the second). In this sense, one legal rule may be more important than another because it has a greater or more important role in regulating behaviour. But we cannot say that one rule is more important than another within the system of rules, so that when two rules conflict one supersedes the other by virtue of its greater weight. If two rules conflict, one of them cannot be valid. The decision as to which is valid, and which must be abandoned or recast, must be made by appealing to considerations beyond the rules themselves. A legal system might regulate such conflict by other rules, which prefer the rule enacted by the higher authority or the rule enacted later, or the more specific rule, or something of that sort. A legal system may also prefer the rule supported by the more important principles. (Our own legal system uses both of these techniques).[72]

---

[72]   Dworkin, Ronald. M. "*Is Law a System of Rules?*" in 'The Philosophy of Law' edited by Ronald Dworkin, [Oxford Readings in Philosophy] (New York: Oxford University Press, 1977) 45 – 49.

Similarly, evidentialism and in particular legal apologetics are not rigidly subject to rules of strict epistemology. It is more practicable. When we say legal apologetics is to an extent the application of the principles of the law of evidence, we meant the flexible characteristics of the *principles* as understood by the legal system, rather than subject to the substantive law per se.

It is the principles and not the law of evidence. We have to be clear that it does not mean our apologetic methods have to follow the statutory provisions passed by Parliament consisting of fallible legislatures. Hence, the legal apologetics have all the advantages of the principles and the moral aim in seeking for the truth. So, it has no legal obligation or legal duties as the legal rules stipulates. Rules operates in an all or nothing fashion.

Although general rules do have exceptions, it is due to the principles of justice, we have these exceptions. The operation of principles on the other hand has a different dimension. For example, as described above, the dimension of weight or importance. As in evidences tendered in court, the ground we based on to believe in God too has a dimension of weight and degree. The amount of one's faith, his rationality, logic, reasoning or evidences cannot be quantified. It depends on each individual on the level of importance and the weight one perceives. Presuppositional apologetics seems to operate in an all or nothing fashion. Their dogmatic hypothesis, "I believe, therefore I understand" has this strong connotation that if you don't believe, you failed the rules of the starting point. If you don't presuppose, is *void ab initio*. In other words, your argument is faulty even from the beginning, if your foundational hypothesis is not the same as theirs.

Such breach of this rigid obligation is considered by them as a total failure to be able to further understand the Word or comprehend whatever Christian reasoning. To them if one begin his starting point from man's understanding, is like a conflict of two rules – which to the presuppositionalist, one of the conflicting rules cannot be valid.

However, in our legal perspective of what *principles* meant, the legal apologists take the flexible stance. If there are conflicting philosophical rules or even principles of logic, we take the principles that guide us to a more practicable and acceptable path understood by both the Christians and the non-Christians. When principles intersect, legal apologists must resolve the conflict and take into account the relative weight of each evidence. We acknowledge that there is no exact measurement, or any judgment that a particular principle or policy is more important than another. This will often be a controversial one. Nevertheless, it is an integral part of the concept of a principle that it has this flexible dimension, that it makes sense to ask how important or how weighty it is. This will eventually play the important role of persuading our target audience to appreciate the evidence and reasons put forth, without setting a presumptuous rule that the Christian theism is prima facie the ultimate truth until proven otherwise. Such rigidity will terminate any discussion from the very beginning.

Once we understood the flexible characteristics of this judicial principle (as oppose to legal rules), it would be apt for us to comprehend the primary conceptual building blocks of evidence scholarship and trial practice which is employed into the more complex evidentiary rules, doctrines, and principles. Most of it can be incorporated into legal apologetics as a better means of religious epistemology. We shall now move on to the most important basic concept of the principles of the law of evidence – relevancy and admissibility in fact-finding.

## The Basic Concept of Fact-Finding: Admissibility of Relevant Evidence

When presenting argument by way of reasoning or evidence, the Christian apologists (like lawyers) will decide the best possible facts to be tendered, either positively to prove or negatively to disprove a fact presented by the opposing parties. The whole process of the right fact-finding would depend on whether the evidence or reasoning are relevant and admissible. These two is the core concepts within the definition of the Law of Evidence.

Professor Adrian Keane begins his introduction on the law of evidence in his book:

> Evidence is information by which facts tend to be proved, and the law of evidence is that body of law and discretion regulating the means by which facts may be proved in both courts of law and tribunals and arbitrations in which the strict rules of evidence apply. It is adjectival rather than subjective law and overlaps with procedural law. At the risk of over simplification, the broad governing principle underlying the English law of evidence can be stated in no more than nine words: all relevant evidence is admissible, subject to the exceptions.[73]

---

[73]    Keane, Adrian. "*The Modern Law of Evidence*" (Oxford: Oxford University Press, 6th ed., 2006), 1.

Resembling Christian evidentialism, the legal principles of evidence embraces all evidences as long they are relevant. Only relevant rational arguments and evidences are allowed to be tendered in court and assessed by the judge and/or jury. The body of law regulating developed through legislations and judicial precedents set forth the principles for the judge to decide which evidences and arguments are admissible or inadmissible. This would sieve out the relevant data from the irrelevant ones. Obviously, the relevant facts are argued rationally to constitute it as the evidence. On the other hand, one should note that there are evidences which are considered as evidence merely on its face value but yet not admissible due to either their irrelevancy or may lead to confusion, biasness, and prejudice or very low in probative value. For example, an accused's confession obtained during interrogation in the police station may be seen as relevant in the eyes of the prosecutor but the mode (if not according to the standard operation procedure) in extracting the confession may imply that piece of confession note is dubious.

Hence, though it may be relevant but there are rules of justice that persuade the judge to reject such confession. Similarly, legal apologists would sift mystical experiences[74] from the other religious experience, admitting only the more reliable and less risky ones as relevant evidence. It is more likely the 'evidence' claims of experiencing the wolf spirit after indulging in an alcoholic binge should be expunged, considering it to be highly unreliable. Like the illegally obtained confession, the mystical experience was obtained through unreliable source of method i.e. consuming intoxicated drinks. Even though the number of alcoholics are many and have similar experiences, relevant as it seems to be, it should be inadmissible as a grounds to be considered.

The advantage of applying the legal principles of evidence is all dodgy evidences are summarily dismissed before it churn towards irrelevant discourse and misleading justification. Seeking a religious truth is similar to the fact-finding process in court litigation, with proper guidelines and rules of legal epistemology to avoid unreliable deliberation:

"... there is the law of evidence itself, much of which comprises rules which exclude relevant evidence for a variety of different reasons. For examples,

---

[74] *"Mysticism usually assume their words are descriptive, as do their critics and defenders. Thus, the concept of ineffability does not do the logical work that some have hoped for. It does not separate the mystical real, cleanly from other forms of experience. Mysticism cannot provide a unique area of evidence on the basis of which other modes of experience may be summarily ignored."* – Clark, David K. and Norman L. Geisler. *"Apologetics in the New Age: A Christian Critique of Pantheism"* (Grand Rapids: Baker, 1990), 182.

evidence may be insufficiently relevant or of only minimal probative force; it may give rise to a multiplicity of essentially subsidiary issues, which could distract the court from the main issue; it may be insufficiently reliable or too unreliable; its potential for prejudice to the party against whom it is introduced may be out of all proportion to its probative value on behalf of the party introducing it; ... Thus the court may aspire to the ascertainment of the truth, but at the end of the day it must come to a decision and settle the dispute even if the evidence introduced is inadequate or inconclusive."[75]

So, whether it is civil or criminal, all courts engaged in applying the law to facts proved or agreed before them. If the courts has got the wrong or irrelevant facts, then the application of any legal principles, be they sound or unsound, is a waste of time. Similarly, the legal apologist, though embraces all kinds of evidence or theory of knowledge but if enter into an irrelevant issue or considering the wrong facts, much time is wasted. Our *apologia* is pointless and leads to no further persuasion. The canons of the judicial evidential law will enhance the apologist's discernment and skill in filtering the relevant from the irrelevant.

Similar to any court's verdict, after all the relevant evidences are considered, there must be a time to make a decision, either to believe or not to believe. A commitment must be made even there is no such thing as 100% certainty. Faith then must be applied to make a decision. All pronouncement of court's decisions are made upon calculated 'faith' on the legally affirmed certainty of relevant and reliable evidences. That legally affirmed certainty is not 100% certainty but recognised certitude as highly probable, beyond a reasonable doubt source of persuasion.

Aquinas said that *"perfect knowledge requires certitude and this is why we cannot be said to know unless we know what cannot be otherwise."*[76] He meant that a strong decision made must be based on something we are certain of. Geisler confirms that there is no certainty and *"if there is to be certainty, then knowledge must be based ultimately on some principles about which there can be no question."*[77] Aquinas and Geisler here are referring to self-evident knowledge that do not need to be proven, so to avoid the impossible demonstration of infinite regression. Likewise, law of evidence recognises the impossibility of proving the certainty of every relevant evidence

[75]   Keane, A., *The Modern Law of Evidence*, 1-2.
[76]   Aquinas, St. Thomas, *Posterior Analytics*, 1.8 quoted in McDowell, Josh, The New Evidence That Demands A Verdict (Here's Life Publishers, 1999), 599.
[77]   Geisler, Norman L. *"Thomas Aquinas: An Evangelical Appraisal"* (Grand Rapids: Baker, 1991) 71 quoted in McDowell, New Evidence, 599.

leading to the certainty of a verdict. Hence, the law develops the principles on the standard of proof which we will discuss in the next chapter.

When a non-believer asks us to give an account for the hope that is in us, we gently provides our reasons. Often there are times after given a simple explanation of our belief in Christ as Savior and Lord, together with some logical and rational clarification,[78] the non-believer may dispute the facts. In an ideal situation, if we are prepared as commanded in 1 Peter 3:15, extra facts will be given to answer the allegation or facts cast by the non-believers. I guess it would be rude to reply by saying that his mind is depraved (whether totally or partially) and he is not one of the elects. It would be even more unacceptable and confusing if we persuade him to presuppose the truth of our hope otherwise he can never receive the ability to understand.

What normally any apologists, including presuppositionalists and reformed epistemologists should do is to provide more evidences or arguments (if any) to rebut the non-believers' allegations. This seems to be natural response by the opposing party. Any circularity or self-defeating arguments would not seem to be legitimate for the other side. Further, it would be considered unacceptable if the reply is not within the normal comprehension of the common people. Similarly, in any truth and fact finding process, the inquirer probing into those facts would take account of all evidences which are relevant to the dispute. Thereafter, scrutinising all evidences that logically goes to substantiate or refute the existence of those facts would thereby get to the truth of the issue.

In the next chapter, we will delve into more details in regards to the basic evidential concept of relevancy and admissibility. After acquire a foundational understanding of relevancy and admissibility, we can thereon discuss on the several types of evidences, such as hearsay evidence, documentary evidence, circumstantial evidence, expert opinion evidence, real evidence, demonstrative evidence, testimonial evidence, etc. The basic rule is that for all evidences of whatever types to be tendered in court, it must first be considered as relevant and admissible. We shall note some of the examples of Christian apologetics which have apply the principles of the law of evidence, whilst we scrutinise each of the types of evidence.

---

[78]   Say for example, the fact that Old Testament prophesized Jesus' death and resurrection.

# CHAPTER 3

## The Basic Modern Concept of Judicial Principles of Evidence and its Application in Apologetics

The exclusionary ethos of the modern legal principles of evidence are to a very great extent developed from the common law history. A large amount of rules evolved at a time when the adjudicator (jurors, lay justices or judge) of facts adopted a paternalistic and protective attitude, excluding irrelevant evidences, such as bad character evidence, opinion of non-experts and hearsay evidence due to the concern that lay persons might overvalue its weight and significance and credulously treat it as conclusive. It is not uncommon that judges fear there might be a possibility of mistaken evidence or an intentional concoction of evidence by the litigating parties or their witnesses. Hence, the courts developed certain general principles with its exception to assess when to admit and not to admit a witness and any of their testimonies. The dread of manufactured evidence went beyond the exclusion of specific kinds of evidence: it involved excluding a whole class of persons with a pecuniary or proprietary interest in the verdict. Prior to the Criminal Evidence Act 1898, the accused himself and his spouse were considered as not competent witness in all criminal cases to give evidence on oath. Over the years, the principles guiding the admissibility of evidences in court have positively evolved, based on new technology, improvement in investigation, psychology and social research on human behavior.

Statutory reforms had led to new and better law governing the procurement of evidence in court. For example, the Human Rights Act 1988 ensures that the scales cannot be unfairly loaded against the accused. The current principles of evidence have been for hundreds of years constructed through the doctrine of judicial precedent by the courts, but which is subject to periodic alteration by parliamentary mechanics through legislations. Parliament has also rationalized and improved many of the criminal rules. Legislations such as Police and Criminal Evidence Act 1984, Criminal Justice and Public Order Act 1994 have been to rationalize the law relating to corroboration and corroboration warnings. There are many more law reforms that led to statutes being passed by

Parliament to improve the criminal justice system especially in procuring evidences.

However, we are not concern with each and every provisions of these statutes. The above is merely to demonstrate that legal science has always in an evolution of constant development to the existing principles of evidence. In this book, we are more concern with the essentials of the principles. One may observe that these principles have some resemblance of epistemology and can be appropriately applied in apologetics. We shall only deal with the more general principles than any specific rules provided in the statutory provisions. We shall now discuss each of the main principle in turn systematically, beginning with preliminary concepts of admissibility and relevancy. Thereon, we shall see a variety of judicial evidences usually tendered in court.

## Admissibility

As mentioned above, what constitute 'evidence' depends on the classification and the admissibility. As an illustration: Upon assuming the possibility of the discovery of the black box of the Malaysian Boeing 777 MH370[79], the Australian and Malaysian authorities responsible for the search of the missing plane are strongly positive about finding the possible location of the aircraft's final resting place. This is due to the several 'pings' detected. However, some of the Chinese victims' relatives are skeptical and argued that they should not rely merely on 'clues' but on 'evidence'. Are these 'pings' merely 'clues' or 'evidence' or both are of equally the same probative force? Obviously, it really depends on what do they meant by 'clues' and 'evidence' and what is the weightage and relevancy in these two words to consider as sufficient facts to convince. It seems the victims' relatives considered the 'pings' are of very low probative value to be concluded as 'evidence'. Hence, they used the word 'clues'. It is solely a problem of semantics but nevertheless whatever the weightage, it is still an important data for the search team to rely on. Classification of these words are important to make clear what they refer to by their use of a particular classifications, why they say that the 'pings' are merely 'clues' which may have no probative force and why it follows that the 'pings' should be admitted as conclusive evidence that the plane clashes at the

---

[79]   Plane went missing sometime about 1.30 a.m. on March 8th 2014 after taking off Kuala Lumpur International Airport bound for Beijing, China carrying 239 people on board. 'Pings' from the black box has been detected, narrowing the search area in the south Indian Ocean about 1,400 miles northwest from Perth.

location where the 'pings' were detected. This merely serve as an illustration on how one perceive a fact within a particular classifications. This will in turn suggest its relevancy and hence its admissibility in the fact-finding process.

Not all evidences are admissible. Generally all relevant evidences are admissible but one has to first argue which evidence can be considered as relevant. Both doctrines of admissibility and relevancy are intertwined. These two are understood as the very 'basic concepts' of the Law of Evidence. They are the primary conceptual building-blocks of Evidence scholarship and trial practice, which may be employed directly in their own right or incorporated into more complex evidentiary rules, doctrines, and principles.[80]

The admissibility of evidence is a matter of law for the judge. In order for the judge to admit any evidence, it must be of sufficiently relevance to prove or disprove a fact in issue and which is not excluded by the judge, either by reason of an exclusionary rule of evidence or in the exercise of judicial discretion. Paul Roberts and Adrian Zuckerman further clarify:

> The admissibility inquiry can be further broken down into two basic questions that judges must ask themselves in order to determine whether proffered evidence should be admitted or excluded:
> 1. Is the evidence relevant?
> 2. Is the evidence subject to any applicable exclusionary rules?
>
> Lawyers sometimes refer to the judicial 'discretion' to exclude evidence, but this unqualified usage is invariably misleading and usually best avoided. Admissibility standards do vary in the extent to which they call for an exercise of judgment in their application. The mandatory effect of some rules is almost automatic, once the conditions for their application have been found to exist, whilst others leave trial judges with much greater room for manoeuvre in deciding whether to admit or exclude contested evidence. The difference, however, is a matter of degree, inadequately encapsulated by a categorical distinction between rules of admissibility and judicial discretion. Provided that it is understood that rules come in different shapes and sizes, with structures capable of accommodating more or less 'discretionary judgment', there is no need to insist on a further, formal dichotomy of admissibility standards.
>
> It is a cardinal legal principle that only relevant evidence can be admitted at trial. Thus, if the answer to the first question of admissibility is 'no',

---

[80]   Roberts, Paul and Adrian Zuckerman., "*Relevance, Admissibility and Fact-Finding*" Chapter 3 of Criminal Evidence (Oxford: Oxford University Press, 2004), 95.

the evidence is definitively inadmissible: it must be excluded for all purposes, and the admissibility inquiry is concluded. If on the other hand the answer is 'yes, the evidence is relevant', then one may proceed to consider the second question. Evidence can be received in the trial only if this second hurdle to admissibility is also successfully cleared. Relevance is therefore a necessary, but not a sufficient condition, of legal admissibility.[81]

There are a variety of exclusionary rules with different objectives, values and policies to promote. One may perceive it as contradictory that on one hand the law is to seek the truth, whilst on the other hand it deprive the jury from receiving extra facts. The strategy of withholding information from the jury is valid and serve the truth-seeking purpose if certain forms of evidence may have a propensity to misrepresent, mislead, and create confusion or a diversion. For example, hearsay statements or evidence of accused's bad character or previous unconnected conviction should be excluded[82], as not to divert juror's attention from the main issue.

Legal apologists, are like judges, withholding irrelevant information not because to hide the truth as seen to be disadvantage to Christianity, but to enhance accuracy in fact-finding. Sometimes relevant ones are also withhold temporarily as not to mislead or divert or waste precious time until certain points of disputes are clarified or proven. Classical apologists are most aware of this, for example the issue of the existence of God or the truthfulness of the Christian Gospel are shelved aside before solving the philosophical question on knowability of truth. It would be wise that evidences on the historicity of the New Testament and the atheist's argument against ever knowing the certainty or reliability of the New Testament be inadmissible, at least at the preliminary stage of evangelism. This will never be relevant if the initial present dispute is on the nature of truth.

For example, before the theologian asks whether what he has come to know or believe is or is not the truth (i.e. is one's theological and religious beliefs *justified* as being true belief – and thus *knowledge*?), he or she must also ask what is meant by the concept of 'truth,' or 'true.' Is truth a *quality* of a thing? A design nation of the relationship between knowledge of something and what is known? Is truth primarily the result of an activity, such as reason and rationality, or of experience and evidence? Is

---

[81] Roberts, P. and A. Zuckerman, 'Relevance, Admissibility and Fact-Finding', 96 – 97.
[82] Other examples or exclusionary rules – rules of privilege which the main aim of the law is to protect relationships founded on mutual reliance and confidentiality, e.g. bond of trust between husband and wife, or lawyer-client confidentiality.

truth mainly a function of the exercise of a mind or minds? Or is truth mainly subjective and personal? Is truth relative to time, location, and the knower? How can one verify that his or her knowledge and beliefs are true?[83] These are some of the preliminary objections that our skeptical friends may tender. At this junction, relevant evidences on Christian theism need to be withheld until the preliminary issues are cleared. Legal apologists, similar to the judicial role is to discard unhelpful, superfluous, tainted information or immaterial facts so as to clear all preliminary obstacles.

The role of the legal apologetics, like the English law of criminal evidence is to ensure adjudication must be fair as well as accurate, so that even highly probative, reliable, evidence (but only relevant until at its appointed time), may have to be excluded. Fairness must not only be presupposed but must be seen to be done. This is what presuppositionalists fail to appreciate. Our classical apologetic brothers have got it right. Hence, classical apologists are to some extent applying legal apologetics too, or vice versa.

Basically, a judge has to strike a balance between the probative value of evidence and its potential or mischief or (the proper legal jargon) 'prejudice'. Legal apologists have to strike a balance between evidences that are relevant having added value to the present argument, irrespective of its weight, with the evidences that may be prejudice to the ultimate issue i.e. the verdict that Jesus is the only way to salvation. In general, the test of admissibility is that the probative value of admissible evidence must outweigh its prejudicial effect – which for simple expression can be represented by this formula, PV ˃ PE.

## Relevancy

The fact that most of the people in the town I lived in are Christians is good supporting evidence that God's existence is highly likely probable. Is this fact relevant? It is only a fact that many people within the same town believe in God. No reasonable thinking man would accept this as relevant fact to the issue on proving or disproving God. Hence, it is not relevant fact and thus inadmissible. For example, the testimony of the neighbour who heard a woman screaming and a sound similar to gun

---

[83]   House, W. and D. Jowers. *"Reasons for Our Hope: An Introduction to Christian Apologetics"* (Nashville, Tennessee: B&H Academic, 2011), 61.

shot in the night when Oscar Pistorius[84] shot his girlfriend, is relevant. However, one may argue that the video tendered by the prosecution showing Oscar laughing loudly after shooting a watermelon in the firing range is totally irrelevant. It is not relevant because it does not directly relate to the fact in issue i.e. the murder. However, the prosecution may argue that it is relevant only to infer that Oscar possibly enjoyed the impact of the watermelon exploding, describing him as a 'zombie-stopper'. An image to visualise the similar impact of the victim's skull made by Mr Pistorius and his probable response. But, how do a court distinguish or determine which facts are relevant and which are not?

The court can take cognisance that a fact may be relevant to the past, present or future existence of another fact. As in the Pistorius case, the prosecution tendered email and WhatsApp messages from Reeva stating that she is afraid of Oscar – a past existence of fact that may be relevant to establish Oscar's motive and bad character. Similarly, in the case of *R v Nethercott*[85], the first defendant (N) testified in his defence that as a result of threats by the co-defendant (G) and evidence that N feared for his own safety because to the way in which G had acted on previous occasions, therefore N had acted under duress. It was held that evidence of the fact that three months later G had stabbed N with a knife was also relevant because it made it more likely that N, at the time of the offence, had genuinely feared for his safety.

Generally, all evidence, in the first instance, must relate to the issue of the case. Relevant evidence is defined by FRE[86] 401 as that "*evidence having tendency to make the existence of any fact that is of consequence to the determination of the action more probable or less probable than it would be without the evidence.*" Whether the existence of the fact of consequence is more or less probable is a question of common sense and logic, rather than an intricate rule of evidence. To be admissible in court, the evidence need only make the existence of a fact of consequence more probable or less probable than it would be without the evidence.[87]

This is a simpler working definition of 'relevant evidence' statutorily laid down in the American Rules of Evidence. A more commonly adopted definition in the UK that relevant facts need only make the matter re-

---

[84]   Oscar Pistorius, the first double amputee runner to compete in the Olympics, charged for premeditated murder of his girlfriend, Reeva Steenkamp in February 14th 2013.

[85]   [2002] 2 Cr App R 117, CA.

[86]   United States Federal Rules of Evidence.

[87]   Garland, Norman and Gilbert Stuckey. "*Criminal Evidence for the Law Enforcement Officer*" (Woodland Hills, California: Glencoe/McGraw-Hill, 1998), 64.

quiring proof more (or less) probable is given by Lord Simon of Glaisdale in *DPP v Kilbourne*[88]:

> Evidence is relevant if it is logically probative or disprobative of some matter which requires proof. I do not pause to analyse what is involved in 'logical probativeness' except to note that the term does not of itself express the element of experience which is so significant of its operation in law, and possible elsewhere. It is sufficient to say, even at the risk of etymological tautology, that relevant (i.e. logically probative or disprobative) evidence is evidence which makes the matter which requires proof more or less probable.[89]

No definition or description of what constitute 'relevant evidence' is perfectly satisfactorily. Basically, we are dealing with natural state of affairs of events happened in past history within space-time dimension not exactly applicable to all cases, even with similar facts. They are not confine to strict application such as a mathematical or scientific formula. Since the Christian faith is based on the life, death and resurrection of Jesus Christ happened within history, it is utmost important to show that the Christian claim really did in fact occurred. Applying Lord Simon of Glaisdale's definition, all evidences are relevant evidences which makes the Christian claim more or less probable. Giving some examples of relevant evidence and its importance to the Christian faith, Yale's distinguished professor of English literature, William Lyon Phelps says,

> In the whole story of Jesus Christ, the most important event is the resurrection. Christian faith depends on this. It is encouraging to know that it is explicitly given by all four evangelists and told also by Paul. The names of those who saw Him after His triumph over death are recorded; and it may be said that the historical evidence for the resurrection is stronger than any other miracle anywhere narrated; for as Paul said, if Christ is not risen from the dead then is our preaching in vain, and your faith is also vain.[90]

Like all civil or criminal disputed events which may occurred in history needed to be proven by relevant facts, the historical resurrection too should be proven by relevant facts. For example, the writings of the four evangelists are relevant as documentary evidence. The names of eyewitnesses who were alive at the time of Jesus' resurrection or had participat-

---

88  [1973] AC 729, HL.
89  Ibid., at 756.
90  Cited in Smith, Wilbur M. "*A Great Certainty in This Hour of World Crises*" (Wheaton Ill: Van Kampen Press, 1951), 18.

ed in the event, and when the information is published and who is able to verify the validity of the writings, the empty tomb, the life transformation of the disciples, though some are circumstantial evidences can be considered as relevant evidences. It is relevant because it denotes a relationship such that these facts, individually or collectively have some bearing on another fact, namely the resurrection of Jesus Christ. But nevertheless one must see how the logic of relevance and relationship are determined before one can conclude that it satisfied the probative criteria for establishing the truth and rendering judgment.

Throughout centuries, judges and legal philosophers have attempted with difficulty to improve the description and criteria, so as to distinguish between relevant and irrelevant evidence. For example, Edmund Powell, barrister-at-law of the Inner temple wrote about the difficulty in 1856:

> As it is the object of pleading to reduce the case of each litigating party to one or more substantial issues which involve the merits of the question; and as for this purpose none but material allegations which tend to the raising of such issues are admitted; so it is the object of evidence to provide that, when such allegations have been made, and such issues selected, they shall be supported by strictly relevant proof. It is impossible to define the distinction between relevant and irrelevant evidence, and even the cases illustrate the difference unsatisfactorily.[91]

Though impossible to put in perfect description but nevertheless Mr Powell emphasized the main criteria is that the evidence offered must correspond with the allegations, and be confined to the points in issue.

On certain type of evidences with specific intention for its admission, there are statutory provisions that guide the judges to consider what evidences are relevant or irrelevant. For example, there are provisions that govern the admissibility of character evidence in civil and criminal cases involving a claim of sexual assault or child molestation.[92] Although Rule 404(a) generally excludes evidence of similar acts when offered to prove the propensity of the criminal defendant or the civil party to commit the act which is charged, Rules 413, 414, and 415 create an exception for such offers in cases involving sexual assault or child molestation. Of course, the admission of such evidence is subject to exclusion if it is prejudicial or confusing, or involves an undue waste of time.

---

[91] Powell, Edmund. *"The Practice of the Law of Evidence"* (London: John Crockford, 1856), 203.
[92] Rules 413, 414, and 415, US Federal Rules of Evidence.

Pursuant to Rule 403, relevant factors to be considered in the balance and factors below have to be taken into consideration:

1) proximity in time to the charged or predicate conduct;
2) similarity to the charged or predicate conduct;
3) frequency of the prior acts;
4) surrounding circumstances;
5) relevant intervening events; and
6) other relevant similarities or differences.

Even though statutory provisions that guide the judges to decide what relevant evidences should be excluded and the grounds for consideration for its exclusionary exceptions, but yet only if the rules are not erroneous. That is why the rules in deciding relevancy is of utmost practical importance. Justice of the Supreme Judicial Court of Maine, John Appleton wrote of this concern in 1860:

> In the whole field of law or of legislation, there is no subject of such vast practical importance as the rules by which the admission or rejection of evidence is determined. The substantive portion of the law, that which prescribes or ordains, may be in the highest degree wise; the criminal code may be framed with the soundest philosophy, and the most judicious combination of the principles of prevention and reformation; perfection, in fine, may be predicated of each and every portion of the substantive branch of the law, yet if the rules of evidence are erroneous, the wisdom of the law is no better than so much folly, the will of the legislator is unheeded, his rewards unreapt, his penalties unimposed.[93]

Prolific writer of many books on Law of Evidence during the mid-19th to early 20th century, William Mawdesley Best[94] explains further about the difficulty on rules of relevancy:

> Of all rules of evidence, the most universal and the most obvious is this, "that the evidence adduced should be alike directed and confined to the matters which are in dispute, or which form the subject of investigation, The theoretical propriety of this rule never can be matter of doubt, whatever difficulties may arise in its application. The tribunal is created to determine matters which either are in dispute between contending parties or otherwise require proof; and anything which is neither directly nor indi-

---

[93] Appleton, John. "*The Rules of Evidence: Stated and Discussed*" (Philadelphia: T. & J. W. Johnson & Co., 1860), 9.
[94] Barrister-at-Law of Gray's Inn.

rectly relevant to those matters ought at once to be put aside as beyond the jurisdiction of the tribunal, and as tending to distract its attention and to waste its time. "*Frustra probatur quod probatum non relevant.*"[95]

Lord Steyn states that '*relevance is a question of degree determined, for the most part, by common sense and experience.*'[96] The principles in regard to relevancy is as simple as common sense and yet the analysis on its profound theoretical and practical importance is beyond the scope of this book. In simple summary, relevancy is any two facts to which it is applied are so related to each other that according to the common course of events one either taken by itself or in connection with other facts proves or renders probable the past, present, or future existence or non-existence of the other.[97] In the next few sections, we shall further discuss on the logic of relevancy in a little bit more detail and its application to legal apologetics. With this brief but clear grasp of the basic evidentiary concepts, we are now ready to embark unto the discussion of other issues and general types of evidential principles.

## Burden of Proof

Primarily, the first general principle will have us ask, "*Which litigant has the first responsibility to prove?*" The law of evidence provides guidelines for the court to detect who should be the one to discharge his or her burden of proof. In other words, unless that person (who has the burden of proof) successfully discharged his burden (i.e. satisfactorily provides adequate evidence to convince the court), he or she will be the losing party to the case. Almost in all criminal cases, it is the prosecutor that bears the burden of proof. Unless the prosecutor discharged this burden, the defence or the accused can fold his hand without even providing a shred of evidence to rebut the allegation. In exceptional criminal cases, where the charge of the offence is under what we called strict liability, then the burden of proof is on the accused.

---

[95] Best, William Mawdesley. "*The Principles of the Law of Evidence: With Elementary Rules for Conducting the Examination and Cross-Examination of Witnesses*" (London: Sweet & Maxwell, 1902), 231.
[96] *R v Randall* [2004] 1 ALL ER 467 at 474.
[97] Stephen, James Fitzjames, "*A Digest of the Law of Evidence*" (Stevens, 12th edn., 1948), Art, 1.

Similarly, in almost all civil cases[98], the plaintiff has the burden of proof. Based on the legal maxim, "*Actori incumbit onus probandi*" i.e. the weight of proof lies on a plaintiff. That means the plaintiff has to produce more evidences that have stronger probative value than the defendant. I remember in year 2008, I was representing the 2nd and 3rd defendants who were sued by a company as guarantors for the 1st defendant. Our clients claimed that a few years ago they have already informed the plaintiff that they have discharged themselves as guarantors for the 1st defendant. The plaintiff alleged that there was no such discussion about the 2nd and 3rd defendants withdrawing as guarantors. However, plaintiff admitted that there was a meeting with 2nd defendant informing them the sale of their total shares to the 1st defendant. The remaining fact in issue was whether any revocation of guarantee communicated at that time of the meeting. Neither the plaintiff nor the defendants can produce any evidence to substantiate their claims. It is more like plaintiff's word against our client's word. Both parties can be considered as equally producing 0% evidence and since based on the legal maxim 'he who assert must prove' (*ei incumbit probatio qui dicit, non qui negat*), the plaintiff bears the burden of proof. Since the plaintiff failed to discharge its burden, our client won the case with costs even though they have not discharged any single evidence except a bare denial.

Apologists faced the problem on who has the obligation to prove. The atheists say if you claim that God exists, then it is your burden to prove His existence. On the contrary, the theists say if you alleged that God does not exist, then the onus is on you to prove His non-existence. So, who has the responsibility to present evidence that persuades the fact-finder of the truth of the claims the evidence is offered to support? The presuppositionalists and the reformed epistemologists most probably will argue that it is the non-believers' obligation to prove. As for the former's view, one generally presuppose that God exists. It is an irrebuttable presumptions. Even if it is a rebuttable presumptions, it is for the other side to discharge his burden with convincing proofs that such presumption is refutable or rebuttable. If the other side cannot furnish convincing proofs, the presuppositionalists can just fold his hands, gratifying the

---

[98]  In most defamation cases, the overall burden of proof lies with the defendant. All the Plaintiff needs to do is produce the prima facie fact that the defendant had published orally or in writing the defamatory statements and such statement has caused harm to his reputation. The overall burden of proof lies with the defendant is to show that the content of the statement concerned is true or he has the qualified privilege to publish the statement concerned.

feelings on his triumph of victory by just saying God exists due to his pre-liminary presumptions. The medieval philosophers called this type of transcendental reasoning – *demonstration quia* i.e. proof that proceeds from consequence to ground.[99]

As for the latter's view, our faith in God is a properly basic justified belief. It would be almost impossible for the non-believers to refute such basic belief. Just as our basic belief that everyone has a mind, no other person are able to discharge his burden (if any) to prove otherwise. Even if it could be determined that belief in God is properly basic and hence all opposing party has the burden to prove otherwise, how do we know that this is the God of Christian theism? Could it be that the Muslim or the theistic Hindu might passionately agree that his belief in god or gods is properly basic? If yes, then the burden of proof lies with any person op-posing to their beliefs, including Christians. Then who shall ultimately bear the burden to prove? Legal apologists appeal to the principle of law of evidence to seek fairness and have a more realistic reasoning.

Lawyers and legal apologists alike must appreciate that there are two principal kinds of burden i.e. the legal burden[100] and the evidential bur-den[101]. Professor of Law of City University in London, Adrian Keane[102] ex-plains and illustrates in simple terms on the *'legal burden'*:

> The legal burden relates to particular facts in issue. Most cases, of course, involve more than one issue and the legal burden of proof in relation to these issues may be distributed between the parties to the action. ... in a criminal case where insanity is raised by way of defence, the legal burden in relation to that issue is borne by the defendant, whereas the prosecution may well bear the legal burden on all the other facts in issue. In civil pro-ceedings ... which the defendant alleges contributory negligence: the claimant bear the legal burden on the issue of negligence, the defendant on contributory negligence. The obligation on the party to prove may oblige that party to negative or disprove a particular fact. In criminal proceed-ings, for example, the prosecution bears the legal burden of proving lack of consent on a charge of rape.
>
> Which party bears the legal burden of proof in relation to any given fact in issue is determined by the rules of substantive law ... Judges some-

---

[99]   St. Thomas Aquinas, *Summa Theologiae* 1a.2.2.

[100]  It also referred to as 'probative burden', 'the persuasive burden' or as 'the ulti-mate burden'. If the burden is indicated by the pleadings, the court may label it as 'the burden of proof of the pleadings'.

[101]  Sometimes referred to as 'the burden of adducing evidence' and 'the duty of passing the judge.'

[102]  Barrister-at-law of the Inner Temple.

times refer to the 'shifting' of a burden of proof from one party to his opponent.[103]

As for 'evidential burden', Professor Keane defines it as:

> ... the obligation on a party to adduce sufficient evidence of a fact to justify a finding on that fact in favour of the party so obliged. In other words, it obliges a party to adduce sufficient evidence for the issue to go before the tribunal of fact. ... Thus in a criminal trial in which the prosecution bears the evidential burden on a particular issue, it must adduce sufficient evidence to prevent the judge from withdrawing that issue from the jury. If the prosecution discharges the evidential burden, it does not necessarily mean that it will succeed on the issue in question. The accused will not necessarily lose on that issue, even if he adduces no evidence in rebuttal, although if he takes that course that is a clear risk he runs.
>
> ... it does not follow that a discharge of the evidential burden necessarily results in a discharge of the legal burden; the issue in question goes before the jury, who may or may not find in favour of the prosecution on that issue.[104]

Before we are tempted to find this part of discussion boring or irrelevant to apologetics and skip to the next topic, let us agree that the logic on the argument of who bears the burden to prove God's existence may be simple and direct. Here, the judicial principles of legal burden and evidential burden can be complicated and a tedious task for a lay legal apologist to comprehend. This is because there are many various criminal offences and civil disputes with thousands of defences, facts and evidences that a judge have to assess and decide which party have to discharge his legal or evidential obligation. Not to mention also the various substantive laws and its many judicial precedents from case laws. It all depends on each individual case. Hence, legal apologists need not have a comprehensive knowledge in this area as not all of them are lawyers. Nevertheless, this book is to draw the attention of apologists that before one embark into an argument on who bears the burden to prove, he or she need to at least get a minimal grasp of the judicial principle of legal burden and evidential burden. Let me give a few simple illustrations distinguishing between legal burden and evidential burden.

Take the Oscar Pistorius case as an example again. The charge against Pistorius is premeditated killing of Reeva Steenkamp on Valentine's Day

---

[103]   Keane, A. *"The Modern Law of Evidence"* (2006), 83.
[104]   Ibid., 84 -85.

2013. The overall legal burden on the prosecution is to prove that Pistorius did pull the trigger (*actus reus*) and has the intention (*mens rea*) to injure or kill Reeva. Since, Pistorius admitted that he was the one who shot Reeva, the prosecutor has discharged his burden on the first element of the crime. However, the prosecutor still need to discharge his burden that Pistorius knows that Reeva was behind the toilet door and at the point of pulling the trigger, he has the *mens rea* i.e. intention with malice aforethought. However, within the trial, many 'side issues' and evidences were tendered. These 'side-issues' if taken collectively can amount to a strong conviction and fully discharged the main fact in issue. Pistorius also tendered a few evidences in his defence e.g. Valentine's card given to him by Reeva to show both of them are a loving couple on that fateful Valentine's day; previous accident that may affect his present fear; forensic expert's opinions demonstrating Pistorius' room was dark on that moonless night, etc. These 'side-issues' are particular facts in issues which are evidential burden the prosecutor and defendant have to bear and discharged. So, the evidential burden in relation to the various 'side-issues' in a given case may be distributed between the parties to the action. The number of the evidential burdens failed to be discharged by the prosecution may affect his chances of success in discharging his legal burden.

Thus, generally the legal burden of proving any fact essential to the prosecution case rest upon the prosecution and remains with the prosecution throughout the trial.[105] '*Throughout the web of the English criminal law one golden thread is always to be seen, that it is the duty of the prosecution to prove the prisoner's guilt.*'[106] However, this general rule is subject to three categories of exception: where the accused raises the defence of insanity[107], where a statute expressly places the legal burden on the defence[108], and where a statute impliedly places the legal burden on the defence[109].

---

[105] Unless subject to three categories of exception in the law of England and Wales, the accused generally bears no legal burden in respect of the essential ingredients of an offence, whether they be positive or negative and whether or not he denies any of them.

[106] Per Lord Sankey LC in *Woolminton v DPP* [1935] AC 462 at 481.

[107] See section 6, Criminal Procedure (Insanity) Act 1964.

[108] For example, section 2(2) Homicide Act 1957 places upon the accused the legal burden of establishing the statutory defence of diminished responsibility on a charge of murder.

[109] For example, section 101 Magistrates' Act 1980, the burden is on the defendant where he to an information or complaint relies for his defence to any exception, exemption, proviso, excuse or qualification, whether or not it accompanies the

The legislature may pass a law defining a crime in such a way as to eliminate certain facts from the elements of the crime. In other words, the prosecutor need not discharge his legal burden to prove the certain facts or elements of the crime to establish an offence had been committed. That would mean the accused is presumed to have committed the offence and hence he bears the legal burden. The legal burden is said to have 'shifted' to the accused to prove otherwise. For example, one of the provisions in the Malaysian Dangerous Drugs Act 1952 (DDA1952) introduces a presumption that the accused had committed a crime of trafficking drugs punishable by death if 'any person who is found to have had in his custody or under his control anything whatsoever containing any dangerous drug shall, until the contrary is proved, be deemed to have been in possession of such drug and shall, *until the contrary is proved*, be deemed to have known the nature of such drug.'[110] Subsequent sections list down the various kind of dangerous drugs and the amount one is found in his custody is presumed to be trafficking the said drugs.[111]

Section 37(e) DDA1952 also provides that 'any person who is found to have had in his possession or under his control or subject to his order any document of title relating to any dangerous drug shall, *until the contrary is proved*, be *deemed* to have known the nature of such drug.' Section 39B (1) DDA1952 is the punishment section – 'No person shall, on his own behalf or on behalf of any other person, whether or not such other person is in Malaysia —

    a)  traffic in a dangerous drug;
    b)  offer to traffic in a dangerous drug; or
    c)  do or offer to do an act preparatory to or for the purpose of trafficking in a dangerous drug.
    2)  Any person who contravenes any of the provisions of subsection (1) shall be guilty of an offence against this Act and shall be punished on conviction with death.

---

description of the offence or matter of complaint in the enactment creating the offence or on which the complaint is founded.

[110]  Section 37 (d) Malaysian Dangerous Drugs Act 1952.

[111]  For example, s. 37(da) any person who is found in possession of—
(i) 15 grammes or more in weight of heroin,
(ii) ...
(iii) ...
otherwise than in accordance with the authority of this Act or any other written law, shall be presumed, until the contrary is proved, to be trafficking in the said drug;

Hence, if the accused is caught with certain drugs of an amount not less than specified, he is deemed to have committed a crime of trafficking. The elements of *mens rea* (i.e. intention of committing that act) need not be proven by the prosecution. The legal burden is said to have shifted to the accused to prove otherwise e.g. the amount of drugs in custody was for his own consumption.

Another example where the defendant is required to prove a 'lawful excuse' because he is expressly required to do so by a particular Act. In one old Malaysian case, *Subramaniam v Public Prosecutor*[112] which the accused's appeal went all the way to the Privy Council. The defendant had been convicted under regulation 4 of the Malayan Emergency Regulations which provided that "(1) *Any person who without lawful excuse the onus of proving which shall be on such person ... has in his possession ... any ammunition ... shall be guilty of an offence and shall on conviction be punishable with death ...*" Regulation 2A provided that "*a person shall be deemed to have lawful authority for the purposes of* this *regulation only if he ...* [fulfils certain conditions]". The defendant relied on the defence of duress which was not among the conditions mentioned in regulation 2A. The Crown argued that the defence of duress was not available but the Privy Council held the 'lawful excuse' in regulation 4 covered a field of its own and that regulation 2A, although restricts the scope of the defence of lawful excuse, did not affect the scope of the defences afforded by the general exceptions – including duress – appearing in the Penal Code.[113]

Fortunately, there is no substantive law or reverse onus provisions compelling which part of arguments the theists or the atheists has or the legal and evidential burden to bear and discharged. In our apologetic task however, it would be imperative for us to take note that a failure to prove a minor premise does not necessary entail the ultimate failure of proving the major premise. In legal terms, if an apologist fails to discharge his evidential burden on a 'side-issue', it does not decisively mean that he is not successful in discharging his legal burden of proving the main message of the gospel. For example, in proving that Jesus is the Son of God who died for our sin, there are several core evidences (e.g. the existence of God, resurrection miracle, historical accuracy of the New Testament) which assist in discharging this burden of proof. Here, it is the Christian that bears the legal burden. However if there are 'side-issues' like for example, proving that religion is compatible with science; that not all Christians

---

[112] [1965] 1 WLR 965.
[113] Smith, J.C. "The Presumption of Innocence", *Northern Ireland Legal Quarterly* (1987) Vol. 38, No. 3, 223 at 235-236.

are hypocrites; how do we know the truth; Jesus did not really suffer pain during crucifixion; young earth theory; attributes of God; contradiction in the moral law; justification for the Canaanite genocide and many more non-essentials including which apologetic methodology is final epistemologically authoritative in proving God, etc. - these issues are just evidential burdens oblige upon the alleging parties which failure to discharge them are not consequence of failure in discharging the ultimate legal burden. Therefore, apologists like judges in distributing evidential burden in relation to various issues, we need to focus on the main fact-in-issue. As an evidentialist, on one hand we ensure our evangelism should be fair, kept within reasonable limits, not be arbitrary but discharging our evidential burdens one relevant issue at a time without letting the opposing party leading us astray away from the main issue.

In all fairness, apologists have to distinguish the major from the minor premise i.e. identifying the main fact in issue from the side-issues in order to identify who has the legal burden (as contrast to evidential burden). Once we identified the major premise, we'll identify the party responsible in discharging the legal burden. I'll give three different scenarios:

1] The first one clearly shows the principle of 'he who asserts must prove' lay the legal burden on the one asserting the existence of that main fact in issue. If Christians claim that Jesus rose from the dead, then it is their legal burden to furnish with sufficient evidences to demonstrate there is a high probability that Jesus resurrected on the third day as proof that He is the Son of God who conquer death, and hence able to save us. However, a non-believer may request to have his questions answered first, say, "why can't God choose another better method to save human kind?" or "Is it possible for anyone to know historical truth?" or "Can God exists?" These three questions are minor side-issues.[114]

The first one may be an important subject for the theologians. The second may be a significant topic for the philosopher. The third is a mix of philosophy and theology. But all three are apologetic in nature. The

---

[114] Consequently, discharging the legal burden of the main issue (Jesus raises from the dead) will indirectly prove this third side-issue (God can exists). So, discharging the third side-issue is only on the level of evidential burden and not necessarily meant that the Christian has that ultimate legal burden to satisfy convincingly the question on the third side issue. However, if the main issue is 'God can exists?', then the evidential burden of proof of Jesus' resurrection can be a supporting evidence for this main issue and if strong enough it can shift the legal burden on the atheists to prove that God does not exists. Evidential burden has lower standard of proof than the legal burden.

classical apologists most probably will say these three questions are highly important groundwork issues or what the lawyers describes in court as *'preliminary objections'* which needed to be dealt with, otherwise the whole case will be dismissed even before the trial begins. No wonder that the classical apologists firmly avers the three step model in their apologetic methodology *to wit* philosophy → theism → theology.

Both the presuppositionalist and reformed epistemologist are the *'presume guilty until proven innocence'* type of strict legal enforcer. To them, there is no preliminary objections or distribution of evidential burdens. By virtue of its strict self-imposed presupposition or *a prior* basic belief, it is presumed that all non-believers are guilty until proven otherwise. Hence, all legal burden rests on the non-believers. Their beliefs are presumed basic and rational until proven irrational. Applying the logic of legal argument of those supporting legal burden should be on the accused, I suppose it can be illustrated in the following:

> Parliament intended the enactment which created the offence to be an enforceable provision.
>
> It would not be enforceable if the onus of proof on this matter lay on the prosecution.
>
> Therefore, Parliament intended the onus of proof to be on the accused.
>
> Presuppositionalists intended his argument to be a very firm reinforcement and fortified argument.
>
> It would not be fortified or reinforcible if the onus of proof on this matter lay on them.
>
> Therefore presuppositionalists intended the onus of proof to be on the non-believers.

How do they do it? By an argument that it is a presumption the non-believers have to be on their side first before they can even discharge their burden of proofs. There are no side-issues for them to be initially proven. Hence, by default, legal burden is on the non-believers.

The legal apologists, as fair as they can be, do not impose any unnecessary or unreasonable presumption. They do not insists that philosophy or theism are a compulsory main issue as the main legal burden that have to be discharged with, otherwise it makes apologetic an uphill task. Legal apologists, applying the judicial principles, identifies the fact in issue or the 'side issue' and thus able to distribute the legal burden and the evidential burden accordingly. Neither do the legal apologists play by the rule of the skeptics or the agnostics, nor do they impose a rigid basis that reason and fact should be grounded on the truth of the Christian faith. This would only lead to a never ending circular argument.

2] The second demonstrates that legal burden may shift to the non-believers after the Christians have forwarded prima facie evidence. For example, upon providing convincing evidence that highly likely Jesus resurrected from the dead – enough to discharge his legal burden but the non-believers attempt to cast doubts by alleging that the disciples came to steal Jesus body away when the guards was asleep. This allegation is a strong one because if they are able to prove them, the resurrection issue will fall altogether. If they could prove beyond a reasonable doubt that the disciples stole the body away, then this is a very strong defeater to the Christians' claim. Because this is a strong allegation, the legal burden shift to the non-believer. This is not a 'side-issue' and therefore is not an evidential burden. Be reminded that if it was only an evidential burden, the legal burden still remain with the Christian. Hence, it is not for the Christian to prove that the disciples did not came by night to steal the body away. On the contrary, the legal burden is on the one suggesting the theft theory and if he fails to show convincing proofs that the body was stolen or explain away how the guard knew it was the disciples who stole the body while their eyes were closed when they were asleep, he stands to lose the argument.

3] The third is to illustrate that shifting of burden was never in the argument but the non-believers hold the legal burden from the very beginning. Say, for example, if the atheists took the first step in the argument by claiming that science is not compatible with any religions (not just only with Christianity), then the legal burden should be on the atheists. Similarly, they bear the legal burden if they alleges that modern scientific theories has ultimately proven the beginning of the universe and thus dispel the creation story. Since sentences beginning with "science has now proves", then such strong allegation will lay the legal burden on the one who asserts it.

Take note that it does not mean that apologists may not appeal to scientific evidence for Christian truth claims. If we do, then it is merely an evidential burden to be discharged by the apologist because the main issue we are alleging is not on the main claims of the scientific discovery but on the claim of Jesus Christ. Yes, we bear the burden to prove Jesus Christ but only discharging the evidential burden of scientific discovery as only a supporting evidence. If we fails to discharge the evidential burden of scientific evidence, it is not necessary we fail to discharge our ultimate burden of proving the Gospel truth claim. This is also because Christians acknowledge that scientific discovery is ever changing and relying on them are merely circumstantial evidence to the existing argument at present. It has only an evidential value and not a strong probative force but yet a corroborating evidence to substantiate our ultimate claim. As for the atheists, their attitude towards the scientific discovery is a total reliance on them to dismiss the ultimate question of God. Then, such reliance on this allegation of scientific truth places a legal burden on them, as it is their fundamental claim.

An inference to this can be taken from C.S Lewis:

> If anything emerges clearly from modern physics, it is that nature is not everlasting. The universe had a beginning, and will have no end. But the great materialistic systems of the past all believed in the eternity; and thence in the self-existence of matter ... This fundamental ground for materialism has now been withdrawn. We should not lean heavily on this, for scientific theories change. But at the moment it appears that the burden of proof rests, not on us, but those who deny that nature has some cause beyond herself.[115]

What if the main issue is on the existence of God? The Christian theists allege that God exists and the atheists assert the non-existence of God. Both are equally fundamental fact in issue? As discussed above, if the atheists seek to rely on scientific discovery, then they bear the legal burden to prove that scientific discovery is the ultimate mode of proof. On the other hand, if they base on an eclectic evidences to accumulate sufficient probabilities, then these evidences or 'side-issues' generally should be at the level of evidential burden that they should be discharging. So, is the Christian theists. If both bears the evidential burden in proving various supporting evidences to clear 'side-issues' leading to the fact in issue, then who bears the legal burden? For this fundamental issue, both theists and atheists bears the legal burden. But in the court of law, both prosecutor and defendant cannot bear the legal burden at the same time. If I am allow to give a simple answer, I would just say he who start the conversation first bears the first legal burden. But we cannot be over-simplifying on this area of law, or to be more equally applicable, legal apologetics.

We, legal apologists do not mind bear the legal burden to prove the existence of God. This is because it is easier to prove a positive than a negative. The atheists would have a problem in discharging his burden because to prove a negative is almost impossible. To say, God does not exists, he must have all the answers throughout history and transcend above the universe to show that there is no such a Being as what we may understand as 'God'. Philosophers understand this problematic proof of

---

[115] Lewis, C. S, "*Dogma and the Universe*", in, *God in the Dock* edited by Walter Hooper (Grand Rapids: Eerdmans, 1970), 39.

negativity. If I say there is such thing as a bright blue mango, all I have to do is just to show only one bright blue mango. However, to say there is no such thing as a bright blue mango, I must have a complete knowledge throughout the history of this planet that every mango tree or tree bearing fruit resembling mangoes are not bright blue in color.

After all, why should legal apologists worry when God provided more than adequate evidence to prove the Christian truth claim? It is the atheists that should worry whether they can successfully discharge their evidential burden adequately. Similarly, one wonders why the presuppositionalists who presuppose the sovereignty of God worry about not able to discharge their burden of proof. If they presume that God is all powerful and the Scripture is inspired by God, why do they rests the legal burden on the depraved minds of the atheists? Could God not given the presuppositionalists the wisdom to discharge this legal burden? If they presuppose the opposite party to be man of depraved mind, why worry that such depraved intellect can defeat the Christians' evidences? If the presumption that the depraved minded opposition are not capable to comprehend their evidences, how could they be able to even comprehend the importance of having faith first? One wonders how a depraved minded individual can intellectually take exclusive cognisance the presumption of "Christian truth is true until proven otherwise" or "atheists are guilty of their non-beliefs until proven innocent."[116]

Several scholars have tried to avoid both of the above alternatives by suggesting that the burden of proof is on each individual whatever his thesis may be. M.D. Hooker is of the similar view that burden of proof depends on each party to give reasonable evidence:

> Yet perhaps a debate about the burden of proof is not very profitable, and is appropriate only if one takes the extreme position that the gospels represent historical reports of the words of Jesus, or the equally extreme view that Jesus himself said nothing sufficiently memorable to have come down

---

[116] I am not suggesting that non-believers are innocent until proven guilty, or otherwise. Neither am I suggesting that they are exonerated from their blameworthiness for not believing in God just because Christians fail to discharge their legal burden to them. Apologetics is about applying the right, fair and effective methodology in defending or supporting the Christian faith. Legal apologetics is to achieve this end by applying much of the principles of the law of evidence commonly administered in the western jurisdiction. Neither a correct or incorrect description & application of apologetics might infer prospective salvific status of the non-believers nor aggravate or mitigate any justification to their eternal judgment.

to us ... It is perhaps more appropriate to suggest that the burden of proof lies upon each scholar who offers a judgement upon any part of the material, to give a reasonable explanation for the existence of that saying, and to suggest a suitable *Sitz im Leben* for every saying or pericope[117].

Again,

The presuppositions come to the surface when one side declares "The burden of proof is on those who maintain that any of the material is authentic", or when the other asks "Who is more likely to have been creative - Jesus or the Church?" But these are not the real alternatives. All the material comes to us via the Church, and is likely to have been coloured by the beliefs of those who have handed it on. But the burden of proof, to prove or disprove authenticity, lies neither on one side nor on the other. It is the duty of every scholar in considering every saying, to give a reasonable account of all the evidence; for he is not entitled to assume, simply in the absence of contrary evidence, either that a saying is genuine or that it is not.[118]

## The Standard of Proof

There is a mathematical theory of probability in which the likelihood that an event will occur can be expressed exactly in quantitative terms. For example, the probability of rolling a dice for the first time and get the number 3 face upwards is 1/6. Mathematically everything that can happen has some degree of probability, ranging from zero to one. Thus even a very unlikely event in common sense terms is probable to some extent in the mathematical sense. However, the probability where it applies to court process cannot be mathematically ascertained.

The view of probability in the court process is what Bishop Butler meant when he said, *"Probability is the guide of life"*. In this sense probability is a quality of belief about human affairs rather than a mathematical statement. It is an expectation that something has happened, so far as criminal trials are concerned. It can be stated in terms of degree or standards of proof, namely a balance of probability which applies excep-

---

[117] Hooker, Morna D. "Christology and Methodology", NTS 17 (1970-71): 485 quoted in Goetz and Blomberg, "The Burden of Proof", *Journal for the Study of the New Testament* Vol. 11 (1981) 39-63.

[118] Idem., "On Using the Wrong Tool", *Theology* 75 (1972): 580.

tionally where there is a limited evidential burden on the accused, and proof beyond reasonable doubt which is required for conviction.[119]

Like making most serious decisions in our lives, the whole trial process is permeated by questions of probability. Should I marry this man, do I need to change career, can I trust my former classmates as business partner, which bottle of wine to buy and even crossing the road are decisions based on facts or evidences we assessed in unquantifiable degree of probability. The decisions about the veracity or accuracy of witnesses or reliability of documentary evidences involve probability. Similarly, the testimony of the evangelists or the historicity of the Scriptures or the trustworthiness of the preachers can never be a matter of logical certainty. We exercise our decisions based on probability, sometimes relying on calculated risk. In reaching for the verdict either of guilt or innocence, the jury's decisions have to be based on a necessary degree of probability, and not certainty even where the evidence is direct and not circumstantial.

To discharge the burden of proof and succeed on that issue the evidence adduced by that party, in the opinion of the trier of fact (either the jury or the judge alone in a non-jury trial), be more cogent or convincing than that adduced by the opponent. How much is considered as cogent or convincing the evidence is required to be is determined by the rules of law relating to the standard of proof.

Generally there are two standard of proofs – *"beyond reasonable doubt"* and on a *"balance of probability"*. Usually, to convict an accused in a criminal case is when the prosecutor had successfully discharged his burden on a 'beyond reasonable doubt' standard of proof. This *"beyond reasonable doubt"* standard of proof is much higher than the *"balance of probability"*. In a criminal case, if the defence discharged any burden of proof on a balance of probability the accused will be acquitted. This will also follow if the defence leaves a reasonable doubt about guilt in the court's mind. In other words, the evidence tendered by the accused (either beyond reasonable doubt or on a balance of probability) had diluted the probative force of the evidence submitted by the prosecution. This would mean that the prosecution did not discharged his legal burden at all, even he had discharged on a balance of probability. In criminal trials, the judge must give a direction to the jury that the prosecution is obligated to meet the standard of proof on a beyond reasonable doubt. How would the jury understand which degree amount to a beyond reasonable doubt standard

---

[119] Stone, Marcus. *"Proof of Fact in Criminal Trials"* (Edinburgh, W, Green & Sons Ltd., 1984), 368.

of proof? Denning J. (as he was then) in *Miller v Minister of Pensions*[120] described the standard of proof required to be met in a criminal case, before an accused may be found guilty in the following terms:

> It need not reach certainty, but it must carry a high degree of probability. Proof beyond a reasonable doubt does not mean proof beyond the shadow of a doubt. The law would fail to protect the community if it admitted fanciful probabilities to deflect the course of justice. If the evidence can be so strong against a man as to leave only remote possibility in his favour, which can be dismissed with the sentence 'of course it is possible but not in the least probable' the case is proved beyond reasonable doubt, but nothing short of that will suffice.

This high degree of standard of proof reflects the intrinsic policy of promoting accurate fact-finding, or, in other words, with what Jeremy Bentham called *'rectitude of decision'*.[121] In the words of Sommer Professor of Law and Philosophy at New York University, Ronald Dworkin:

> People have a profound right not to be convicted of crimes of which they are innocent.[122]

No person of reasonable mind would take issue with Dworkin's view of the fundamental nature of the right of an innocent person not to be convicted. A 15th century Chief Justice, Sir John Fortesque once said:

> One would much rather than twenty guilty persons should escape the punishment of death, than that one innocent person should be condemned, and suffer capitally.[123]

In judicial practice, this does not mean weight to be attached to the right of the innocent not to be convicted. It is not maximum protection of the

---

[120] [1947] 2 All ER 372 at 373-4.

[121] Bentham, Jeremy. *"Rationale of Judicial Evidence: Specially Applied to English Practice: From the Manuscripts of Jeremy Bentham"* (London: Hunt and Clarke, 1827), [reprinted 1978], 1.

[122] Dworkin, Ronald. *"A Matter of Principle"* (New York: Oxford University Press, 1986), 72.

[123] Grigor, Francis. *Sir John Fortesque's Commendations of the Laws of England: The Translation into English of 'De Laudibus Legum Angliae'* (Sweet & Maxwell, 1917), 45 (emphasis removed). See also Sir Matthew Hale. *"The Testimony of the Pleas of the Crown"* (published posthumously by Sollom Emlyn, 1736) (Vol. 2) (reprinted 1971), 289 who favoured a lower ratio: *"it is better five guilty persons should escape unpunished, than one innocent person should die."*

innocent as though it is an absolute right. Justice is *as much concerned* with the conviction of the guilty as the acquittal of the innocent.[124]

A blanket ban on evidence probably have the effect of leading to the widespread 'acquittal' or 'guilt' on all opposing parties of any theistic or atheistic presuppositionalists, if you know what I mean. There must be a fair evaluation of the other side's argument. It is where when we understand the allegation or criticism of the atheists, we began to acknowledge the value of the evidence, rationality and the intellect God has given us.

Like judges having a 'clear, distinct and essential role to ensure, as best can be achieved, that the innocent are not convicted,'[125] the task of legal apologetics is also to ensure the Christian faith are not being condemned as an irrational faith based on a lower standard of proof through the atheists' scrawny and insubstantial arguments. Applying the Court of Appeal in R v *Ward* which states that 'the law, practice and methods of trial should be developed so as to reduce the risk of conviction of the innocent to an *absolute minimum*,'[126] legal apologists should endeavor to expound epistemological methods drawing from all field of studies to reduce the risk of credulous faith to an absolute minimum.

Christians should have no fear to bear the legal burden with a higher standard of proof. God has not left us with no proof or less convincing evidences. Applying the principles, if matters of important fact-in-issue was first alleged by the other side, the legal burden should be with them. Hence, we would expect the non-believers to discharge their obligation to the beyond reasonable doubt standard of proof. As mentioned above, if a single 'side-issues' that do not necessarily affect the ultimate legal burden, then whoever has the evidential burden has to discharge his onus of proof on the standard of balance of probability. How do we describe this balance of probability standard of proof?

As for civil proceedings, the standard of proof required to be met by either the plaintiff or the defendant seeking to discharge a legal burden is proof on a balance of probabilities. This same standard on balance of probabilities should also be applied in deciding on a submission of no case to answer when the defendant has elected not to adduce any evidence.[127] In the case of Miller v Minister of Pensions, Denning J. as well

---

124  R v McIlkenny [1992] 2 All ER 417 at 425, CA (emphasis added).
125  Mills, B. QC. "Justice For All – All For Justice" (1994) 144 *New Law Journal*, 1670 & 1672.
126  R v Ward [1993] 2 All ER 577 at 628 (emphasis added).
127  Miller v Cawley [2002] The Times 6 Sept 2002, CA.

resolved the description on the degree of cogency required in a civil case
for the party seeking to win to discharge:

> It must carry a reasonable degree of probability, but not so high as is re-
> quired in a criminal case. If the evidence is such that the tribunal can say:
> 'we think it more probable than not', the burden is discharged, but if the
> probabilities are equal it is not.[128]

As mentioned above, the probability in the court process cannot be expressed exactly in quantitative terms. Unlike mathematical certainty, the
degree of cogency and standards of proof are based on common sense,
usually described through words, concepts or analogies. Even one cannot
describes the taste of a durian or strawberry in quantitative terms. The
degree of love and faithfulness of anyone's spouse cannot be expressed
with mathematical certainty, except through words in qualitative terms
understood by experience. Given the enormous difficulty of defining degrees of probability clearly and precisely, Denning J's dictum might fairly
be regarded as a model. Many times judges describes the standards by
way of analogy easily understood by the jury. One example for describing
balance of probabilities is *"assuming that you have a balance scale and you
place all our evidence on one side of the scale and you place all the defendant's
evidence on the other side. If one side of the scale is heavier even by the weight of
a single feather, we have proved our case by a preponderance of the evidence."*[129]

Analogies are powerful legal reasoning tools, fundamental to common
law development. Apologists sometimes uses them so that his target audiences are able to weigh the probative force of the evidences tendered.
Jesus Himself also uses parables as an analogy to describe the Kingdom of
God and even the degree of God's love. The parables of the lost sheep[130];
the lost coin[131]; the prodigal son which was once lost but now found[132] are
analogies describing the degree or extent of God's happiness over one
sinner who repents. The parables of the two debtors[133] or the labourers in
the vineyard[134] though cannot express exactly God's mercy, Jesus uses
them as parallel description.

---

[128]   [1947] 2 All ER 372 at 374.
[129]   Bergman, Paul. *"Trial Advocacy in a Nutshell"* (Thompson West, 2003), 258.
[130]   Luke 15: 3 – 7.
[131]   Luke 15: 8 – 10.
[132]   Luke 15: 11 – 32.
[133]   Luke 7: 41 – 48.
[134]   Matthew 20: 1 – 16.

Legal apologists acknowledge that our religious quest cannot demand a verdict of absolute certainty. Applying the judicial principles of evidence, legal apologists seek to discharge the evidence to the highest probability as the real world would possibly allow. The Holy Spirit will do the ultimate conviction of the heart. Fair description in explaining our standard of proof and the cogency of the evidence or reasoning tendered are not base on some incomprehensible mystical explanation. Presupposition that cannot be experienced beforehand or self-imposed belief that's not possible to pre-empt genuinely are only described in words that is not recognised by common sense. The basic notion of warrant of belief are only confine to philosophers well versed with epistemological vocabulary.

## Hearsay Evidence

Basically, a party may want to prove a particular content or incident by tendering testimonial evidence from a witness who heard someone (who are not present in court to testify due to some reasons) said he wrote the content or saw the incident is generally not admissible in court. Such an evidence is called 'hearsay' evidence. The law of evidence from time to time had developed principles to ensure fairness in admitting hearsay evidences by way of exceptions. In other words, generally, hearsay evidences are inadmissible unless it falls under several exceptions. The reason hearsay are generally inadmissible is due to the preference for the presence of the declarant so that the fact-finder (trial judge or the jury) is in the position to evaluate the declarant's ability of initial perception, accurate memory, and correctly narrate the event. If the declarant is present as a witness in court, the judge and jury are able to observe his demeanor during chief-examination and cross-examination. Thus, the fact-finder are in a better position to decide what weigh to give to the testimony. These safeguards will be lost if the declarant is not present but hearsay evidence is admitted.

In the United States Constitution, an accused has the right "to be confronted with witnesses against him" as guaranteed by the Sixth Amendment. The accused will be able to cross-examine that person under oath. If this 'confrontation clause' were applied literally, no hearsay evidence could ever be admitted in any criminal trial. Fortunately, the Supreme Court of the United States on several occasions considered the constitutionality of the hearsay exceptions in connection with an accused's right of confrontation, and had found most of the exceptions to be constitutional.[135]

In seeking the truth of the Christian claim, if all hearsay evidences are strictly inadmissible, then no testimony from the four evangelists, writings of the prophets or any statements from Jesus are admissible as none of them are able to come to court to testify or verify their claims in court. None of them are around to be confronted and be cross-examined. Apologists and historians recognises this fact that no dead person can come forward to testify the content or the incident of which he said or involved. Hence, on one hand the judicial principles wants to ensure hearsay statements do not fall into the risky characteristics of a gossip or rumour, but on the other hand, the admission of the evidence is particularly necessary to ensure proper outcome of the trial. Like the "Chinese whisper" game played when we were kids, each time the message transfers to the other person's ears, it increases the probability that the content of the message might had changed. At the end, the ultimate hearers will give an almost completely distorted version from the original message.

This bring us to mind a poem by Alexander Pope (21 May 1688 – 30 May 1744) an 18th-century English poet:

> The flying Rumours gather'd as they roll'd,
> Scarce any Tale was sooner heard than told;
> And all who told it, added something new,
> And all who heard it, made Enlargements too,
> In ev'ry Ear it spread, on ev'ry Tongue it grew.[136]

Even though there is the risk of potential unreliability, if such hearsay evidence is relevant and there are no other way to obtain the original document or maker of the content, then in all fairness and practical pur-

---

[135] For example, in *Crawford v. Washington*, 541 U.S. 36 (2004), the court reformulated the standard for determining when the admission of hearsay statements in criminal cases is permitted under the Confrontation Clause of the Sixth Amendment. *Crawford* gives enhanced protection to defendants when the hearsay offered against them is testimonial in nature. When a statement is deliberately accusatory, or when the declarant knows that the statement is likely to be used in the prosecution of the defendant for a crime, the need for face-to-face confrontation is at its highest. When statements are directly accusatory, the defense needs an opportunity to explore the accuser's motives. Where statements are the product of police interrogation, it is necessary to ensure that the testimony is not the product of improper coercion or intimidation.

[136] Lines 468-472, *The Temple of Fame* (1711).

poses, the court may allow hearsay evidence but of course with much caution.[137] There are several reasons to justify the rule against hearsay, including the danger of manufactured evidence, and in case of oral hearsay, especially multiple oral hearsays as the 'Chinese whisper' we discussed above, the danger of distortion, inaccuracy or mistake by reason of repetition. Christian apologists faces such similar problem on the issue of textual transmission (the path from the original writings to today's printed copies) in verifying the historical reliability of the Old Testament. To be fair, Christians must understand the concern of the non-Christians to this risk of hearsay evidence as we are also concern to their religious scriptures. Lord Bridge explained the rationale of this common-law rule in *R v Blastland*:[138]

> Hearsay evidence is not excluded because it has no logically probative value ... The rationale of excluding it as inadmissible, rooted as it is in the system of trial by jury, is a recognition of the great difficulty, even more acute for a juror than for a trained judicial mind, of assessing what, if any, weight can properly be given to a statement by a person whom the jury have not seen or heard and who has not been subject to any test of reliability by cross-examination ... The danger against which this fundamental rule provides a safeguard is that untested hearsay evidence will be treated as having a probative force which it does not deserve.

The common-law rules on hearsay evidence have come a long way through recommendations of Law Commission. Finally, the provisions relating to hearsay in the UK are governed in Chapter 2 of Part II of the Criminal Justice Act 2003. Whilst in the United States, hearsay rule is governed in the Federal Rules of Evidence. Section 801(c) FRE defines hearsay as "*a statement, other than one made by the declarant while testifying at trial or hearing, offered in evidence to prove the truth of the matter asserted.*" The hearsay rule grew out of the fear of convicting an accused person based upon the untested, out-of-court statements of those not present in front of the jury and subject to observation. Hence, the rule on hearsay evidence was developed by the common law to prevent the miscarriage of justice that would result from the acceptance of extreme forms of untested, unsworn

---

[137] At common law, hearsay can only be received by the court as admissible evidence exceptionally. Under the modern law, in civil cases the rule has been abrogated; in criminal cases there are a variety of statutory exceptions; and in both civil and criminal cases a number of common law exceptions have been preserved and given statutory force.

[138] [1985] 2 All ER 1095, HL at 1099.

statements by persons not present in court.[139] Since the days of Sir Walter Raleigh in England, the rule against hearsay has evolved into a considerable body of law, and have gradually influenced the law in America and also many Commonwealth countries.

The trial of Sir Walter Raleigh in 1603 exemplifies the freedom, historically, with which hearsay evidence was admitted in courts. Raleigh was on trial for conspiring to overthrow the King of England. The prosecution relied almost exclusively on witnesses testifying statements made by a particular individual, Lord Cobham. Raleigh objected to this evidence, demanding the production of the witness against him. Raleigh was unsuccessful in his own defence and was found guilty of high treason. Although he was released to conduct a second exploratory expedition to Guiana, he ultimately was executed after the expedition failed.[140] Since then, the hearsay rule in England and subsequently influenced American legal system, was evident that not all hearsay evidence should be condemned and considered inadmissible, but with numerous exceptions. In fact, the lawyers concentrate on its exceptions rather than the rule itself. Similarly, Christian apologetics recognises the historical evidences, Old Testament prophecies, the content from the Scriptures, the witness of the resurrection, etc. are admissible hearsay evidences fall under the exceptions.

According to the definition of hearsay in United States' FRE, only evidence that is in the form of a 'statement' not presently made in court can be hearsay. In other words, if evidence is in any other tangible form such as a fragment of a parchment, wooden cross or a blood-stained shroud, then there is no application of the hearsay rule. The FRE definition focus on what is known as an "assertion-based" test i.e. evidence is a statement, and therefore may be hearsay, only if the declarant's intention is that the utterance, writing, or conduct is for the purpose of asserting something.[141]

Similarly under the common-law rule, any assertion, other than one made by a person while giving oral evidence in the proceedings, was in-

---

[139]  Or while still alive, his statements had not been affirmed as an Affidavit recognised as admissible document.

[140]  Phillmore, J.G. "*History and Principles of the Law of Evidence*", 357 (1850), as cited and presented in Waltz, John R. and Roger C. Park, "*Evidence, Cases and Materials*" 82 (8th ed. 1995), cited in Garland and Stuckey, *Criminal Evidence for the Law Enforcement Officer* (Glencoe/McGraw-Hill, 1998), 204.

[141]  See section 801(a) FRE.

admissible hearsay, if tendered as evidence of the facts asserted.[142] The description of the hearsay rule from various case examples need much more attention than the definition. Let us assume that A, who witnessed an act of murder by a man with a scorpion tattoo on his left arm. Several days later, A informed B orally that the murderer in question had the said tattoo. On the same day, A emailed C to the same effect. B and C reported it to their school principal, D of what A had saw. If A is subsequently called as a witness in the criminal trial concerned with the incident in question, his statement from the witness box would be admissible to the effect that there was tattoo in the accused's left arm and the tattoo is a picture of a scorpion. However, evidence may not be given by either A, B, C or D, for the purpose of establishing the picture of the tattoo through the statement made by A out of court. In criminal cases, the meaning of hearsay and the circumstances in which it is admissible, are now governed by Chapter 2 of Part II of the Criminal Justice Act 2003 (CJA 2003).

Since this book is not for the law students or legal practitioners, we shall merely confine to the basic explanation of the hearsay exceptions and its justification. Within the statutory definition of the UK hearsay law, it provides categories of hearsay exceptions that are admissible.

Section 114(1) CJA 2003 defines 'hearsay' as 'a statement not made in oral evidence in the proceedings is admissible as evidence of any matter stated if', but only if –

a) any provision of this Chapter or any other statutory provision makes it admissible,
b) any rule of law preserved by s.118 makes it admissible,
c) all parties to the proceedings agree to it being admissible, or
d) the court is satisfied that it is in the interests of justice for it to be admissible.

"*Any provision of this Chapter*" in s.114 (1) (a) refers to the provisions of Chapter 2 of Part II of CJA2003 which list the categories of hearsay that are admissible. They are:

(i) statements made by persons who are not available as witnesses;
(ii) statements in business and other documents;
(iii) certain inconsistent and other previous statements of witnesses;

---

[142] See explanation of hearsay assertion by Lord Havers in *R v Sharp* [1988] 1 WLR 7; and Lords Ackner and Oliver in *R v Kearley* [1992] 2 All ER 345 at 363 and 366 respectively.

(iv) statements on which an expert will in evidence base on opinion;[143]
(v) confessions admissible on behalf of a co-accused.

"... *any rule of law preserved by s.118*" in s.114 (1) (b) are mostly common-law rules rendered admissible. For example, statements in public documents, works of reference, evidence of age, evidence of reputation, and statements forming part of the *res gestae*.[144]

There are many common-law exceptions to hearsay restriction generally adopted by the United States. Statutory exemptions from the hearsay rule are provided in FRE 803 and 804, which includes dying declarations pertaining to the cause of death; spontaneous declarations or excited utterances; state of mind; statements for purposes of medical diagnosis or treatment; former testimony; business records and public records; pedigree or family history; past memory recorded; prior statements of witnesses; admissions and confessions; and declaration against interest.

Obviously, all authors of the Scriptures and eyewitnesses concerned in both the Old and New Testaments are dead, their testimonies are hearsay. Since we do not have the luxury to have them present in court for us to cross-examine them or observe their demeanour, nevertheless like any other authors of ancient documents and historical characters, we can only verify their reliability under the exceptions of the hearsay rule. Even if there are able to be present, we cannot expect them to be observed and cross-examined by every single potential believer or non-believer.

It is not only impossible but impracticable to have them present at everyone's sight whenever their reliability and their truth content are call into question. That is why the exceptions to the inadmissible hearsay are formulated to circumvent where witnesses are unavailable, especially when they are dead. The British CJA 2003 provides statutory rule to admit hearsay evidence where the maker of the original content is not available.

For example, Section 116(1), (2) and (3) provides as follows:

1) In criminal proceedings a statement not made in oral evidence in the proceedings is admissible as evidence of any matter stated if –

---

[143] And, by virtue of section 128 (1) CJA2003.
[144] Literally, *res gestae* means "the thing done" – a term commonly used to refer to the spontaneous utterance exceptions to the hearsay rule but could be meant to encompass any number of other exceptions. Therefore, it is ambiguous and its use should be avoided.

a) oral evidence given in the proceedings by the person who made the statement would be admissible as evidence of that matter,

b) the person who made the statement (the relevant person) is identified to the court's satisfaction, and

c) any of the five conditions mentioned in subsection (2) is satisfied.

2) The conditions are –

a) that the relevant person is **dead**;

b) that the relevant person is unfit to be a witness because of his bodily or mental conditions;

c) that the relevant person is outside the United Kingdom and it is not reasonably practicable to secure his attendance;

d) that the relevant person cannot be found although such steps as it is reasonably practicable to take to find him have been taken;

e) that through fear the relevant person does not give (or does not continue to give) oral evidence in the proceedings, either at all or in connection with the subject matter of the statement, and the court gives leaves for the statement to be given in evidence.

3) For the purposes of subsection 2(e) 'fear' is to be widely construed and (for example) includes fear of the death or injury of another person or of financial loss.

The above is only a statutory example where the court allows hearsay evidence to be admitted.

For the purposes of verifying the Christian truth, especially the reliability and authenticity of the relevant authors, section 116 (2) (a) applies for obvious reason. Before we wander off into bewilderment and wonder what's the relevance of the law, note of reminder. When we subscribe to legal apologetic as application of the principles of the law of evidence, we do not mean our fact-finding process are governed exactly by the complete existing modern law of evidence. Otherwise, it will be self-defeating to say legal apologetics follow the strict tenets and provisions of the law. For example, the opening word of section 116 (1), it refers to 'criminal proceedings.' It would be doubtful that anyone would wish to take issue that our search is for the religious truth of Christianity and not a criminal proceedings. If legal apologetics is to follow exactly the rules of evidence, then it is exactly not applicable because our quest is not within the classification of a 'criminal proceedings'. But we are saying it is 'as though similar to a criminal proceedings.' Legal apologetics emphasizes the similar method and principles for the fact-finding process commonly accepted by the courts as though it is seeking for the verdict of either guilty or not guilty. Such legal methodology are more commonly appreciated and understood by most people, as compare with the very subjective philosophical concepts and theological biasness of the other schools of apologetics. Such apologetic schools usually have no initial starting point to agree on by both parties.

Another example whereby hearsay evidence are admissible is hearsay statements contained in business and other documents as provided under section 117 CJA 2003. The circumstances here admitting hearsay evidence if the document was created by a person in the course of a *trade, business, profession or other occupation or as the holder of a paid or unpaid office*.[145] In addition the person who supplied the information, who may be the same person as the creator or receiver of the document, had or may reasonably be supposed to have had personal knowledge of the matters dealt with.[146] Not only this would be tedious but disputable whether the four Gospels, the epistles and other writings by the early fathers supporting the canonicity of the 66 books and the authenticity of the biblical authors can be classified under any of the categories listed in section 117. It is debatable whether the biblical authors such as the prophets, apostles or the church early fathers are considered as a *'profession'* or *'other occupation'* either paid or unpaid describes under section 117 (2) (a). If not, and since the Bible and its other corroborative extrinsic manuscripts are publicly available to matters of public interest, can we classify them under statements in public documents? If yes, then our Christian documentary evidences are admissible under the exception provided in section 7, Civil Evidence Act 1995 (CEA1995).

Section 7(2) (b) and (c) of the CEA1995 preserve any rule of law whereby in civil proceedings –

> b) public documents (for example, public registers, and returns made under public authority with respect to matters of public interest) are admissible as evidence of the facts stated in them, or
> c) records for example, the records of certain courts, treaties, Crown grants, pardons and commission) are admissible as evidence of facts stated in them.

Section 118(1)1(b) and (c) CJA2003 preserve the same rules in criminal proceedings. Since the Bible is a religious book, we could safely submit that it should be an admissible public document or at least a document of public interest. Lord Blackburn expressed the opinion in *Sturla v Freccia*[147] that *'public'*, in this context, should not be taken to mean the whole

---

[145]  Section 117(2) (a) Criminal Justice Act 2003.
[146]  Section 117(2) (b) Criminal Justice Act 2003.
[147]  [1880] 5 App Cas 623.

world: the matter in question may concern either the public at large or a section of the public. For example, in *Heath v Deane*[148], it was held that an entry in the books of a manor may be public as concerning all the people interested in the manor. If our Christian scriptures are public documents, it is thus admissible in the sense it concern the Christian public at large or a section of the public. Applying the case laws above, it is still admissible even if not everybody in the world, especially the opposing non-believers, are interested in its existence or content.

However, even if it is still contentious about its admissibility as a public document, then it should nevertheless fall under the category of works of reference based on its historical value. Section 7(2) (a) CEA1995 preserves any rule of law whereby in civil proceedings –

    a)  published works dealing with matters of a public nature (for example, histories, scientific works, dictionaries and maps) are admissible as evidence of facts of a public nature stated in them.

Clearly the Christian scriptures can be considered as authoritative published works of reference dealing with matters of a public nature. Court may take judicial notice of its facts of a public nature in them. Such documents may also include historical works concerning ancient public facts[149], of which the ancient Christian manuscripts are definitely under this category of hearsay exception.

The principles of law of evidence applied to apologetics will help us understand the nature of historical evidences, its admissibility and how one balance the fairness and the risk of untested statements by person not present. Even the Apostle Paul recognises this hearsay problem during the first century when he wanted to tender the claims of the Scriptures, Jesus' resurrection and His appearance to five hundred eye-witnesses. Paul impliedly informs the Corinthians even those eye-witnesses are dead, there are still others that are still alive that can corroborate the apostles.[150] It is as if the Apostle Paul is saying: '*Most are still alive and if you don't believe me go and ask them. You can get them to corroborate.*' This kind of testimony i.e. the testimony that presumes that the hearer can check the details for him or herself, is very convincing evidence of a past incident or hearsay statement. It falls under one of the exclusionary rules and thus admissible, even though most probably they are testifying what they heard from the Apostles or Jesus, who are not

---

148  [1905] 2 Ch 86 (manorial rolls).
149  *Read v Bishop of Lincoln* [1892] AC 644.
150  1 Corinthians 15: 6–7.

present. Under the modern law of evidence, it is admissible not with the purpose of proving the truth of the content, but is relevant and for the purpose of proving many who are still alive heard and saw. It is also admissible if those corroborating testimonies' prejudicial effect outweighed by its probative value[151]. This supporting evidence are justified on the ground that they are reliable value. Two relevant statutory provisions seem to be applicable here are section 121 and 114(2) of the CJA2003.

Section 121 (1) provides that:

1) A hearsay statement is not admissible to prove the fact that an earlier hearsay statement was made unless –
   c) the courts is satisfied that the value of the evidence in question, taking into account how reliable the statements appear to be, is so high that the interests of justice require the statement to be admissible for that purpose.

And in the interest of preventing injustice, the court has the discretion to have the hearsay evidence admitted. The court must have regard to the non-exhaustive list of factors set out in section 114(2) of the CJA2003, which provides as follows:

2) In deciding whether a statement not made in oral evidence should be admitted under subsection (1) (d), the court must have regard to the following factors (and to any others it consider relevant) –
   a) how much probative value the statement has (assuming it to be true) in relation to a matter in issue in the proceedings, or how valuable it is for the understanding of other evidence in the case;
   b) what other evidence has been, or can be, given on the matter or evidence mentioned in paragraph (a);
   c) how important the matter of evidence mentioned in paragraph (a) is in the context of the case as a whole;
   d) the circumstances in which the statement was made;
   e) how reliable the maker of the statement appears to be;
   f) how reliable the evidence of the making of the statement appears to be;
   g) whether oral evidence of the matter stated can be given and, if not, why it cannot;
   h) the amount of difficulty involved in challenging the statement;
   i) the extent to which that difficulty would be likely to prejudice the party facing it.

---

[151] *DPP v Boardman* [1975] AC 421; *DPP v P* [1991] 2 AC 447.

In such circumstances, Paul's hearsay evidences are admissible not only during his time but also should be admissible in our present day. In addition to the original maker and Paul's death as exception to the hearsay rule, their statements are also admissible satisfying the factors listed under section 114(2), especially the reliability of the maker; probative value of their hearsay evidences and the amount of difficulty involved in challenging the statement.

Another example is the Apostle Paul's defence before King Agrippa, where he said: The king knows about these matters, and I speak to him also with confidence that none of this has escaped his notice, because it was not done in a corner. On the basis of what was public knowledge Paul was able to challenge the King, "Do you believe the prophets? I know you do." Agrippa replied, "Do you think that in such a short time you can persuade me to be a Christian?" Paul's passion is evident. "Short time or long, I pray to God that not only you but all who are listening to me today may become what I am, except for these chains."[152] Again although much of what Paul claims are hearsay in nature, it is nevertheless admissible as this is of public knowledge. Under the principles of evidence, Paul may tender such evidence, admissible not with the purpose of proving the truth of the hearsay statement, but maybe for the purpose that it is also of public knowledge. Assuming none of those information 'has escaped his notice' are written as public records accessible by King Agrippa and those written about the prophets whom Agrippa believes are not kept away from the public, they are admissible to corroborate what Paul is claiming. Similarly, one of the admissible exceptions of hearsay is public records as provided in United States FRE 803 (8) which encompasses: "records, reports, statements, or data compilations, in any form."[153]

The fundamental principles of the law of evidence and some examples how it is applied in legal apologetics have been discussed above. The 'basic key concepts' on judicial evidential principles i.e. relevance and admissibility should be understood by legal apologists when deciding which evidence is relevant in our religious truth seeking process. The principle of hearsay evidence is utmost important for the obvious reason that all makers of statements in the Scriptures are already dead. Skeptics may argue that hearsay evidence are not admissible due to the potential unreliability but we have seen that the both common-law and statutory laws allow admissibility of hearsay evidence if it falls under its excep-

---

[152] Acts 26:26-29.
[153] Or under the British law of Section 118(1)1(b) and (c) CJA2003; and Section 7(2) (a) CEA1995 discussed above.

tions. It is usually admissible if the prejudicial effect of the evidence out-weighed by its probative value. In summary, considerations of fairness (both to the Christian theists and the atheists) become crucial to deter-minations of admissibility of relevant evidences. We also have taken note on who shall bear the legal or evidential burden of proof and on which standard of proof should it be discharged.

At this juncture we should have some vivid perception on the meth-odological question of how the legal evidential criteria used by the legal apologists to test the admissibility and credibility of the evidence gener-ally, applies to the Christian truth claim, particularly on the case of Christ's death and resurrection.

## Other varieties and Classifications of Evidence

We shall now just very briefly introduce some of the varieties or classifi-cations of evidence, of which hearsay evidence is one of them already discussed above. Adrian Keane plainly introduces that:

> The evidence by which facts may be proved or disproved in court is known as 'judicial evidence'. Judicial evidence takes only three forms, namely oral evidence, documentary evidence and things. Judicial evidence, however, is open to classification not only in terms of the form in which it may be pre-sented and the rules by which its admissibility is determined. Thus, any given item of judicial evidence may attract more than one of the labels by which the varieties of evidence have been classified. The principal labels are 'testimony', 'hearsay evidence', 'documentary evidence', 'real evidence' and circumstantial evidence'.[154]

## Testimony Evidence

Testimony usually refer as the oral statement made in court by a witness or the litigant party. In contrast with hearsay evidence, a witness testify in court of what he perceived a fact in issue directly via one of his five senses. This personal knowledge or first-hand knowledge is termed as 'direct testimony'. John says he saw Jesus took the five barley loaves and two fish, distributed it to the five thousand[155] is direct testimony of what he had perceived with his sight. However, when we want to tender John's statement of what is true, we are tendering a hearsay evidence because the original maker is not present to testify. Similarly, when John wants to

---

[154]   Keane, *The Modern Law of Evidence*, 10.
[155]   John 6: 9 – 14.

quote Jesus saying that *'I and the Father are one'*[156], he is tendering hearsay evidence if the purpose of that testimony is to show the truth of that content. However, if the intention of his testimony is to show that this is what he perceived with his ear, John is giving a direct testimony. By submitting the direct testimony of seeing the feeding of the five thousand and the hearsay evidence of what Jesus said, John is indirectly providing *'circumstantial evidence'* that if taken collectively with other evidences, it may raise the probative value to a higher degree that in most probability what Jesus claimed is true. The credibility of the testimony and the one who testify are also to be examined.

## Documentary Evidence

This usually mean proving the truth of the content written in a document or a copy of a document, including data presented electronically. These are produced in court for inspection. The production of documentary evidence is for the intention which may either to prove the truth of their contents, their existence or their physical appearance. More than one century ago, Darling J in R v Daye[157] defined *'document'* as:

> ... any written thing capable of being evidence is properly described as a document and ... it is immaterial on what the writing may be inscribed. It might be inscribed on paper, as is the common case now; but the common case once was on stone, marble, on clay, and it might be, and often was, on metal.

This does not exhaustively apply to present day as now information can be electronically stored in a tape, disc, diskette, film, and microchip or somewhere in the World Wide Web. Hence, the word *'document'* should be of a broader meaning. Since there is no single definition of *'document'* for the general law of evidence, its meaning varies depending on the nature of the proceedings and the particular context in question. In this regard, the admissibility of historical documents e.g. Old Testament Hebrew manuscripts or the Midrash[158] (whether written on stones, clay tablets, parchment, vellum[159], ostraca[160], or papyrus) are not to be subjected to

---

[156]   John 10:30.
[157]   [1908] 2 KB 333 at 340.
[158]   Midrash (100 B.C. – A.D. 300) was actually a formal doctrinal and homiletical exposition of the Hebrew Scriptures written in Hebrew and Aramaic.
[159]   Calf skin often dyed purple. Writing on it was usually gold or silver.
[160]   Unglazed pottery found in abundance in Palestine and Egypt (e.g. Job 2:8).

any narrowed legal definition of '*document*'. The United States FRE Rule 1001(1) defines documents, writings, or recordings as "*letters, typewriting, printing, photostating, photographing, magnetic impulse, mechanical or electronic recording, or other form of data compilation.*" Unless can be proven otherwise, this '*other form of data compilation*' generally covers all types and methods of recording information. The generic is so comprehensive, it may be safe to say all ancient manuscripts or futuristic data downloads fall under this definition. Christian apologists would not have any problem in concluding the biblical manuscripts compiled in whatever materials since it can be considered as '*documents*' in the legal sense.

As it is impossible to have the Apostle John or the other authors of the New Testament books to give oral testimony, at best we have now their writings to be tendered as documentary evidence, admissible under the exception of the hearsay rule. It may also be admissible for some other relevant purpose, for example, to identify the document; assess the status or existence of the document; or to shows what its author thought or believed. However, there are two additional requirements relating to the proof of documents on the contents of which a party seeks to rely. The first relates to proof of the contents, the essential question being whether the party relying on the document must produce primary evidence, for example the original, as opposed to secondary evidence, for example a copy of the original. The second relates to proof of the fact that the document was properly executed.[161] This implies two fundamental aspects of the rules of evidence i.e. (i) authenticity and (ii) the best evidence rule.

It is apparent that authorship and genuineness of the document be verified. Similarly, the biblical books and its supporting extrinsic documents must satisfy the foundational requirement of authentication. Some of the authorship of the biblical books may be in dispute amongst theologians. However, it does not mean that it fails the test of authentication just because there is no certainty of the authorship. The rule of authentication requires that the party introducing the document shows that the document is what the party claims it to be. The Christian apologists are not claiming authenticity by virtue that they know exactly who the author were for every books in the Bible. They are claiming that collectively all the biblical books are inspired by God and during the Old Testament days and even Jesus Himself acknowledge of its authenticity and reliability. So, in the sense the Christian apologists introducing the biblical documents will have to show that the said document is what they claim it to be, and not the identity of the authors. In addition, authentication re-

---

[161]   Keane, *The Modern Law of Evidence*, 262.

quires the party to prove that there is a highly probability that the document was in fact genuine and not fabricated or its content distorted.

The United States modern evidential rules expressly allow an unlimited number of ways to authenticate a piece of evidence[162]. The theistic evidentialists or the legal apologists, as mentioned above whom embrace all relevant methodological epistemologies and fields of studies will take advantage of this unlimited number of ways to authenticate any piece of documentary evidence they might want to introduce. If the judge agrees that the evidence of the document's genuineness is sufficient to convince and the document is relevant to the fact in issue, the judge will admit it into evidence, and the document will then speak for itself. It is doubtful any reasonable people will take issue to this common sense procedure.

Unfortunately, the presuppositionalists seems to lay a presumption that their document (the Scripture) is admissible and its genuineness is to be presupposed in advance. By this presupposition, the document will just speak for itself and self-authenticate its genuineness with less or no evidence at all, only able to be convinced by selected non depraved minded juries. This is utmost contradictory, illogical and at variance to objective justice in the legal sense.

The second implied fundamental requirement is the satisfaction of the best evidence rule. Generally, the rule says that if the truth of the content compiled in a document is to be proven, obviously tendering the original document is the best proof. This best evidence rule originated during the times when copying of a document was made by hand. There is great tendency that copying by hand may create a likelihood of mistakes and inaccuracies. In addition, it opened opportunities for possible fraud and deceit. This is of great concern when Christians only possesses duplicates of the manuscripts being copied by human beings and its accuracy are in question.

In our present modern generation, this best evidence rule may not be very compelling in light of modern technology. Today, most modern copies of the original documents can be allowed. Its duplicates are to be admitted in the same manner as the original, unless there is a question as to authenticity or if it would be unfair to do so. Deprived of modern printing technology, many of the ancient handwritten manuscripts have been long lost since. We do not have the originals since it were made in perishable materials. In this sense, to satisfy the best evidence rule is not to produce the original but its duplicates. The US FRE Rule 1001(4)[163] de-

---

[162]   FRE Rule 901(b).
[163]   Advisory committee note.

scribes 'duplicate' as a copy "produced by methods possessing an accuracy which virtually eliminates the possibility of error." Fortunately, God did not allow His words to be lost in oblivion but have it preserved through careful textual transmission.[164] Its 'duplicates' are no doubt produced by methods which virtually eliminates the possibility of error. Hence, it surpasses the test of authenticity and the best evidence rule. Here, I do not intend to give a thorough explanation on the astonishing accuracy of the Hebrew copyists into reliable manuscripts, as compared with other literature of antiquity. There are many literature written on the reliability and historicity of the biblical books.[165] This book is generally to discuss

---

[164]  The path from the original writings to today's printed copies.

[165]  Josh McDowell had compiled many relevant quotations from a collection of great works on the reliability of the Scriptures in Chapter 3 and 4 of *New Evidence That Demands a Verdict* (Here's Life Publishers, 1999). For more academic research on the substantial historicity of the biblical manuscripts, other works include J.P. Moreland, "The Rationality of Belief in Inerrancy" *Trinity Journal* 7 (Spring 1986), 75-86; Archer, Gleason L. Jr. "*A Survey of Old Testament Introduction*" (Chicago: Moody Press, 1974); Yamauchi, Edwin M. "*Archaeology and the New Testament*" in Introductory Articles, in Frank E. Gaebelein (ed.), Expositor's Bible Commentary, Volume 1 (Grand Rapids: Zondervan, 1979), 645-669; Sproul, R.C. "*The Case for Inerrancy: A Methodological Analysis*" in 'God's Inerrant Word: An International Symposium on the Trustworthiness of Scripture' edited by John Warwick Montgomery (Minneapolis: Bethany Fellowship, 1974), 242-261; Geisler, Norman L. "*Christian Apologetics*" (Grand Rapids: Baker, 1976) 285 – 304; Wilson, Robert Dick, "*A Scientific Investigation of the Old Testament*" (Chicago: Moody Press, 1959); Bruce, F.F. "*The Books and the Parchments: How We Got Our English Bible*" (Old Tappan, New Jersey: Fleming H. Revell Co., 1950, reprint 1984); Bruce, F.F. "*Archaeological Confirmation of the New Testament*" in 'Revelation and the Bible' edited by Carl Henry (Grand Rapids: Baker Book House, 1969); Bruce F.F. "*The New Testament Documents: Are They Reliable?*" (Downer Grove; Illinois: InterVarsity Press, 1964); Geisler, Norman, L. and William E. Nix, "*A General Introduction to the Bible*" (Chicago: Moody Press, 1968); Kenyon, Frederic. "*Our Bible and the Ancient Manuscript*" (London: Eyre and Spottiswoode, 1939); Kenyon, Frederic, "*The Bible and Archaeology*" (New York: Harper & Row, 1940); Kenyon, Frederic "*The Bible and Modern Scholarship*" (London: John Murray, 1948); Skilton, John. "*The Transmission of the Scriptures*" in Ned B. Stonehouse & Paul Wooley (eds.), Infallible Word (Philadelphia: Presbyterian and Reformed, 1946); Metzger, "*The Text of the New Testament: Its Transmission, Corruption and Restoration*" (New York: Oxford University Press, 1964); Gerhardsson, Birger, "*Memory and Manuscript: Oral Tradition and Written Transmission in Rabbinic Judaism and Early*" (Uppsala: Gleerup, 1961); France, R.T. "*The Authenticity of the Sayings of Jesus*" in 'History, Criticism, and Faith' edited by Colin Brown (Downers Grove: Inter-Varsity, 1976), 101-143; Turner, H.E.W. "*Historicity and the Gospels*" (London: A. R. Mowbray and Co., 1963); etc.

the modern legal evidential methodology in admitting our Christian manuscripts as reliable evidence.

Duplicate extrinsic documentary evidences and archaeology discoveries are also admissible to support the authenticity of the copies of Scriptures. For example, the writings of first century Jewish historian Flavius Josephus, supporting the authenticity of the Old Testament:

> We have given practical proof of our reverence for our own Scriptures. For, although such long ages have now passed, no one has ventured either to add, or to remove, or to alter a syllable; and it is an instinct with every Jew, from the day of his birth, to regard them as decrees of God, to abide by them, and if need be, cheerfully to die for them. Time and again ere now the sight has been witnessed of prisoners enduring tortures and death in every form in the theatres, rather than utter a single word against the laws and the allied documents.[166]

The principles' logic and rules are almost similar in the UK. Its admissibility of documents for the party seeking to rely on its contents is now mostly governed by section 133 of CJA2003 and section 71 of the Police and Criminal Evidence Act 1984 (PACE1984).[167] Section 133 of the CJA2003 provides that:

> Where a statement in a document is admissible as evidence in criminal proceedings, the statement may be proved by producing either –
> a)  the document, or
> b)  (either or not the document exists) a copy of the document or of the material part of it,
> authenticated in whatever way the court may approve.

Section 71 PACE1984 deals with 'production of an enlargement of a microfilm' and is 'authenticated in such manner as the court may approve.' The copies of the biblical manuscripts fall under the definition of 'documents' and 'copies'[168] and will find no problem under the CJA2003 provision as the Court are given wide discretionary power to approve its method of authentication. Whilst we exercise the similar judicial authentication process, legal apologists may refer to the test laid down by historians and archaeologists in verifying the historicity of ancient documents.

---

[166]  Josephus, Flavius, "*Flavius Josephus Against Apion*" in William Whiston (trans.), Josephus Complete Works (Grand Rapids: Kregel Publications, 1960), 179-180.

[167]  In civil cases, it is governed under Section 8 and 9 of the Civil Evidence Act 1995.

[168]  As defined in sections 115(2) and 134(1) of the CJA2003, Chapter 10.

The last general principle to take note here is the difference between primary and secondary evidence. As seen above on best evidence rule, the party seeking to rely upon the contents of a document must adduce primary evidence. Obviously, the best kind of primary evidence is the production of the original document, or at least both parties agreed to its admission. Since we do not have the original manuscript and the opposing parties may or may not agree to admit it as authentic, and based on the modern judicial evidential law, secondary evidence may be allowed. For example, if it is either impossible or impracticable, (as in our apologetic task) to produce the original document, a party may prove the contents of the document by way of exception to the best evidence rule - such as by any other form of the writing (a copy or a copy of the copy[169]), and if possible, even oral testimony.

Secondary evidence are allowed by the courts usually in light of circumstances of the case if any weight are attach to that evidence, as the court considers appropriate.[170] The most frequently encountered situations in which secondary evidence of the contents of the writing may be submitted in court are where the original document concerned is:-

a) lost or destroyed;
b) unobtainable by any available judicial process or procedure;
c) in the possession of an adverse party and after a notice to produce it, the adverse party fails to do so;
d) in the custody of a public officer;
e) relating to a collateral matter; and
f) voluminous and cannot be examined without a great loss of time, making a summary of the writing's contents sufficient.

Circumstance [a] applies to the original writings of the biblical authors. All originals are either lost or destroyed. During a real trial, usually the court will expect the party seeking to rely on the secondary evidence must have first diligently searched for the documents. The extensiveness of the search will vary depending upon the kind of document involved and its importance to the case. It would be doubtful for reasonable thinking person to insist proofs that the historians and archaeologists or theologians to have extensively search for the originals. Where a copy is produced, proof is required that it is a true copy of the original. This is where the non-believers demand the apologists to furnish adequate supporting proofs of the biblical manuscripts as true copy of the original. A bare re-

169   See *Lafone v Griffin* [1909] 25 TLR 308; *R v Collins* [1960] 44 CR App R 170.
170   See *Springsteen v Flute International Ltd.* [2001] EMLR 654, CA.

ply that one has to presuppose its authenticity or believing without any verification is basic belief, will not suffice to those sincerely seeking for the truth. Evidentialism will seek at every relevant angle to provide reasonable corroboration to substantiate the genuineness of the secondary evidence. Here, the law does not provide specific measurement to confirm admissibility and authenticity. Adrian Keane explains:

> Where secondary evidence is admissible, there is a general rule that 'there are no degrees of secondary evidence'[171]. Thus, although less weigh may attach to inferior forms of secondary evidence, there is no obligation to tender the 'best' copy, rather than an inferior copy or a copy of a copy ... is admissible even if a copy or some other more satisfactory type of secondary evidence is available. To this general rule there is a variety of exceptions.[172]

## Real Evidence

Real evidence or also referred as physical evidence (or material objects) which themselves are sources of legal rights or liabilities. It is admitted in court for inspection in order for the fact finder to draw an inference from its own, their own observation as to the existence, condition or value of the object in question. For example, in a murder case, real evidence can be a blood-stained blouse, a latent fingerprint, photograph of the victim, bullet casing or weapon. Unless some accompanying testimony identifying the material objection question or some kind of explanation connected to it, little weigh will be attached to it. This explanation may also include demonstrative evidence (or illustrative evidence) whereby lawyers often create for trial and which illuminate and clarify oral testimony.[173] Real evidence can come in a variety of forms, such as material objects, person's physical appearance, demeanour of witnesses, lip-reading and facial mapping, tape recordings, films, photographs, views, demonstration and even documents tendered as evidence for a variety of purposes. Just as other evidences we discussed above, the court will only admit real evidences if it is relevant to the fact in issue.

One Christian example of real evidence to support the existence of the resurrection is the church. The church undergone great persecution during the first century is a fact of history. The early Christians would not have suffered torture or death if they knew that Christ had not risen

---

[171] *Doe d Gilbert v Ross* [1840] 7 M&W 102, per Lord Abinger CB.

[172] Keane, *The Modern Law of Evidence*, 267.

[173] E.g. diagrams, photos of the scenes of auto accidents, pictures from CCTV, medical report, etc.

from the grave. This existing real evidence would not have survived even to this day had the story of Jesus ended at His crucifixion. Professor Wilbur Smith emphasizes the church as an important real evidence, having its foundation rest upon the resurrection:

> There would have been no Christianity if the belief in the resurrection had not been founded and systematized ... The whole of the soteriology and the essential teachings of Christianity rests on the belief of the Resurrection, and on the first page of any account of Christian dogma must be written as a motto, Paul's declaration: "And if Christ be not risen, then is our preaching also vain, and your faith is also vain." From the strictly historical point of view, the importance of the belief in the resurrection is scarcely less ... By means of that belief, faith in Jesus and in His mission became the fundamental element of a new religion which, after separating from, became the opponent of Judaism, and set out to conquer the world.[174]

Although essentially only relevant evidence are admissible, the court has the discretion to exclude it if it is unduly prejudicial, confuses the issue, misleads the jury, or is a waste of the court's time.[175] Legal apologists, similar to the trial court, will identify the relevancy of real evidences and thereon balance the worth of the evidence in question to prove or disprove some facts against its potential for unfair impact on the truth seekers. Generally, one should exclude the evidence if its prejudicial value substantially outweighs its probative value. Sometimes this is just common sense but on many occasions, some expert knowledge is required to assess its relevancy and probative value or prejudicial effect. Say, for example, the fact in issue is on the authenticity and the truth claim of the biblical flood account in Genesis. There are many real evidences acting as corroborative evidences substantiating the probability of the flood account. Should one admit the flood account from other historical religious writings or if it is admissible should much weight be attached to it? If consider as relevant and admissible, the probative value may be added to show the similarities point toward a historical core of events that gave rise to all flood accounts. It may also demonstrate that the flood narrative in Genesis is more realistic and less mythological than other ancient or religious versions, and thus infer authenticity of Genesis. However, the prejudicial effect is Moses may have plagiarized the ancient flood account. Moses may have changed the name to 'Noah' from 'Ziusudra' of

---

[174] Smith, Wilbur M. "*A Great Certainty in This Hour of World Crises*" (Wheaton, Ill.: Van Kampen Press, 1951), 20 – 21.
[175] FRE Rule 403.

the Sumerians or 'Utnapishtim' of the Babylon flood account. On whether its probative value outweigh its prejudicial effect or the other way round depends on the nexus of the fact in issue. Either way not much weigh can be attached to it. Further debate on it may draw more confusion, misleading inference and a waste of time. This is the prejudicial effect that legal apologists should take note of.

Specializing both in botany and biblical studies, John C. Studenroth also noted the balancing of relevant evidence between its probative value and prejudicial effect in evaluating biblical truth claims. On the relevancy and genuineness of real evidence where the fact in issue was on the authenticity of Genesis 14, he wrote:

> ... In light of the accumulating evidence for the historical reliability of the patriarchal narratives in the Old Testament, a plea is made here to abandon the fruitless, outdated, unscientific, and hyperskeptical methodologies still prevailing in certain quarters of biblical studies. Freedom to follow the evidence where it leads is not only exhilarating but also can have profound and beneficial effects on one's ability to evaluate Christianity's truth claim.[176]

From Studenroth's conclusion, it can be inferred that he take cognisance of the probative value of evidence but too much or irrelevant or even relevant evidences can be viewed as prejudicial to any 'unwilling seekers' who is hyperskeptical. He summarises:

> As one ponders the hyperskepticism that sometimes emerges in so-called biblical 'scholarship', one wonders what level of evidence would persuade the skeptic. Would a personal visit from Abraham (return from the dead, and appearing to a roomful of Bible scholars all at one time) suffice? Could even Abraham make an acceptable case for the historicity of the patriarchal narratives in Genesis? Perhaps the problems are other than intellectual. A certain involvement of the will seems apparent, which colors the so-called 'scholarly' results. Aldous L. Huxley makes a surprisingly frank and revealing confession in his book Ends and Means that is relevant to our point: "Most ignorance is vincible ignorance. We don't know because we don't want to know. It is our will that decides how and upon what subjects we shall use our intelligence."[177] Is it possible that some Bible scholars are less willing to exercise their intelligence in dealing with their subject mat-

[176] Studenroth, John C., *Archaeology and the Higher Criticism of Genesis 14* in Montgomery, J. W., Ed. Evidence for Faith: Deciding the God Question. (Dallas: Probe Books, 1991), 155.

[177] Huxley, Aldous L., *Ends and Means* (New York: Harper, 1937), 312.

ter than scholars in other fields, and hence the unusual degree of scepticism ... [178]

Apologist will discern, taking note of his target audience as one of the factor to decide whether an admission of a relevant real evidence may have a prejudicial effect. For any sincere and objective truth seekers, most relevant real evidence has its probative value. The only thing is how much weigh one should attach to it. However, apologists must take note that the opposing party may argue that a non-production of the real evidence in question may go to the weight of the oral evidence adduced and give rise to an adverse inference. Here, we are not talking about a material object that is hidden but more towards the refusal to discuss or explain away a particular real evidence. Again this would depend on the relevancy and any outweighing of prejudicial effect over its probative force. Say, for example, the real evidence in question is on the discovery that the universe is expanding and some inferences to the existence of the Big Bang. The discussion on this evidence can go either way – it may infer science has the last answer to everything or God was the cause of Big Bang since He can create the universe out of nothing. The prejudicial effect may even confuse further on the never-ending debate whether God did create the world in six days, literally. By refusing to admit any discussion on this real evidence may draw an adverse inference against the party seeking to prove creationism.

It is here we appreciate the judicial principles, advising us to evaluate when to or not to admit such relevant evidences. Sometimes allowing the opposite party to draw adverse inference is better to display publicly our ignorance or participate in their equally ignorant 'knowledge' of the Big Bang. Unnecessary real evidence may stray us away from the main fact in issue i.e. the Gospel.

## Lay Opinion Evidence[179]

In contrast to expert opinion given by specialist, lay or ordinary witnesses are discouraged to give their opinions during trial. Since 'opinion' are merely judgment or belief not founded on certainty of proof, it is generally inadmissible in court even if it was a prevailing public opinion. The phrase 'two wrongs does not make a right' is apt to illustrate this logic. Otherwise, if majority's opinion that an immanent God is part of the nature,

---

[178] Studenroth, *Archaeology and the Higher Criticism of Genesis 14*, 165.
[179] Also refer as 'non-expert opinion evidence'.

it does not logically follow that such a worldview is correct. Similarly, an opinion of almost everybody that 600 billion years ago, an alien from another world had sown the 'seeds of life' and allow it to grow and evolve on this planet, do not warrant that this belief or opinion is rational and veridical. Correspondingly, we cannot jump into conclusion that the view God exist within the opinion of many communities, necessarily entail a deduction that it is a basic belief, requiring no justification. Evidence rules normally prevent witnesses from giving opinions about the significance of evidence, since they do not acquire a direct evidence i.e. a direct sensory perception.

It is imperative to distinguish between a witness giving unjustified opinion and giving a fact that are based on personal knowledge. The law restrict opinions or inferences that are "rationally based on the perception of the witness and ... helpful to a clear understanding of a witness'[s] testimony or the determination of a fact in issue."[180] If the testimony of a lay witness are inferences drawn from a fact observed, the court may allow it as admissible opinion evidence. For example, a witness may testify her observation that the lady she saw rushing out from a hotel room full of men was in a sense of fear and distress. Consequently, the law has set guidelines by which a lay witness may relate information in the form of an opinion. First, the opinion must be rationally based on a witness's perception. Second, such opinion must be helpful to a clear understanding of the witness testimony or the determination of a fact in issue. In a California case, the court held that:

> The exception [to the rule prohibiting opinion testimony by a lay witness] ... applies to questions of identity, handwriting, quantity, value, weight, measure, time, distance, velocity, form, size, age, strength, heat, cold, sickness, and health; questions also concerning various mental and moral aspects of humanity, such as disposition and temper, anger, fear, excitement, intoxication, veracity, general character, etc. ... We identify men. We cannot tell how, because expressions of the face, gestures, motions, and even form are beyond the power of accurate description. Love, hatred, sorrow, joy, and various other mental and moral operations, find outward expression, as clear to the observer as any fact coming to his observation, but he can only give expression to the fact by giving what to him is the ultimate fact, and which, for want of a more accurate expression, we call opinion.[181]

---

[180]  United States FRE Rule 701.

[181]  *Holland v Zollner*, 102 Cal. 633, 638-39 (1894) cited in Garland and Stuckey, *"Criminal Evidence for the Law Enforcement Officer"*, 144.

The witness must prove that he has personal knowledge of the facts upon which the opinion is formed, usually something that he had observed or from prior experience. When the disciples were asked of their opinion about the identity of Jesus, Peter answered, "*You are the Christ.*"[182] Peter did not have theological academic qualification of messiahship to render him an expert witness. Neither Peter has direct prior knowledge nor experience before he was chosen by Jesus. Hence, his opinion cannot be considered as an expert opinion evidence on Jesus' true identity. However, due to the time he spent with Jesus and had observed the miracles Jesus performed, Peter's personal knowledge of the facts would allow him to be an appropriate witness to tender a layman opinion evidence. After getting the opinion right, Jesus warned the disciples to tell no one about His identity[183]. This is probably Jesus knows that no weight will be attached on Peter's opinion evidence. It would be better not to tender such evidence at the moment, though relevant, but due to the people's ignorance, the prejudicial effect outweigh the probative value. After the warning, Jesus straightaway taught the disciples "*that the Son of Man must suffer many things and be rejected by the elders and the chief priests and the scribes, and be killed, and after three days rise again.*"[184] Jesus foresaw that only when the strongest corroborative real evidence (i.e. the crucifixion and resurrection of Jesus) are tendered, greater weight will be attached on Peter's opinion. Greater weight would also mean greater faith on the disciples and their credibility as eyewitnesses.

Another example from the Gospel on how an inference was drawn to produce an admissible opinion. The apostle John tendered his opinion that Jesus was deeply moved in spirit and was troubled.[185] John was also in the opinion that Jesus loved Martha and her sister and Lazarus.[186] John's opinion was formed through his close encounter with Jesus and personal observation of Jesus' gesture and expression. The apostle personally observed "*Jesus wept*"[187] and overheard the Jews were saying "*see how He loved him.*"[188]

The admissibility of layman opinion evidence may serve a variety of purposes. John's tendered his opinion may serve the purpose in showing the love of Jesus or the fact that he wept indicates that Jesus had the

---

[182]  Mark 8: 27-29; Luke 9:18-20.
[183]  Mark 8: 30; Luke 9: 21.
[184]  Mark 8: 31; Luke 9: 22.
[185]  John 11: 33 & 38.
[186]  John 11: 5.
[187]  John 11: 35.
[188]  John 11: 36.

characteristic of a human nature. John may have an indirect intention to demonstrate that he was close to Jesus and thereon has the competency of a witness to the resurrection of both Lazarus and Jesus Himself. John may intended to prove Jesus' sanity since He just gave an outrageous claim, *"I am the resurrection and the life; he who believes in Me will live even if he dies, and everyone who believes in Me will never die."*[189] It becomes the ultimate fact in issue when Jesus asked, *"Do you believe this?"*[190] In Wright v Doe d Thantam, it was held that although a person's sanity is a matter calling for expertise, it would appear that a close acquaintance may express his opinion as a convenient way of conveying the results of his observations of that person's behaviour.[191] John's close acquaintance with Jesus allows him to tender such opinion to serve the intention to impliedly prove the ultimate fact in issue.

The admissibility of lay opinion evidence is largely a question of degree and the matters open to proof by such evidence defy comprehensive classification. As for civil matters, section 3(2) of the Civil Evidence Act 1972 provides that –

> Where a person is called as a witness in any civil proceedings, a statement of opinion by him on any *relevant matter*[192] on which he is not qualified to give evidence, if made as a way of conveying relevant facts personally perceived by him, is admissible as evidence of what he perceived.

## Expert Opinion Evidence

This type of evidence is particularly significant for the task of Christian apologetics. Much extrinsic evidences from an array of expertise are able to assist objectively to substantiate the many claims of the Christian theology. For example, in case of being criticised for circular reasoning, expert evidences outside of the New Testament documents are available to confirm the biblical text. John Warwick Montgomery summarises in his *Tractatus*:

> The external test of documentary attribution and authenticity focuses on material outside of the texts in question which may be capable of confirming what those texts say about themselves. It is always possible in theory

---

[189]  John 11: 25-26a.
[190]  John 11: 26b.
[191]  [1838] 4 Bing NC 489 at 543-544, as per Parke B.
[192]  Section 3(3) CEA 1972 defines *'relevant matter'* as including an issue in the proceedings in question.

for a document, like a witness, to make claims that are not true; external confirmation is therefore an important avenue for eliminating such mendacity. The external assistance ... is readily available.[193]

What is the legal principles of evidence and the function in regards to expert evidence? An expert witness specializing in some art, trade, science, or profession called to give his opinion (which usually beyond what lay witnesses are capable of) in court are classified as 'expert opinion evidence.' The legal maxim *"cuilibet in sua arte perito credendum"* i.e. whosoever is skilled in his profession is to believed is one of the foundation of accepting an expert opinion evidence. However, it is not necessarily that all expert opinion are admissible in court as evidence. Generally, expert opinion is admissible if the trial court is satisfied that the subject matter of the expert's proposed testimony must be relevant and can help the jury "to understand the evidence or to determine a fact in issue."[194] The judge must also be satisfied if the expert's field must be one requiring scientific, technical, or specialized knowledge and he has the background necessary to qualify as an expert in the field.

The foundational rules governing opinion evidence by expert was very well laid by Lord Mansfield in Folkes v Chadd (1782)[195] and cited by Lawton LJ:

> ... the opinion of scientific men upon proven facts may be given by men of science within their own science. An expert's opinion is admissible to furnish the court with scientific information which is likely to be outside the experience and knowledge of a judge or jury. If on the proven facts a judge or jury can form their own conclusions without help, then the opinion of an expert is unnecessary. In such a case if it is given dressed up in scientific jargon it may make judgment more difficult. The fact that an expert witness has impressive scientific qualifications does not by that fact alone make his opinion on matters of human nature and behaviour within the limits of normality and more helpful than that of the jurors themselves; but there is a danger that they may think it does.[196]

Unless the expert witness opinion is beyond the understanding of the jury panel or the trial judge, the services of the expert witness is not necessarily needed. In other words, however specialize their opinion is, will be

---

[193]  Paras 3.27, 3.271, 3.272 and 3.273 in Montgomery, J. W. *"Tractatus Logico-Theologicus"* (Bonn, Germany: Verlag fur Kultur und Wissenschaft, 2002), 77.
[194]  FRE Rule 702.
[195]  3 Doug. K.B. 157.
[196]  *R v Turner* [1975] 1 QB 834 at 841.

excluded if the jury or the trial judge are able to decide without them. The rule as can be seen in Lord Justice Lawton's judgment in R v Turner (1975)[197] is used principally to exclude the evidence of psychologists and psychiatrists, typically on the grounds that their evidence cannot contribute anything value to the jury's deliberations. The facts in the case of *Turner* is interesting for us to get a clear grasp of the court's reasoning for not allowing expert's opinion as admissible evidence.

Terence Turner was charged with murder of a girl whom he had battered fifteen times with a hammer inside a car. At trial, he claimed the defence of provocation.[198] Turner told the court that he suddenly got angry and struck the girl whom he deeply loved told him, with a grin, that the child she was carrying was not pregnant by him but was by other men whom she had been sleeping during his recent stay in prison. Turner testified, '*It was never in my mind to do her any harm ... I did not realize what I had in my hand.*'[199] This defence of provocation was challenged by the prosecution. Turner was convicted by the trial court but he appealed to the Court of Appeal on the grounds that the trial judge had refused to admit expert opinion i.e. psychiatric evidence on the issues of credibility and provocation. The expert opinion was to show that Turner had a deep emotional relationship with the girl which was likely to have caused a fiery eruption of uncontrollable fury when she confessed her infidelity to him. The psychiatrist's report concluded that the accused was not suffering from mental illness; but had observed that:

> [The accused's] homicidal behaviour would appear to be understandable in terms of his relationship with [the victim] which ... was such as to make him particularly vulnerable to be overwhelmed by anger if she confirmed the accusation that had been made about her. If his statements are true that he was taken completely by surprised by her confession he would appear to have killed her in an explosive release of blind rage. His personality structure is consistent with someone who could behave in this way.[200]

The Court of Appeal held that the jury needed no assistance of any expert opinion in deciding either what reliance they could put upon the accused's evidence or the likelihood of his having been provoked, a matter which was well within normal experience of any human being. Even

---

[197]  Ibid., or [1975] 1 All ER 70; [1975] 2 WLR 56, 60 Cr App Rep 80.
[198]  Although provocation is governed as provided in section 3 of the Homicide Act 1957, this defence is subject to substantial interpretation by the case law.
[199]  *Supra* n. 196, 838.
[200]  Quoted in *supra* n. 196, 839.

though Lawton LJ justifies that the relevance of the expert evidence was supposedly established, he further asked whether the evidence was admissible on the rules governing opinion evidence. He thereon asked whether the proffered psychiatric evidence can be applied. He concludes the expert opinion cannot be admissible because it deals with a matter:

> ... well within ordinary human experience. We all know that both men and women who are deeply in love can, and sometimes do, have outbursts of blind rage when discovering unexpected wantonness on the part of their loved ones; the wife taken in adultery is the classic example of the application of the defence of provocation. ... Jurors do not need psychiatrists to tell them how ordinary folk who are not suffering from any mental illness are likely to react to the stresses and strains of life. It follows that the proposed evidence was not admissible to establish that the defendant was likely to have been provoked.[201]

There is an assumption from this reasoning that the relevance of expert opinion *per se* is insufficient to establish its admissibility. Generally, there are justifications in excluding expert evidence, usually is the negative effects if such evidence are admissible. Lawton LJ attempted to justify, but not immediately clear what dangers would involve:

> ... the fact that an expert witness has impressive scientific qualifications does not by that fact alone make his opinion on matters of human nature and behaviour within the limits of normality any more helpful than that of the juror themselves; but there is a danger that they may think it does."[202]

In other words, the danger may seems to be that the jury will disregard their own everyday experience or common knowledge of human behaviour, when deciding what happened in the car, and solely rely on the psychiatrist's observation. Mike Redmayne[203] suggested another possible danger:

> The evidence was not, at the time, relevant to the legal test of provocation. Perhaps there was a danger that the jury might have thought it was. The psychiatrist's opinion could have undermined the objective standard of the law of provocation through the jury's taking the defendant's emotional immaturity into account when considering whether his response to the girl's conduct was reasonable. ...The jury is a passive fact-finder; lacking

---

[201]   Ibid. 841-842.
[202]   *Supra* n. 196, 841.
[203]   Professor in Law at The London School of Economics and Political Science.

control over the presentation of evidence, it may presume that any evidence the court has allowed it to hear is relevant.[204]

We again are reminded that evidentialism, in particular to legal apologetics, embraces every relevant field of expertise. The apologists and his target audience may rely on the opinion of the expert witness if it is relevant in the sense that it will assist us to understand the evidence or to determine a fact in issue. To determine whether the supporting evidence is proof of Jesus' death, we may rely on an expert of physiology to give his opinion the physical cause of Christ's death. This physiological knowledge goes beyond our normal experience and knowledge. For example, how does the 'blood and water'[205] came out of the pierced side of Jesus can assist in our defence against the accusation that Jesus was not dead? We rely on expert evidence such as Dr Samuel Houghton M.D. from University of Dublin:

> When the soldier pierced with his spear the side of Christ, he was already dead; and the flow of blood and water that followed was either a natural phenomenon explicable by natural causes or it was a miracle. That St. John thought it, if not for the miraculous, at least to be unusual, appears plainly from the comment he makes upon it, and from the emphatic manner in which he solemnly declares his accuracy in narrating it.
>
> Repeated observation and experiments made upon men and animals have let me to the following results – When the left side is freely pierced after death by a large knife, comparable in size with a Roman spear, three distinct cases may be noted:
>
> 1st No flow of any kind follows the wound, except a slight trickling of blood.
>
> 2nd A copious flow of blood only follows the wound.
>
> 3rd A flow of water only, succeeded by a few drops of blood, follows the wound.
>
> Of these three cases, the first is that which usually occurs; the second is found in cases of death by drowning and by strychnia, and may be demonstrated by destroying an animal with that poison, and it can be proved to be the natural case of a crucified person; and the third is found in cases of death from pleurisy, pericarditis, and rupture of the heart. With the foregoing cases most anatomists who have devoted their attention to this subject are familiar; but the two following cases, although readily explicable

---

[204] Redmayne, M. 'The Admissibility of Expert Evidence: (2) the Rule in R v Turner', Chapter 6 of Expert Evidence and Criminal Justice (Oxford: Oxford University Press, 2001), 147.

[205] See John 19: 34-35.

on physiological principles, are not recorded in the books (except by St. John). Nor have I fortunate enough to meet with them.

4th A copious flow of water, succeeded by a copious flow of blood, follows the wound.

5th A copious flow of blood, succeeded by a copious flow of water, follows the wound.

Death by crucifixion causes a condition of blood in the lungs similar to that produced by drowning and strychnia; the fourth case would occur in a crucified person who had previously to crucifixion suffered from pleuritic effusion; and the fifth case would occur in a crucified person, who died upon the cross from rupture of the heart. The history of the days preceding our Lord's crucifixion effectually excludes the supposition of pleurisy, which is also out of the question if blood first and water afterwards followed the wound. There remains, therefore, no supposition possible to explain the recorded phenomenon except *the combination of the crucifixion and rupture of the heart.*

That rupture of the heart was the cause of the death of Christ is ably maintained by Dr. William Stroud; and that rupture of the heart actually occurred I firmly believed."[206]

Expert evidence can also be obtained from expert's opinion published in recognised academic journals as source of authority. This remind us of another legal maxim, "*Argumentum ab authoritate fortissimum est in lege*" i.e. an argument from authority is most powerful in law. Cases like Davie v Edinburgh Magistrates[207] and Seyfang v GD Searle & Co.[208] agrees that experts may fortify their opinions by referring not only to any relevant research, tests or experiments which they have personally carried out, but also to works of authority, learned articles, research papers, letters and other similar materials written by others and comprising part of the general body of knowledge falling within the field of expertise of the expert in question.

Assuming the fact in issue is on the criticism that writers of the Gospel may had credulously believed on the physical cause of Jesus' death. Medical expert reports in official journals can be utilised to dispel the probability of a mistaken belief by the disciples. For example, an article in the Journal of the American Medical provided a medical account on the certainty of Jesus' death before the removal of His body from the cross:

---

[206] Cited in Cook, Frederick Charles, ed. *Commentary on the Holy Bible* (London: John Murray, 1878), 349-350.
[207] [1953] SC 34. Court of Sessions.
[208] [1973] QB 148 at 151.

Clearly, the ... historical and medical evidence indicates that Jesus was dead before the wound to His side was inflicted and supports the traditional view that the spear, thrust between His right ribs, probably perforated not only the right lung but also the pericardium and heart and thereby ensured His death. Accordingly, interpretations based on the assumption that Jesus did not die on the cross appear to be at odds with modern medical knowledge.[209]

In a pharmaceutical negligent case in H v Schering Chemicals Ltd,[210] it was held that expert witnesses were entitled to refer to the results of research into the drug and articles and letters about the drug published in medical journals. Bingham J said:

> If an expert refers to the results of research published by a reputable authority in a reputable journal the court would, I think, ordinarily regard those results as supporting inferences fairly to be drawn from them, unless or until a different approach was shown to be proper.[211]

Other expert evidence such as archaeology also confirms the authenticity of the gospel. Archaeological and historical expertise can provide a host of supporting evidences for the search of Christian truth claim in a variety of disputed fact in issue introduced by the non-believers. Archaeological discoveries have contributed much expert evidences in analysis of manuscripts, the understanding of technical words, and the development of more dependable lexicons. Archaeology had corroborated other evidences against negative results of radical criticism. Nelson Glueck, the reformed Jewish archaeologist, affirmed:

> "It may be stated categorically that no archaeological discovery has ever controverted a biblical reference."[212]

The world most foremost contemporary biblical archaeologist, William F. Albright of John Hopkins University has identified the New Testament materials as primary source documents for the life of Jesus dating all of them (including John's Gospel) 'between the forties and the eighties of the first century A.D. (very probably sometime between about 50 and 70

---

[209] Edwards, William D., M.D., et al. "On the Physical Death of Jesus Christ" *Journal of the American Medical Association* [255:11, March 21, 1986], 1463.

[210] [1983] 1 All ER 849.

[211] [1983] 1 All ER 849 at 853.

[212] Glueck, N. *"Rivers in the Dessert: History of Negev"* (New York: Farrar, Straus, and Cadahy, 1959), 31.

A.D.)"[213] These are supported by archaeological expert evidences which according to the principles of judicial evidence as admissible. To prove the historical reliability of the Old Testaments too requires expert evidence that can assist in our apologetic task. Dr. Albright confirms that:

> There can be no doubt that archaeology has confirmed the substantial historicity of Old Testament tradition.[214]

Christian apologists should not shun scientific evidences. It is one of the best expert evidences we can rely on. Surprisingly, many scientific claims are more 'presuppositionalistic' in nature, acting on faith rather than evidences. Some of its so-called scientific claims based on flawed methodologies. Classical apologist Norman Geisler and Frank Turek concur with the legal apologists that when come to fact in issue such as proving the origin of first life, legal principles of evidence as applied in the law courts are appropriate methodology:

> Many evolutionists as well as many creationists speaks as if they know, beyond any doubt, how the first life came into existence. Both, of course, cannot be right. If one is right, the other is wrong. So how can we discover who's right?
>
> The following fact is obvious but often overlooked: no human observed the origin of the first life. The emergence of the first life on earth was a one-time, unrepeatable historical event. No one was present to see it – neither evolutionists nor creationists were there, and we certainly can't travel back in time and directly observe whether the first life was created by some kind of intelligence or arose by natural laws from non-living materials.
>
> That raises an important question: if we can't directly observe the past, then what scientific principles can we use to help us discover what caused the first life? We use the same principles that are utilized every day in our criminal justice system – forensic principles. In other words, the origin of life is a forensic question that requires us to piece together evidence [*corroborated by admissible expert opinion evidences*] much like the detectives piece together evidence from a murder. Detectives can't go back in time

---

[213] Interview in Christianity Today, January 18th, 1963 cited in Montgomery, John Warwick, "*Is Man His Own God*" in Montgomery, J. W. (ed.) Christianity for the Tough Minded (Edmonton, Canadian Institute for Law, Theology, and Public Policy Inc., 2001), 31.

[214] Albright, William F. "*Archaeology and the Religion of Israel*" (Baltimore: John Hopkins Press, 1942), 176.

and witness the murder again. Neither can they revive the victim and go into the laboratory to conduct some kind of experiment that will allow them to observe and repeat the crime over and over again. Instead, they must use the principles of forensic science [*as applied in the court of law*] to discover what really happened.[215]

As mentioned above, especially in the case of *Turner*, not all expert opinion are admissible evidence. They may or may not be relevant but could be excluded for a variety of reasons, in particularly where the triers of fact can form their own opinion without the assistance of an expert. If the matter in question is within the jury's own experience and knowledge, the opinion evidence of an expert is inadmissible because it is unnecessary. Otherwise, the non-believers will request from the Christian apologists to supply expert opinion for each and every fact in issue dealing with the Christian claims. In fact, if every matters requires an expert opinion, it will lead to an infinite regression – can we have an expert evidence to support the credibility of the expert's opinion that had just corroborated the expert witness and so on? Impossibility in proving a religious experience is another reason expert opinion evidence is irrelevant unless maybe the expert has the similar personal religious experience. In that case, that wouldn't be an expert evidence but may just be a lay witness testimony.

Assuming the fact in issue is on the allegation that Jesus was in fact either lunatic or a compulsive liar. Testimony and documentary evidences from the narratives of the four Gospels are furnished to the seeker of truth to show His trustworthiness. However, this may be argued as circular reasoning or self-attestation. So, should expert opinion be tendered to show that Jesus did not suffer any psychological problem that caused Him to give outrageous claims or He had the tendency to lie?

Before we move on to discuss on the relevance of expert evidences, one will remember the legal maxim '*he who asserts must prove*'. Any nonbeliever alleges that Jesus is either mad or a charlatan, then the burden of proof is on him. It is his obligation to discharge this burden and to achieve a high standard of proof, he has to furnish with credible expert evidences to prove Jesus was suffering from insanity. The question then would be whether it is relevant and admissible for that '*prosecuting*' nonbeliever's expert witness to be tendered in court[216]. Usually, it would be

---

[215]  Geisler, N. and Frank Turek. "*I Don't Have Enough Faith to Be an Atheist*" (Wheaton, Ill.: Crossway Books, 2004), 117 [*emphasis is mine*].

[216]  I.e. should it be a relevant and significant evidence for consideration in our apologetic task?

the accused that seek to put a defence of insanity and not the prosecutor.[217] Case laws imposes the necessity[218] and admissibility of expert evidence (e.g. psychologists) to assist in order to establish insanity.[219]

But instead of the defendant (Christian) claiming the defence of insanity, and assuming it was the 'prosecuting' atheist that submitted a convincing prima facie expert evidence, it is only an evidential burden standard of proof needed to be sufficiently discharged in casting doubt against that allegation. In fact, it was once attempted by the atheist to furnish expert evidence that Jesus was insane,[220] but if not, honestly misunderstood His nature. Formerly dean and Professor of Jurisprudence at Simon Greenleaf School of Law, Dr. John Warwick Montgomery in his *History and Christianity*,[221] first introduces those atheist so-called psychiatric expert opinions:

> This is the position taken by Schweitzer in 1906 in his *Quest of the Historical Jesus*, a work which was epochal because of its recognition of the eschatological character of Jesus' message, but which is almost universally regarded by New Testament scholars today as setting out a "historical Jesus" who reflects Schweitzer's own rationalistic presuppositions.
>
> Schweitzer felt it necessary to vindicate his Jesus (who misunderstood his own nature) from the charge of psychiatric illness. Schweitzer's Psychiatric Study of Jesus (his Strasburg M.D. dissertation of 1913) is a Herculean but ineffective attempt to show that Schweitzer's purely human Jesus could be sane and yet think of himself as the eschatological Son of man who would come again at the end of the age, with the heavenly host, to judge the world. In actuality, as Dr. Winfred Overholster, past president of the American Psychiatric Association, has noted in his foreword to the latest English edition of Schweitzer's thesis, Schweitzer has not ruled out paranoia in the case of a purely human Jesus: *"Some paranoids manifest ideas of grandeur almost entirely, and we find patients whose grandeur is very largely of a*

---

[217]  See ss. 1(1) and 2 of the Criminal Procedure (Insanity and Unfitness to Plead) Act 1991.

[218]  *R v Byrne* [1960] 2 QB 396 at 402, applied in *R v Dix* [1981] 74 Cr App R 306, CA held that expert psychiatric evidence is a practical necessity in order to establish the defence of insanity or diminished responsibility.

[219]  In *R v Strudwick* [1993] 99 Cr App R 326, CA at 332, Farquharson LJ observed that "The law is in a state of development in this area. There may well be other mental conditions about which a jury might require expert assistance in order to understand and evaluate their effect on the issues in a case."

[220]  John 10:20; Mark 3:21.

[221]  Montgomery, J. W., *History and Christianity* (Minneapolis, Minnesota: Bethany House Publishers, 1965), 63-64.

*religious nature, such as their belief that they are directly instructed by God to convert the world or perform miracles.*"[222]

We cannot avoid the conclusion that Jesus was deranged if he thought of himself as God incarnate and yet was not. Noyes and Kolb, in the latest (5th) edition of their standard medical text, *Modern Clinical Psychiatric*, characterize the schizophrenic as one whose behavior becomes autistic rather than realistic – as one who allows himself to "*retreat from the world of reality.*"[223] What greater retreat from reality is there than a belief in one's divinity, if one is not in fact God? I know that you would immediately summon the men in white coats if I seriously made the claims for myself that Jesus did.

John Warwick Montgomery thereon relied on expert evidence to refute these atheists' expert opinion:

Yet in view of the eminent soundness of Jesus' teachings, few have been able to give credence to the idea of mental aberration. Indeed, the psychiatrist J.T. Fisher has asserted recently what many others have been implicitly convinced of:

"*If you were to take the sum total of all authoritative articles ever written by the most qualified of psychologists and psychiatrists on the subject of mental hygiene – if you were to combine them and refine them and cleave out the excess verbiage – if you were to take the whole of the meat and none of the parsley, and if you were to have these unadulterated bits of pure scientific knowledge concisely expressed by the most capable of living poets, you would have an awkward and incomplete summation of the Sermon on the Mount. And it would suffer immeasurably through comparison. For nearly two thousand years the Christian world has been holding in its hands the complete answer to its restless and fruitless yearnings. Here ... rests the blueprint for successful human life with optimum mental health and contentment.*"[224]

But one cannot very well have it both ways: If Jesus' teachings provide "the blueprint for successful human life with optimum mental health," then the teacher cannot be a lunatic who totally misunderstand the nature of his own personality ...[225]

---

[222]  Schweitzer, A. "*The Psychiatric Study of Jesus*" Trans. By Charles R. Joy (Boston: Beacon Press, 1948), 15.

[223]  Noyes & Kolb. "*Modern Clinical Psychiatry*" (Philadelphia and London: Saunders, 1958), 401.

[224]  Fisher J.T., and Hawley, L.S. "*A Few Buttons Missing*" (Philadelphia: J.B. Lippincott, 1951), 273.

[225]  Montgomery, *History and Christianity*, 65-66.

Professor Keane observes that the distinction between matters calling for expertise and matters within the experience and knowledge of the jury are often illustrated by cases concerning a person's mental state. Many of the decisions reflect the view that expertise is only called for in the case of a person suffering from a mental illness.[226] Even on that note, it is for the non-believers who alleges that Jesus was a loony to prove by furnishing expert evidences. The legal burden rest on them and not the Christian apologists. In cases in which expert opinion evidence is properly adduced, the weight to be attached to it is a matter entirely for the tribunal of facts.

As for establishing whether the accused (Jesus) was lying, it should not be a matter calling for expertise because this does not go beyond the jury's own experience and common knowledge. The jury (or the person whom we are evangelizing to) are able to decide the mental state of a liar (Jesus) unless that liar concerned is not able to control himself due to some psychological impairment. In such a case, expert psychiatric evidence may be admissible to assist in deciding the existence of the psychological disorder.[227] In other words, generally expert medical or psychiatric evidence are not admissible on the question of *mens rea* unless it is for deciding whether the accused fall under the class of mental defective or is inflicted by some medical condition affecting his mental state. We can draw a similar justification the case in Re S (a child)(adoption: psychological evidence)[228] whereby at first instance, the trial judge had relied on the results of personality questionnaire, including a 'Lie-Scale' measuring the mother's willingness to distort her responses in order to create a good impression. Overturned the trial court's decision, the Court of Appeal held that the results of personality or psychometric tests should only rarely have any place in such cases because it is for judges to decide questions of credibility.

Psychology is gaining popularity in recent times and often experts in psychology are called to assist in criminal investigation. Psychologists as expert witness also have special valuable knowledge about testimony given during trial, which is denied to common sense. Psychologists may test witnesses for reliability and give their opinions about the accuracy of

---

[226]  Keane, 557.

[227]  For example, in deciding the intention of a thief, the jury also has to consider his defence that he is suffering from *kleptomania* – a psychological disorder compelling defendant to steal.

[228]  [2004] EWCA Civ 1029; [2004] All ER (D) 593 (Jul).

other evidences. Writing in the bulletin of the British Psychological Society, M. King is of the view that:

> Many psychologists writing about the legal system appear more concerned with the promotion of psychologists as people qualified to educate lawyers than with the advancement of reliable knowledge about behaviour. ... legal psychology ... attempts to define the problems more precisely than hitherto and to establish criteria by which claims as to the generalisability of research results may be assessed. It also seeks to establish principles and develop strategies for future research to avoid extravagant claims and to build a sound basis for psychological knowledge relevant to the legal system.[229]

Although they can contribute in various ways, they cannot conclude the verdict as this is the job of the trial judge and/or jury. They may assist the jury in deciding whether a witness is credible or of intelligent level to testify but question cannot be put forward to seek their opinion whether the accused is guilty or innocent. In one infamous rape case, the Court of Appeal held that, if an accused comes into the class of mental defective, with an IQ of 69 or below, then insofar as that defectiveness is relevant to an issue, expert evidence may be admitted, provided that it is confined to an assessment of the accused's IQ and an explanation of any relevant abnormal characteristics, to enlighten the jury on a matter that is abnormal and *ex hypothesi* outside their experience; but where an accused is within the scale of normality; albeit at the lower end, as the appellant was, expert evidence should generally be excluded.[230] Leading modern psychologist in the field of eyewitness testimony and Professor of Psychology in the University of Washington in Seattle, Elizabeth Loftus is of the similar view. She said psychology can contribute to the courts in America:

> In addition to being beyond the common knowledge of the jury, expert testimony, to be proper, should not evade the province of the jury ... the expert testimony that is being proposed does not involve an opinion on the credibility of any particular witness's testimony. The psychologist does not say whether he believes a particular piece of testimony to be accurate or not. Rather, the expert task is to review the psychological findings and enumerate the various factors affecting the reliability of eyewitness ac-

[229] King, M. "Understanding the Legal System: A Job for Psychologists", *Bulletin of the British Psychological Society*, Vol. 35, December 1982, A92-A108 quoted in Stone, M., *Proof of Fact in Criminal Trials* Edinburgh, W, Green & Sons Ltd., 1984), 7.

[230] *R v Masih* [1986] Crim LR 395, CA; see also *R v Hall* [1987] The Times, 15 July, CA cited in Keane, 558.

counts. The psychologist is speaking about the powers of observation and recollection the typical witness. The jury then decides what weight to give both the eyewitness testimony and the expert testimony.[231]

And again,

> Any psychologist who attempted to offer an exact probability for the likelihood that a witness was accurate be going far beyond what is possible. But a psychologist can show the operation of a relevant factor ... without giving an opinion as to the magnitude of the effect in the case being tried.[232]

Unless the psychologist's expert opinion goes beyond the ordinary jury or the trial judge's ability to offer an exact probability of various factors for the likelihood that a witness's testimony is believable or not, his opinion is deemed inadmissible. Even if it is admissible, it is not for the psychologist to play the role of the jury. For example, we have to distinguish the psychologist's role in enumerate the various factors affecting the reliability of accused's accounts that he was under stress and the jury's role in deciding to believe whether the accused's testimony was true due to the stress factor. However, if the court is of the opinion that the jury are able to assess the simple facts whether the accused was under stress, there is no necessity for experts to tell them that.

In R v Wood, the Court of Appeal rightly upheld the trial judge's decision for excluding the psychiatric evidence attempting to demonstrate the accused had a personality which to some extent was abnormal and liable to give way to excesses of behaviour under stress, and thus susceptible in entering a suicide pact[233] It was excluded because this matter in deciding whether the accused was under such stress is not being outside the ordinary experience of the average juror.[234]

Let's say the Christian apologist is facing this not-so-common disputed issue in Luke 22:44 – "*And being in agony He was praying very fervently; and His sweat became like drops of blood, falling down upon the ground.*"[235] There is no necessity for us to adduce expert evidence from psychologist that Jesus was under stress. Anyone appreciating the situation in the

---

[231] Loftus, Elizabeth F. "*Eyewitness Testimony*" (Harvard University Press, 1979), 196 quoted in Stone, *Proof of Fact in Criminal Trials*, 7-8.
[232] Ibid., 200-201.
[233] This being a partial defence to murder under section 4 of the Homicide Act 1957.
[234] *R v Wood* [1990] Crim LR 264, CA.
[235] Updated New American Standard Bible.

Garden of Gethsemane that night Jesus knew He was about to be betrayed by Judas and will be taken to several quick trials and then to be crucified, are within the ordinary reasonable man's knowledge and experience to decide Jesus was under much stress and therefore He was in agony. If anyone's sweat became like drops of blood, it does not take a psychologist to tell us that this is stress. However, if the side-issue was whether such stress can really cause sweat to become 'like drops of blood', then expert evidence should be admissible. This expert opinions will assists to show that Luke's account is possibly authentic. Medical experts today know that this apparent sweating of blood resembles a medical condition triggered by extreme stress called hematidrosis, which causes subcutaneous blood vessels to rupture into the exocrine sweat glands.[236]

The judicial principles in regards to expert evidence similarly applies to our apologetic task. Like the jury, the truth seeker ultimately has to by faith make a decision based on all available relevant evidences. There are expert opinion evidences which is of value that offer the probability of likelihood that certain issues are authentic. It is not for these expert evidences to make a decision for us. Say, for example, whether we should abide in Christ to bear much fruit,[237] it is not for the archaeologists or biblical historical theologians to give us the verdict that apart from Christ, we cannot bear fruit.

We may decide what weight to put on the eyewitness or the trustworthiness of John the apostle but are all based on the expert evidences provided for us to evaluate. However, when deciding issues that go beyond our personal knowledge, we have to rely on those who are of more knowledgeable and experience than us. Expert evidences guides the mind, Holy Spirit convicts the heart but we, as jury decides with our will. Thence, our body and soul totally commits in faith.

## Circumstantial Evidence

Circumstantial evidence are often relied by the prosecution in criminal trials through a variety of ways to obtain a guilty verdict. Usually when the prosecution does not have eyewitness to present direct evidence, it will try to tender other evidences that are connected to the series of

---

[236] Wilson, Ian. "*Jesus: The Evidence*" (HarperSanFrancisco, 1996), 124 quoting Dr. Frederick Zugibe, a forensic pathologist and chief medical examiner of Rockland County, New York, cited in Ewen, Pamela B. "*Faith On Trial: An Attorney Analyzes the Evidence For the Death and Resurrection of Jesus*" (Nashville, Tennessee: Broadman & Holman Publishers, 1999), 96.

[237] John 15: 4-5.

events from which the jury could draw an inference of guilt. In other words, circumstantial evidence is an indirect approach to proving a fact in issue. Not surprisingly, a collective circumstantial evidences can be as convincing as or more convincing in proving a fact than direct evidence. A witness who testified he directly saw the accused pulled the trigger with the gun aiming at the victim may not be convincing if the jury is of the opinion that the witness concerned is not credible or may have a vested interest in the verdict. However, a compilation of various scientific evidences presented by forensic experts e.g. accused's fingerprints on the gun; the trace of gunpowder on the accused's hand; accused's bloodstain found in the accused's car boot; a few threatening text messages from the accused in the victim's mobile phone; or someone saw the accused sped off in a hurry after the sound of a gunfire may be more convincing.

Lord Simon in DPP v Kilbourne[238] said that circumstantial evidences are *"works by cumulative, in geometrical progression, eliminating other possibilities."* It is actually plain common sense and derives from daily experience. We gather evidence and through induction, we eliminate possible propositions less convincing but left with one or two factual propositions of higher probative value to reach a conclusion. Similarly, the nature of the case for theism and Christianity can at most demonstrated by sound argument drawing inferences from logic and available evidences. They can never be proven with 100% mathematical certainty. In other words, there is no direct evidence. The best available evidences are mostly circumstantial evidences. Collectively, we can make an inference towards a probable objective case.

Professor of Biblical and Systematic Theology at Trinity Evangelical Divinity Schools, Dr. Paul Feinberg comprehend this when he contributed his view on 'cumulative case apologetics'[239] or the 'inference to the best explanation approach.' Although unlike the jury weighing the probability of truthfulness, Feinberg agrees that such argument does not take the form of a proof or argument for probability in any strict sense of these words but yet it is a rational argument. Whether he had intentionally or inadvertently applied legal apologetics, he sure had intertwined classical and evidential apologetics. Though Feinberg had not used the word *'circumstantial evidence'* per se, his approach are like lawyers starting with a

---

[238] [1973] AC 729 at 758, HL.
[239] Feinberg, Paul D. *"Cumulative Case Apologetics"* in chapter 3 of Steven B. Cowan. 'Five Views on Apologetics' (Grand Rapids, Michigan: Zondervan Publishing House, 2000).

system acceptable by all parties and thence working *through cumulative, in geometrical progression, eliminating other possibilities* to achieve a probable verdict. Feinberg affirms that:

> This approach understands Christian theism, other theistic religions, and atheism as systems of belief. Such systems are rationally supported by a variety of considerations or data. The model for defending Christianity is not to be found in the domain of philosophy or logic, but law, history, and literature.[240]

Feinberg describes this informal argument for theism and Christianity is more like a lawyer brings, or an explanation that a historian proposes, or an interpretation in literature. It is a broadly based argument that is drawn from a number of elements in our experience, which in turn either require explanation or point beyond themselves. In addition, none of the elements that constitute this case has any priority over any other. Feinberg continues:

> Such an argument is cumulative in the sense that Christianity is defended in terms of more than a single argument. It is ... the approach ... one may start with any element of the case, and depending on the response, appeal may be made to some other element to support or reinforce the claim that Christianity is true.[241]

This is similar with the approach in the principles of the law of evidence. A lawyer's approach never rigidly or always starts from the same element of the case but depending on the fact in issue concerned and any other allegation casts by the other side. With other types of relevant and admissible evidences, especially circumstantial evidences, they are reinforced to raise the probative value of their argument to reach a favourable verdict. This is the practical task of legal apologists. They are realistic in nature. Neither beyond fideism that insist justification by faith alone nor presuppose premises in the argument that the nontheists will refuse to accept. The legal apologists explain it in some legal jargons with much emphasis on the accepted rules of legal evidence as applied in the court of law. Feinberg and friends[242] indirectly explain the value of circumstantial evidence in philosophical and literary argots with much rational il-

---

[240] Ibid., 151.
[241] Ibid., 152.
[242] Distinguished apologists and philosophers such as C.S. Lewis, G.K. Chesterton, Elton Trueblood, F.R. Tennant, William Abraham, Basil Mitchel and Richard Swinburne.

lustrations easily understood by many. Circumstantial evidence as understood by lawyers can also be appreciated through a parable as illustrated by Basil Mitchell[243]

> Two explorers ... come to a hole in the ground. One explorer finds nothing unusual about it, while the other thinks there is something odd about it. They find some other holes in the vicinity. Then they come upon a papyrus fragment in a cave that looks as if it might be a part of the plan for a building. The large hole could be for the center post, and the other holes for poles that gave support to the sides of the building. They even try to reconstruct the building. One explorer thinks that he can see how a building once sat on that spot. He theorizes that there is some order or plan in the location of the holes. Though he lacks the complete plan, he thinks that the fragment supports his view. The other explorer, by contrast, sees the placing of the holes as accidental and argues that there are unexplained and missing elements in the data. The first explorer, in turn, thinks it is possible to explain why certain elements are missing.[244]

Feinberg explains that Mitchell holds this parable to be a good example of a cumulative case. There is a need for ultimate and overarching explanations, but attempts to give such explanations may conflict. The data at certain points may even be capable of a number of different interpretations. However, the theory that best accounts for the data is to be preferred. Feinberg continues to explain:

> Mitchell tries to relate the parable to the question of God's existence and the truth of Christianity. He suggests that the large hole could be the need to explain certain aspects of the universe and reality, which natural theology is an attempt to address. Some of the smaller holes represent religious experiences, the experience of God's presence, of sin, and of grace. Finally, the fragment of the plan is analogous to the concept of the Bible or Christian revelation. In this example, it is possible to see how the various elements help to reinforce one another.[245]

In *Five Views*, Paul Feinberg thereon propound his tests for truth how one can settle conflicting truth claims and determine what is the best expla-

---

[243] Basil George Mitchell, D.D., FBA (9 April 1917 – 23 June 2011) was a British philosopher and one-time Nolloth Professor of the Philosophy of the Christian Religion at the University of Oxford.

[244] Mitchell, Basil. *"The Justification of Religious Belief"* (New York: Seabury, 1973), 43-44.

[245] Feinberg, *Cumulative Case Apologetics* in Five Views on Apologetics, 153.

nation for all the data. Some of the tests are not specifically used in the court of law as the spiritual matters may be irrelevant but the general principles in his seven tests of truth[246] are very much similar with the judicial principles of relevancy. For example, Feinberg's first test of consistency[247] is plainly common sense to the operation of justice. The law of evidence accepts the principle of non-contradiction e.g. a defendant cannot be guilty and innocent at the same time. Evidence tendered must be believed or not believed by the jury but cannot be both. The only difference is how much the jury puts weight on the probative value of each evidence tendered. In judicial principles, the more corroborating evidences that supports a piece of evidence, the more consistent and credible that piece of evidence it should be. Whether the test of correspondence or livability should be admissible really depends on its relevancy fit to the particular fact in issue. For example, Feinberg's test of conservation reminds us whenever we face some anomaly to our theory, we first choose solutions that require the least radical revision of our view of the world. But this cannot be considered as a test of truth. It doesn't support or strengthen the theory or evidence put forth. It only act as a principle not to discard truth at the first sight of anomaly. As for legal apologists, these tests reminds us for not making prejudicial presumptions but will seek other relevant circumstantial evidences to corroborate our argument.

Feinberg admits that these tests for truth are tests that would be used throughout rational discourse but not all of these criteria are of equal importance.[248] As the legal apologists embraces all evidences, these tests are also helpful. Legal apologists recognise all evidences, including the internal witness of the Holy Spirit,[249] as long they are relevant, credible and consistent, easily understood even to the more or less depraved minded. One relevant circumstantial evidence is the consistency which goes beyond mere coincidence is the fact that throughout human history, many individuals from different community and cultures claimed to have known and had a personal relationship with God. The opposition will

---

[246]  Ibid., 153-156.

[247]  Ibid., 153-154.

[248]  Ibid., 156.

[249]  Religious experience can be considered as one of the evidence depending on the methodology of introducing it into the argument. The extent of its relevancy depends on the issue in question. In fact, in proving the existence of God, religious experience play a very important role in the task of apologetics. But it is beyond the scope of this book. Legal apologetics will not insist that anybody including atheists must have this religious experience as a prerequisite to his or her justification of belief.

have to bear the burden to prove that each and every one of them are not credible witness. It would be impossible, if not, difficult for the atheists to introduce any single individual to claim they have an inner experience that God does not exists. The atheist would have to find other type of evidence to disprove the collective probative force of our circumstantial evidence.

However, it is also plausible that evidence can be falsified. Circumstantial evidences are not by default to be immediately believable at first instance. The evidence and its witnesses have to be relevant and shown to be highly credible. Lord Normand took a story from Genesis 44:1-8 to illustrate the value of but caution the risk of circumstantial evidence:

> Circumstantial evidence may sometimes be conclusive, but it must always be narrowly examined, if only because evidence of this kind may be fabricated to cast suspicion on another. Joseph commanded the steward of his house, 'put my cup, the silver cup in the sack's mouth of the youngest', and when the cup was found there Benjamin's brethren too hastily assumed that he must have stolen it. It is also necessary before drawing the inference of the accused's guilt from circumstantial evidence to be sure that there are no other co-existing circumstances which would weaken or destroyed the inference ....[250]

Just because there is a slight possibility of fabricating circumstantial evidences, it does not warrant a total rejection for its admissibility in court. In criminal cases, most of the evidences tendered by the prosecutor are circumstantial evidences. The jury will have to assess each and every witness of their credibility and the relevancy of the circumstantial evidence tendered before they put a probative value to its weight. The United States Federal Rules of Evidence provides that *"every person is competent to be a witness except as otherwise provided in these rules."* [251]

In other words, the evidential burden moves away from the party seeking to rely on the witness and that circumstantial evidence but shift towards the person alleging that the witness is not competent. Otherwise in our daily lives, there will be no witness or any circumstantial evidence for anyone to rely to make any judgment. The more circumstantial evidence based on similar facts, the stronger its probative value. However, some may object that all the circumstantial evidences are defective i.e. false. Truly indeed 10 wrongs does not make a right. That is why a direc-

---

[250]  *Teper v R* [1952] AC 480 at 489, Privy Council.
[251]  FRE Rule 601.

tion from the judge to the jury was to be given of this risk. For example, in the case of R v Goodway.[252]

In the fact of Goodway, the defendant lies to the police as to his whereabouts at the time of the offence. This alibi was a circumstantial evidence attempt to convince the jury that the identification adduced by the prosecution is probably wrong. The Court of Appeal held that whenever a lie told by an accused is relied on by the Crown, or may be used by the jury to support evidence of guilt, as opposed merely to reflecting on his credibility (and not only when it is relied on as corroboration or as support for identification evidence), a direction should be given to the jury that (1) the lie must be deliberate and must relate to a material issue; (2) they must be satisfied that there was no innocent motive for the lie, reminding them that people sometimes lie, for example, in an attempt to bolster up a just cause, or out of shame or a wish to conceal disgraceful behaviour; and in cases where the lie is relied upon as corroboration, (3) the lie must be established by evidence other than that of the witness who is to be corroborated. From this case, we can appreciate that although there might be risk, we must take note whether is there a possibility of the lie to be deliberately done and whether there are other established evidence that corroborate the credibility of the witness.

Of course, in our apologetic activity, there isn't any judge to direct any jury. We just have to direct ourselves – in other words to take note what the jury should have noted. Sometimes there is no necessity for such a direction where it is otiose or clearly a common sense. For example, where the rejection (or acceptance) of the explanation by the accused almost necessarily leaves the jury no choice but to convict (or acquit) as a matter of logic.[253]

In the most often quoted works dealing with legal apologetics, *"Testimony of the Evangelists, Examined by the Rules of Evidence Administered in Courts of Justice"*,[254] its author, the Professor of Law in Harvard University, Simon Greenleaf[255] established a five-part test for determining credibility, taken from the common law principles of evidence before the enactment of the Federal Rules of Evidence. Greenleaf wrote that the credibility of

---

[252] [1993] 4 All ER 894, CA.

[253] *R v Dehar* [1969] NZLR 763, New Zealand Court of Appeal. See also *R v Barsoum* [1994] Crim LR 194, CA.

[254] Published in 1846. The whole work is published in the appendix in Montgomery, John Warwick, *The Law Above the Law* (Minneapolis, Minnesota: Bethany House Publisher, 1975), 91-140.

[255] The principal founder of the Harvard Law School. Also authored *Treatise on the Law of Evidence*.

these witnesses depends, *first*, upon their honesty; *second*, upon their ability; *third*, on the number of witnesses and the consistency of their testimony; *fourth*, on the conformity of the testimony with experience; and *fifth*, on the coincidence of their testimony with collateral facts and circumstance.[256]

Former partner and lawyer of prestigious international law firm Baker & Botts, L.L.P. in Houston, Texas, Pamela Binnings Ewen elaborates:

> It is not necessary under our system of law for each item of evidence to stand on its own as proof of the issue that we are examining. Evidence is introduced to the jury item by item, with each item of evidence creating a link in the entire chain of proof, to build the case cumulatively. It is enough with each item of evidence that it reasonably shows that a fact is slightly more probable than it would appear without the evidence. As we have recognised previously, the jury may consider both direct and circumstantial evidence.[257]

In our apologetic task in proving the existence of God and the Christian claim, there is no one single evidence or best argument to bring about the best conviction. Different circumstantial evidences or different set of accumulated circumstantial evidence works well with a variety of target audiences. However, we take exclusive cognizance that proving the existence of God is not exactly the same as proving a crime committed by somebody. We have to be involved in the spiritual realm. But yet, one may only be convinced with adequate evidence to agree with you to enter into a religious experience to understand more. This will almost never happen if we refuse to provide adequate rational reasons and/or evidence. As for the Christian truth claim, Christianity like some of those religions with its historical roots, are based on time-space dimension. It requires a collection of circumstantial evidences to reach a high probability of convincing value. In my article[258] in the Global Journal of Classical Theology, I wrote and quote:

> All religion, unless it is based on mythology, has a historical origin, the claims of its founder and the process of its establishment. These are all past

---

[256] For clearer explanation and its application, see Ewen, Pamela. B., chapter 5 in *"Faith On Trial: An Attorney Analyzes the Evidence for the Death and Resurrection of Jesus"* (Nashville, Tennessee: Broadman & Holman Publishers, 1999) 85-106.

[257] Ewen, P.B., *Faith On Trial*, 87.

[258] Teh, Henry Hock Guan, "Legal Apologetics: Principles of Legal Evidence as Applied to the Quest for Religious Truth", *Global Journal of Classical Theology* 5(1) (July 2005).

events occurred in history. Merely proving the existence of both the teacher and his teaching are not enough. Its claims, the life and circumstances of its founder, reliability of its scriptures/ religious writings, the coherence of its philosophy, the fulfilment of prophesies and performance of miracles (if any), and as for Christianity, the death and resurrection of Jesus Christ are all relevant historical events that need to be proven. Thus, the legal evidential principles would be a guide to the inquiry of the respective religion's past events and claims. The main purpose of which is to establish to an acceptable degree of probability those past events which it is claimed entitling the adjudicator to come to a reasonable verdict.

Stressing the point again, it is a fact from human experience that it is impossible to ascertain the truth of past events with scientific or mathematical certainty. Although certain scientific proof (deduced from repeated experiments within a closed and controlled environment) provides much contribution in a trial, the law of evidence recognise that it is not possible to ascertain the ultimate truth of the past events inquired into, which happened once within a specific time and space. However, in a court of law, it use a variety of evidences and especially reliable historical evidences such as documentary evidence written in the past or testimony of witnesses who explain the facts they experienced in the past. All the various evidences admissible in court may be fragmentary but so long it is sufficient and consistent enough to outweigh any reasonable doubt, the court can come to a reliable decision. It would be wrong to say that because there is no certainty or the evidences are fragmentary in nature, we should not and cannot come to an objective conclusion. Just because we cannot prove with 100% certainty any food place before us is safe for consumption, that does not necessary mean we refrain from eating at all. Even to the point that assuming everybody has a cupbearer (human or an animal), for every meal, still there will never be a 100% certainty that the food is not poisonous to their stomach alone. Our decision to eat derives from the fragmentary evidences we subconsciously evaluated. You have consistently eaten this type of food, many others have tried before, the aroma was pleasant to the nose, the cook was your wife whom all this while is trustworthy (though cannot prove that she'll be trustworthy forever), the expiry date shown on the can, the unlikelihood of mass murder by poison, etc. are all fragmentary evidences.

These fragmentary evidences are the accumulation of circumstantial evidences dove-tailed together like a jigsaw puzzle, even if it is not complete, one may guess from the almost completed picture puzzle and come to a conclusion its probable image. This is one of the strength of legal apologetics. In fact, it is the only strength available for us in our daily investigative pursuit of making decision. The more reliable circumstantial evidences cohere with each other, the stronger the probative value.

Employing the analogy of a rope in the case of R v Exall, which Pollock CB said, '*One strand of the cord might be insufficient to sustain the weights, but three stranded together may be quite of sufficient strength. Thus, it may be in circumstantial evidence – there may be a combination of circumstances, no one of which would raise a reasonable conviction, or more than a mere suspicion; but the whole, taken together, may create a strong conclusion of guilt, that is, with as much certainty as human affairs can require or admit of.*'[259]

Former Australian Solicitor & Barrister Dr Ross Clifford[260] confirms that for circumstantial evidence to be sufficient, the 'rope' of evidence must be more probable than any other alternative and the inference sought must outweigh all other contrary inferences.[261] Furthermore, applying this judicial principles of circumstantial evidence on the reliability of the Gospel writers, Simon Greenleaf in his *Testimony of the Evangelists* explains:

> The increased number of witnesses to circumstances, and the increased number of the circumstances themselves, all tend to increase the probability of detection if the witnesses are false, because thereby the points are multiplied in which their statements may be compared with each other, as well as with the truth itself, and in the same proportion is increased the danger of variance and inconsistency. Thus, the force of circumstantial evidence is found to depend on the number of particulars involved in the narrative; the difficulty of fabricating them all, if false, and the great facility of detection; the nature of the circumstances to be compared, and from which the dates and other facts are to be collected; the intricacy of the comparison; the number of the immediate steps in the process of deduction; and the circuity of the investigation. The more largely the narrative partakes of these characters, the further it will be found removed from all suspicion of contrivance or design, and the more profoundly the mind will repose on the conviction of its truth.[262]

[259] [1866] 4 F & F 922 at p. 929.
[260] Principal of Morling Theological College, Sydney.
[261] Clifford, Ross. "*John Warwick Montgomery's Legal Apologetic: An Apologetic for all Seasons*" (Bond, Germany: Verlag für Kultur und Wissenschaft Culture and Science Publ., 2004), 148.
[262] Republished in Montgomery, *The Law Above the Law*, 130-131.

## Presumptions

Legal apologetics also take note on presumptive evidence recognised by the court of law as practise in the commonwealth legal jurisdiction. Briefly, presumption here means proof of a fact without evidence. There are certain situations recognised by the courts that evidence is not necessary to prove the existence of a fact which may substantiate that situation in question. In other words, certain facts may be presumed to be true in the absence of proof or certain conclusion must be drawn by the court in the absence of evidence in rebuttal. At first sight, the law of presumption seems like the philosophical logic of an *a priori* proposition. An *a prior* proposition is one that can be determined to be true independently of sense experience. For example, "All bachelors are unmarried" can be known *a prior*, because the truth cannot be affected by any empirical observations.[263] *A prior* propositions may be considered as a subset of presumptions[264] but the law of presumptions goes much beyond the rigidity of logic. It also involves situations which the facts may be rebutted and empirically experienced.

Professor Keane explains the effect of presumptions:

> The effect of this is to assist a party bearing a burden of proof, the degree of assistance varying from presumption to presumption. In some cases the proof required to establish the fact in question may be less than it otherwise would have been. In other cases no proof may be required at all or the other party may be barred from adducing any evidence in rebuttal.[265]

---

[263] Evans, Stephens C. "*Pocket Dictionary of Apologetics & Philosophy of Religion*" (Downers Grove, Illinois: InterVarsity Press, 2002), 7.

[264] *A prior* propositions may be closer to (but they are not) the evidential concept of 'irrebuttable presumptions of law' i.e. a conclusive presumption, applies, on the proof or admission of a basic fact (basic belief?), another fact must be presumed and the party against whom the presumption operates is barred from adducing any evidence in rebuttal. It appears similar to the familiar philosophy illustration of basic belief that other people has minds. If one presume that he has a mind, then it should be irrebuttably presumed that other people has a mind too. However, in the presumption of law, there is a possibility of refuting the presumption but due to the difficulty in proving and based on public policy and common sense, the law disallow any rebuttal to the presumptions. For example, section 50 of the Children and Young Persons Act 1933 provides that: "it shall be conclusively presumed that no child under the age of ten years can be guilty of an offence." (as amended by s.16 (1) CYPA 1969) which formerly the age was set at 8 years).

[265] Keane, 685.

For example, the courts will always take exclusive cognisance of the presumption of innocence. The fact that the customer did not steal the can of tomato soup from the shelf must be first presumed to be true in the absence of proof. It is for the supermarket security officer to prove.

Unsurprisingly, presumption of innocence finds a place in every known human rights documents. It may be assumed that it is one of the least controversial rights. This presumption appears to operate in two different levels – (i) in the criminal trial and (ii) criminal process in general. In criminal trials, the legal burden lies with the prosecutor and the standard of proof is beyond a reasonable doubt. In the criminal process, compulsory detention is only justifiable if there is at least 'reasonable suspicion' that the detainee has committed an offence, and that even the detainee must be brought promptly before the judge.[266] Similarly, if Christian apologists faced with the issue about accusation that the eyewitnesses or the authors of the Gospels probably had lied, the burden to prove their lies is on the other side to discharge. Presumption of innocence will work in favour for us and hence no requirement to provide evidence that the evangelists are honest.

As to the honesty of the evangelists, Simon Greenleaf explains the application of the presumption of innocence:

> Here, they are entitled to the benefit of the general course of human experience, that men ordinarily speaks the truth, when they have no prevailing motive or inducement to the contrary. This presumption, to which we have before alluded, is applied in the courts of justice, even to witnesses whose integrity is not wholly free from suspicion; much more is it applicable to the evangelists, whose testimony went against all the worldly interests.[267]
>
> ... But we may well suppose that in these respects they were like the generality of their countrymen, until the contrary is shown by an objector. It is always to be presumed that men are honest, and of sound mind, and of the average and ordinary degree of intelligence. This is not the judgment of mere charity; it is also the uniform presumption of the law of the land; a presumption which is always allowed freely and fully to operate, until the fact is shown to be otherwise, by the party who denies the applicability of this presumption to the particular case in question. Whenever an objection

[266] For more detail on the rationale of presumption of innocence, see Ashworth, Andrew. "Four Threats to the Presumption of Innocence", *International Journal of Evidence & Proof* (2006) Vol. 10(4), 241-279; or Hamer, David. "The Presumptions of Innocence and Reverse Burdens: A Balancing Act", *Cambridge Law Journal* 66(1), March 2007, 142-171.

[267] Greenleaf, *Testimony of the Evangelists* reproduced in Montgomery, The Law Above the Law, 118.

is raised in opposition to ordinary presumptions of law, or to the ordinary experience of mankind, the burden of proof is devolved on the objector, by the common and ordinary rules of evidence, and of practice in courts.[268]

Assuming the objector accuses that the New Testament is not reliable because the eyewitnesses is not competent and/or credible, it is also for him to prove. About 300 years before Christ, this legal concept already existed since Aristotle. This Greek philosopher's dictum states that the benefit of the doubt is to be given to the document itself, not arrogated by the critic to herself.[269] Quoting from Stark on Evidence[270], Professor Simon Greenleaf agrees that:

> In the absence of circumstances which generate suspicion, every witness is to be presumed credible, until the contrary is shown; the burden of impeaching his credibility lying on the objector.[271]

The judicial concept of presumption guides the apologists to ascertain who shall bear the burden of proof. Unlike presuppositionalism, the law of presumptions are based on considerations of common sense and public policy but not necessarily logic. Most of the presumptions are what we term it as *rebuttable presumptions* i.e. the party relying on the presumption bears the burden of establishing the basic fact. Once he has adduced sufficient evidence on that fact, his adversary bears the legal burden of disproving the presumed fact. As for presuppositionalism, they insists that not a shred of evidence shall be given. Their apologetics seems to imply that unless the objector stops objecting but accept (the opposite of what he is objecting?), he can never comprehend the truth with or without evidence. Since legal apologetics embrace all relevant evidence and principles, the presumptions need not be applied strictly as not all presumptions are applicable. Furthermore, presumptions are not necessarily logical because the subjective situations in life are not like mathematical formula that needs to be rigidly adhered to. Certain facts or combinations of facts can give rise to inferences which justify legal rules that in such circumstances a conclusion may or must be drawn. Professor Keane[272] gives two examples of presumptions from case laws:

---

[268]  Ibid., 122.
[269]  Aristotle, *De Arte Poetica*, 1460b-1461b.
[270]  1 Stark on Evidence, pp. 16, 480, 521.
[271]  Montgomery, *The Law Above the Law*, 116.
[272]  Keane, 684.

For example, if after an operation a swab is found to have been left in a patient's body, it seems reasonable enough to infer, in the absence of explanation by the surgeon, that the accident arose through negligence.[273] If a surgeon uses proper care, such an accident does not, in the ordinary course of things, occur; negligence may be presumed. However, there is another presumption that a person is dead if he has not been heard of for over seven years. There is, of course, no logic in the choice of 2,556 days' absence of these purposes as opposed to say 2,560 days' absence.[274]

Another presumption of law in support of our apologetics task when we rely on our Scriptures. Since Christianity is based on the New Testament and the sayings of Christ as written in the gospels, the Christians undoubtedly will rely on them as the primary source of evidence. But we do not have the primary documents to be tendered as the best evidence. Neither do we have the eyewitnesses to be in court to testify through tendering the secondary documentary evidence. Hence, the objector definitely would wish to submit a preliminary objection at the preliminary stage, to get a ruling on its inadmissibility. However, the objector would face an uphill task because his preliminary objection will be ruled out because of the law of presumptions on ancient documents. As the manuscripts concerned are nearly two thousand years old and together with the circumstances surrounding it, they fall under the category of ancient documents which is admissible in court through the law of presumptions.

This law presumes that private documents of 20 years or more[275] produced from proper custody, and otherwise free from suspicion, prove themselves, and no evidence of the handwriting, signature, sealing or delivery need, in general, be given. The rule applies to wills, deeds requiring attestation, accounts, letters, entries, receipts and settlement certificates,[276] as well as, it has been through, to all other documents, public of private.[277] Naturally, the New Testament fall under this principle as it could be considered as a collection of letters and documents, private and/or public. It was held in Bishop of Meath v Marquis of Winchester[278] that such ancient documents would be sufficient to be in the proper custody that is deposit with a person and in a place where, if authentic, it might naturally and reasonably be expected to be found, even though

---

[273]  *Mahon v Osborne* [1939] 2 KB 14, CA.
[274]  *Chard v Chard* [1956] P 259 at 272 as per Sachs J.
[275]  Section 4 of the Evidence Act 1938.
[276]  Stark. Ev. (4th ed.) pp. 521 – 524.
[277]  *Wynne v Trywhitt* [1821] 4 B. & Ald. 376.
[278]  [1836] 4 Cl. & F. 445; 3 Bing. N.C. 183.

there might be another which would be more strictly and absolutely proper. This is precisely the case with the NT manuscripts. They have been used in the church from time immemorial, and thus are found in the place where might naturally and reasonably be expected to be found. Simon Greenleaf concisely explained that these Sacred Writings are:

'... found in familiar use in all the churches of Christendom, as the sacred books to which all denominations of Christians refer, as the standard of their faith. There are no pretense that they were engraven on plates of gold and discovered in a cave, nor that they were brought from heaven by angels; but they are received as the plain narratives and writings of the men whose names they respectively bear, made public at the time they were written; and though there were some slight discrepancies among the copies subsequently made, there is no pretense that the originals were anywhere corrupted. If it be objected that the originals are lost, and that copies are now produced, the principles of the municipal law here also afford a satisfactory answer. For the multiplication of copies was a public fact, in the faithfulness of which all the Christian community had an interest ...'[279]

It is clear that if these ancient documents 'come from such a place, and bear no evident mark of forgery, the law presumes that they are genuine, unless the opposing party is able successfully to impeach them. The burden of showing them to be false and unworthy of credit,'[280] rest on the objector whereas the party relying on the ancient document merely have to show that writings are found in the proper custody that is deposit with a person and in a place where, if authentic, it might naturally and reasonably be expected to be found.

Another presumptions clearly applicable to our apologetic task is the principle of res ipsa loquitor i.e. 'the facts speaks for itself'.[281] In Scott v London & St Katherine Docks Co.,[282] the court defined res ipsa loquitor as follows: on the proof or admission of the basic facts that

---

[279]  Montgomery, *The Law Above the Law*, 99

[280]  Ibid., 98.

[281]  Some precedents of *res ipsa loquitor* from case laws. It is presumed in advance without supporting evidences that a failure to exercise proper care committed by those who have the management of the things or situation in question e.g. *Ward v Tesco Stores Ltd* [1976] 1 WLR 810, CA presumed that slippery substances are not left on shop floors; *Ellor v Selfridge & Co Ltd* [1930] 46 TLR 236 presumed that cars do not mount the pavement; *Chapronière v Mason* [1905] 21 TLR 633, CA presumed that in the ordinary course of things, stones are not found in buns; or bags of flour do not fall from warehouse windows as in *Byrne v Boadle* [1863] 2 H&C 722.

[282]  [1865] 3 H&C 596.

i) something was under the management of the defendant or his
servant and

ii) an accident occurred, being an accident which is in the ordinary
course of things does not happen if those who have the management use proper care, it may or must be presumed, in the
absence of sufficient evidence to the contrary, that an accident
was caused by the negligence of the defendant.[283]

The application of the maxim *res ipsa loquitor* as circumstantial evidence
exceedingly can point towards Christ's resurrection. Professor John
Warwick Montgomery illustrates by showing *res ipsa* entails the following
syllogism:

*Res ipsa loquitor* in typical negligent case:

1) Accident does not normally occur in the absence of negligence.
2) Instrumentality causing injury was under the defendant's exclusive
control.
3) Plaintiff did not himself contribute to the injury.

Therefore, defendant negligent: "the event speaks for itself".

*Res ipsa loquitor* as applied to Christ's resurrection:

1) Dead bodies do not leave tombs in the absence of some agency affecting
the removal.
2) The tomb was under God's exclusive control, for it had been sealed, and
Jesus, the sole occupant of it was dead.
3) The Romans and the Jewish religious leaders did not contribute to the
removal of the body (they had been responsible for sealing and guard-
ing the tomb to prevent anyone from stealing the body, and the disciples would not have stolen it, then prevaricated, and finally died for
what they knew to be untrue).

Therefore, only God was in a position to empty the tomb, which He did, as
Jesus Himself had predicted, by raising Him from the dead: "*the events
speaks for itself.*"[284]

---

[283] [1865] 3 H&C as per Sir William Erle CJ at 601.

[284] Montgomery, John Warwick. "*Law & Gospel: A Study Integrating Faith and Practice*"
(Edmunton, 1994), 35; also see Montgomery, *Tractatus Logico-Theologicus* [Bonn,
Germany: Verlag fur Kultur und Wissenschaft, 2002], paras 3.666 – 3.67.

As discussed above on the accusation or suggestion that Jesus may be a charlatan or crazy when He gave such outrageous claims, the actual onus of proof should be on the one proposing it. Based on this judicial principles of evidence on presumptions, it should be presumed first that Jesus was telling the truth and was of sound mind at the time He claimed to be the Son of God. Let us remind ourselves that presumptions without basic facts come into operation without the proof or admission of any basic fact; they are merely conclusions which must be drawn in the absence of evidence in rebuttal. Even if the atheists are able to discharge their burden by proving prima facie evidences, it is not a problem from the Christians to tender a host of evidences to prove that Jesus was neither a liar nor a loony.[285] Professor Keane explains the relevance of presumptions of innocence and sanity:

> They are rules relating to the incidence of the legal and evidential burdens expressed in the language pertaining to presumptions. The following examples may be given. In criminal proceedings, reference is often made to the presumptions of innocence and sanity. Both are more meaningfully expressed in terms of the incidence of the burden of proof. The presumptions of innocence is a convenient abbreviation of the rule that the prosecution bear the legal burden of proving any fact essential to their case.[286] Likewise the presumption of sanity refers to the rule that the accused bears the legal burden of proving insanity when he raises it as a defence.[287]

Some judicial members of the House of Lords referred them as "*the presumption of mental capacity.*"[288] Truly, this presumption of mental capacity is adequate to show that Jesus was in fact of sound mind without any ne-

---

[285] Many great works have been written to explain away the possibility that Jesus was a liar or a lunatic. The more popular amongst the many are such as Lewis, C.S., "*Mere Christianity*" (New York: MacMillan, 1952); Hort, Fenton John Anthony. "*Way, Truth and the Life*" (New York: MacMillan, 1894); Latourette, Kenneth Scott. "*A History of Christianity*" (New York: Harper & Row, 1953); Schaff, Phillip. "*The Person of Christ*" (New York: American Tract Society, 1913); Montgomery, John Warwick. "*History and Christianity Minneapolis*" (Minnesota: Bethany House Publishers, 1965); Strobel, Lee. "*The Case for Christ: A Journalist's Personal Investigation of the Evidence for Jesus*" (Grand Rapids, Michigan: Zondervan, 1998); Geisler, N & F. Turek. "*I Don't Have Enough Faith To Be an Atheist*" (Wheaton, Illinois: Crossway Books, 2004); and McDowell, Josh, "*The New Evidence That Demands A Verdict*" (Here's Life Publishers, 1999).

[286] See *Woolminton v DPP* [1935] AC 462.

[287] Keane, 689.

[288] *Bratty v A-G for Northern Ireland* [1963] AC 386 per Viscount Kilmuir LC at 407 and per Lord Denning at 413.

cessity on the part of the Christians to provide evidences. Lastly, it should be noted that the atheists bears the burden of proof in any of the allegation such as the above examples. However, evidential apologists must agree that the ultimate burden on proving the existence of God and Jesus is the incarnate Son of God who died for our sins rests on us.

The constant suppression of the truth and the intentionally aggravate one's own existing depraved minds to further harden their hearts is not the failure of the apologists in discharging their legal burden. As long with integrity and the proper use of a fair methodology, we have taken a few steps ahead in persuading the other side to consider the probability of the Christian truth claim and assist in deciding to open their hearts to the constant prompting of the Holy Spirit.

## Conclusion

The legal maxim familiar to legal philosophers – "*Ubi eadem ratio ibi idem lex*" can simply be said that the law is founded upon reason, and is the perfection thereof, and what is contrary to reason is contrary to law. For the purpose of this book, this maxim could be equally applied to mean that the principles of the law of evidence is founded upon reason. Hence what is contrary to reason is contrary to the judicial principles of evidence. To a large extent then, what is contrary to the basic principles of legal evidence, is contrary to basic apologetic methodology. I intentionally use the word 'basic' inferring that man's restricted capability in seeking the truth is merely basic and in the sense, limited to their finite mind. What is contrary to the finite reason is contrary to the finite law within their capacity to comprehend. What is contrary to the basic apologetic methodology is contrary to their basic reason. Any other apologetic methodology that goes beyond their finite reasoning is contrary to the basic principles of evidence only understood within our physical realm. By no means can it persuade man to understand the things of the spirit as they have not yet converted into '*spiritual man*' by the Holy Spirit. It only act as a basic tool of apologetics adequately persuade man of basic mind.

Maintaining any apologetics that presupposes a belief that goes beyond the basic mind is liken to any mystical imprudent persuasion of the irrationals.

The law will not admit any presumption against reason, for the law is reason and equity; to do right to all and to keep men from wrong and mischief; therefore the law will not make any construction against the law, equity and right. Whenever there is the like reason, there is the like law. "*Nihil quad et contra rationem est licitum*" i.e. for the reason is the life of the law; and the common law is nothing but the reason. This reasons which have been gotten by long experience, and not each individual man's natural reason. It derives from a long process of experiences and collective knowledge of many heads united into one to make up the ever developing principles of the law of evidence. These methodological principles of seeking the truth, may not be perfect, but has the substance of authority, proving rules of sieving out irrelevant evidences from the relevant ones.

Another legal maxim bring us to mind, "*Duo sunt instrumenta ad omnes res aut confirmandas aut impugnandas - ratio et auetoritas*" i.e. there are two instruments either to confirm or impugn all things - reason and authority. It is the collection of reasons and legal authorities in furnishing an acceptable rule of the game in achieving an answer of which one would be accountable if fail to accept.

This is the law of nature and the law of order evident within mankind. Any true epistemology and any true knowledge are the creation of God within the natural order of things. This is the general revelation and natural theology sanctioned by God. Paul tells us in Romans 1:19-20 the truth which is revealed from heaven is '*evident within them; God made it evident to them. For since the creation of the world His invisible attributes, His eternal and divine nature, have been clearly seen, being understood through what has been made, so that they are without excuse.*' In other words, the epistemological knowledge as reflected in the principles of judicial evidence are part and parcel of the natural created order of which all person are responsible for inferring the truth. William Lane Craig remind us:

> A person who rejects all theistic arguments may be said to be "rational" in this technically defined sense, but the fact remains that he rejects without justification a theistic conclusion that he knows to be probable with respect to the deliverance of reason. He thereby reveals his hardened heart and renders himself "without excuse" before God. If the Christian apologist can show Christian theism to be probable with respect to premises that are either deliverances of reason or themselves ultimately probable with respect to them, then his task is complete.[289]

In addition, God is not a God of confusion,[290] He makes laws that corresponds with the logical reason he had set up for this universe, especially for man who is made in His image. He appoints man and provides wisdom to them to develop right argument and principles of epistemology. As

---

[289] Craig, W. L., *Classical Apologetics* in Five Views, 47-48.
[290] 1 Corinthians 14:33a.

'there is no authority except from God, and those which exist are established by God. Therefore whoever resists authority has opposed the ordinances of God; and they who opposed will receive condemnation upon themselves'[291], similarly all good logic and principles of evidences belongs to God. As the saying goes, "All truths are God's truth." There is no good legal authority or wisdom except from God.

At this juncture, one may argue that the author of this book seems to sound like a presuppositionalists. Yes, but in a different sense. We presupposes that all authority and reason of procuring truth comes from God. Hence, legal apologists embrace all good authority and reason ordained by God in our apologetic task. God must have given each of us, and at different degrees, the faculty of reasoning and the common sense to assess the probative value of an evidence when He made us in His image,[292] otherwise He wouldn't have invited us to reason together with Him.[293]

---

[291]   Romans 13: 1a-2 [NASB].
[292]   See Genesis 1: 26-28.
[293]   Isaiah 1:18.

# CHAPTER 4

## Legal Apologetic Methodology of the Fourth Gospel

From the last chapter's long discourse of various type of evidences, one may come to realize that the dominant approach to analyzing the principles on the law of evidence focuses on how the trial system are structured to guard against error. Similarly, the task of legal apologetics is to our best endeavors to ensure our defense are structured to guard against wrong accusation of unfair methodology which may be manifestly seen as irrational to the non-Christians. Whilst taking note of the complex and intertwining moral, spiritual and epistemic considerations, legal apologists must come into view by departing from the standpoint of a detached observer and taking the perspective of the person responsible for making findings of fact. Through exploring the nature and content of deliberative responsibility that the role and purpose of much of the evidential law can be fully understood. Going through the principles of evidence either propounded through case laws or govern by statutes will give us a rough comprehension of how the courts discharge its deliberative responsibility to achieve a right verdict.

Any litigant does not merely have a right that the substantive evidential law be correctly applied to objectively true findings of fact, but also a right to have the case tried under rationally structured rules. Similarly, a religious truth seeker should applies the judicial evidential principles to achieve objectively true finding of fact and have his process of decision making operates under rationally structured arguments. The litigant has, more broadly, a right to a just verdict, where justice must be understood to incorporate a moral evaluation of the process which led to the outcome. Similarly, any of the potential believers has a right to a just verdict, where a judicious decision in making the Christian commitment must be understood to have involve the incorporation of an honest, logical and coherent process.

There must be an important sense in which truth and justice are applied in the apologetic task of evangelism. The principles of the law of evidence governs the court process in finding truth and justice. Christian apologists must not only find the truth to do justice, they must do justice in finding the truth. By applying the similar judicial evidential principle, it immensely will help our apologetic task in declaring the Word of God in a just and fair manner. Evidentialism is not out to declare every beliefs are irrational if it was made without adequate evidence. Evidentialism, especially legal apologetics endeavors to make beliefs more rational and have faith strengthened even to a higher level as more evidence are provided through rational epistemological mode. Evidentialism is to ensure justice is done in the process of seeking the truth, applying whatever relevant available sources at the right time, and a right place to the appropriate target audience. Through this fair and just epistemological mode, it entails a belief we can consider as rational. Sadly, presuppositionalism neither have such judicious mechanism nor a common acceptable contact point even at the initial stage of evangelism.

The previous chapter may had whetted our appetite in appreciating how some basic principles of the law of evidence can be applied in the task of apologetics. In this chapter we shall answer whether legal apologetics was applied by the author in the fourth gospel. Consequently, it will indirectly defend evidentialism, as oppose to presuppositionalism. As stated elsewhere legal apologetics is not the only or perfect method of executing the apologetic task. Basically, in appreciating legal science, one can see that it indirectly demonstrates the 'common sense' of our human make-up in assessing the truth. In other words, the normal commonality of investigation as understood by many of us in assessing any fact in issue should be similarly applied in our investigation of the Christian truth claims. If the presuppositionalists assume that the Scriptures should be the sole authority, it would mean that the Scripture's epistemological methodology also act as a model for Christian apologists to comply. Hence, this chapter will conclude that if the Apostle John had consciously and intentionally assessed the logical flow and evidence (but unconsciously applied the principles of the law of evidence) to rationally convince his readers, then legal apologetics should be the method and should not be ridiculed by the presuppositionalists or reformed epistemologists. If this were true, then the Apostle John is truly indeed an evidential apologist and one who love God with all his mind. Then, our Christian apologetic task should not be plainly fideistic.

## Evidence of Authorship

We shall not delve unto a protracted discourse on the authorship of the fourth gospel. However, it is noted that similar to the Synoptic, the fourth gospel is formally anonymous.[294] Carson & Moo were careful to state that as far as we can prove, the title "According to John" was attached to it as soon as the four canonical gospels began to circulate together as "the fourfold gospel." In part, no doubt, this was to distinguish it from the rest of the collection; but it may have served as the title from the beginning.[295] But even if the attribution "According to John" was added two or three decades after the book was published, the observation of F.F. Bruce is suggestive: *"It is noteworthy that, while the four canonical gospels could afford to be published anonymously, the apocryphal gospels which began to appear from the mid-second century onwards claimed (falsely) to be written by apostles or other persons associated with the Lord."*[296]

There are adequate internal and external evidences that point towards the Apostle John as the author of the fourth gospel. General Editor of Biblical Theology of the New Testament, Andreas J. Köstenberger[297] wrote in regards to the internal evidence:

> ... the author leaves tantalizing clues in his gospel, which, when examined in conjunction with the testimony of the early church fathers, points convincingly to authorship of John, the son of Zebedee and an apostle of Jesus Christ. The author identifies himself as *"the disciple whom Jesus loved"* (John 21:20, 24), a prominent figure in the Johannine narrative (13:23; 19:26; 20:2; 21:7, 20). Although this disciple's identity is elusive, he leaves sufficient clues in the narratives to ascertain it beyond reasonable doubt. The initial such clues appear in 1:14 and 2:11. The author uses the first person in 1:14, *"We have seen His glory,"* revealing that he was an eyewitness to the accounts contained in his gospel. The "we" of 1:14 are identified in 2:11 as Jesus' disciples. The writer, then, is both an apostolic eyewitness and one of Jesus' first followers.[298]

There are also sufficient extra biblical sources to indicate that the Apostle John was the author of the fourth gospel. University of London Professor

[294] For a brief treatment of the 'anonymity' of John's gospel, see Köstenberger, Andreas. J. *"Encountering John: The Gospel in Historical, Literary, and Theological Perspective"* (EBS; Grand Rapids: Baker, 1999), 27.

[295] Carson, D.A. & Douglas J. Moo. *"An Introduction to the New Testament"* (Grand Rapids, Michigan: Zondervan, 2005), 229.

[296] Bruce, F.F., *"The Gospel of John"* (Basingstoke: Pickering & Inglis, 1983), 1 cited in Carson & Moo, 229.

[297] Senior Research Professor of New Testament and Biblical Theology at Southeastern Baptist Theological Seminary at Wake Forest, North Carolina.

[298] Köstenberger, Andreas. J. *"A Theology of John's Gospel and Letters"* (Grand Rapids, Michigan: Zondervan, 2009), 72.

of New Testament Exegesis, R.V.G. Tasker listed a few of the earliest external evidences with regard to the authorship of the fourth Gospel. Amongst others, he noted that:

> Irenaeus, who became bishop of Lyon in AD 177, speaks of 'John the disciple of the Lord ...who reclined on His breast and himself issued (*exedōke*, 'gave out' or 'published') the Gospel at Ephesus'. This statement of Irenaeus was founded on reliable information, for he tells us that he had often heard Polycarp the saintly bishop of Smyrna, who was martyred at the age of eighty-five in AD 155, relate what he had heard from the lips of John and other disciples about Jesus. It is significant that Irenaeus does not say that John wrote the Gospel, but his language clearly implies that it was published with his authority.[299]
>
> Polycrates, bishop of Ephesus, in a letter to Victor, bishop of Rome, which is usually, dated about AD 190, states that 'John who reclined on the breast of the Lord' was a 'witness ... and a teacher.[300]
>
> From Rome about the year AD 170 comes the evidence of what is known as the Muratorian Fragment, which gives a list of Christian books which should be accepted as Scripture with a brief account of the origin of some of them. It clearly regards John as the virtual author of the Fourth Gospel, but the language used suggests that others besides him were concerned with its production.[301]

The apostle John shall be assumed as the author of the fourth gospel in this book. The Gospel of John as inspired word of God and its historical authenticity shall also be presupposed. Whether the Gospel in question was composed in John's name and with his approval by one who based his work on the evidence of the apostle or not, for the purposes of this book we shall pursue only the apologetic methodology applied by the author of the fourth Gospel.

## Why John?

Basically, John is chosen because his gospel reflects himself as the actual eyewitness testimony from one of the key participants in the actual events leading to Jesus' crucifixion. John's purpose of writing is unequivocal affirmed in 20:31, as though he is saying the ultimate fact in issue that needed to be proven is *"Jesus is the Christ, the Son of God; and that be-*

[299] Tasker, R. V. G. *"Tyndale New Testament Commentaries: John"* (Grand Rapids, Michigan: Inter-Varsity Press, 1983), 17.
[300] Ibid.
[301] Ibid., 18-19.

*lieving you may have life in His name.*" The Gospel he wrote exhibits the solemnity of a documentary evidence as reflected in his affirmation in 19:35 – "*And he who has seen has testified, and his testimony is true; and he knows that he is telling the truth, so that you may believe.*" John affirmed again before he 'close his case' as though he is asked to stand to take the oath to say '*the truth and nothing but the truth*', by admitting that he was the disciple who is testifying – "*This is the disciple who is testifying to these things and wrote these things, and we know that his testimony is true.*"[302]

It is said that the Gospel of John has every reason to be considered as a "spiritual gospel".[303] Professor Köstenberger describes the fourth Gospel as "*being an interpretive account that brings out more fully the spiritual significance of the events and teachings its features – is grounded firmly in actual historical events, for it is only on such that theological reflection can properly be based.*"[304] Although the genre is closer towards spirituality, grounded on a profound theological reflection, John still need to have an approach to convince his readers that this is truly based on real historical events through which God acted in salvation history. In other words, John has to meticulously frame his narrative so as not to be interpreted as a myth or cult legend. Hence, John uses eyewitness language as though testifying in court to what he and other disciples had seen. For example, we see in John 1:14, "And the Word became flesh and dwelt *among us*, and *we saw* His glory as of the only begotten from the Father, full of grace and truth." In other words, his readers need to be intellectually convinced before they make a decision to enter this good news of spirituality John wants them to experience in Christ. Nowhere can we infer from John's writings insisting his readers to presuppose or experience the spirituality first before understanding or accepting the actual historical value of his narrative. Instead John, similar to a lawyer, framed his argument on relevant evidences and reasoning, whilst leaving out the irrelevant ones. This is to ensure adequate evidences and rationale arguments put forward are explained convincingly beyond a reasonable doubt, so as not to fall under future criticism for being precariously unjustified.

Professor Köstenberger further explains:

> If ...the Johannine narratives were found to rest on a precarious historical foundation, this would have a major negative consequences for the veraci-

---

302   John 21:24 [NASB].
303   See Clement of Alexandria's *Hypotyposes*, cited in Eusebius, HE, vi. 14. 7 briefly quoted in Guthrie, Donald. "*New Testament Introduction*" (Leicester, England: Apollos/IVP, 1990), 285-286.
304   Köstenberger, "*A Theology of John's Gospel and Letters*", 39.

ty of its theological, Christological, and soteriological assertions. It is therefore imperative to assess the historical value of John's gospel, not least because mere literary readings fall short of doing full justice to the historical nature of Christianity and the gospel's claim of eyewitness testimony.[305]

Besides being the eyewitness, one can look at the angle of John as the lawyer presenting his case by forwarding evidences and testimony to the readers of his time. On the other hand, one may look at the angle as a judge/jury deciding the reliability of John as a witness and the testimony he presented to us in our present time. However, we will concentrate on the methodology John adopt for the conviction of belief.

We are not here to prove how reliable is the writings of John. We assume that John's Gospel are prima facie reliable but we are more concern with the methodology used by John to convince his readers. We envisage that John is the defense lawyer making a defense for the allegation that Jesus was not the Messiah. John laid down his logical argument systematically both based on rationality and evidences to convince the reader that *"Jesus is Christ, the Son of God"*. He applied the principles of logic understood by the Greek philosophers and the evidences easily comprehended by the Jews, which can be considered as common sense and admissible by the modern trial courts of the Anglo-American principles law of evidence.

Nowhere in John's writing was there any extolment of blind faith over rationality. In fact, in almost all the chapters in John's gospel, we can see the constant application of evidence and reasons. John clearly understood that the belief in Jesus as the Son of God does not merely rest on faith but such belief must be justified by responsible knowledge. A proper concentration on John's writing will convince us that his apologetic and Jesus' approach is closer to evidentialist apologetics than other school of apologetics. This is not because of John's and Jesus' predilection on such methodology but because man is generally created to have a mind to rationalize and the free-will to decide. Since God is not a cruel God that left us with nothing except blind speculations and fallible philosophies over His redemption plan for mankind through a Person who had once walked on earth within space and time, by His grace He has left us with abundance of historical evidence. There are ample of evidences, individually or collectively which are adequately persuasive for man to be convinced. Through the reliance of these evidences, it will prompt him to apply his faith on Jesus Christ.

---

[305]   Ibid., 41.

The Apostle John truly understood the requirement for an objective explanation supported by reasoned argument and evidence. While feelings may be plausible criteria to use in deciding which church or temple has a better worship team or inspiring songs, emotions certainly should have little place in our search for truth in religion. Similarly, the judge may use her subjective feelings in deciding whether which blouse to wear beneath her judiciary robe, her heart's preference cannot be relied on as the measurement for the test she use to pronounce the verdict of the accused she is trying that morning in court. Similarly, our decision to accept Jesus as the second person in the Trinity and as the only way to salvation requires us to rationalize the logic and evidence objectively. One may or may not presuppose the existence of God, but unless the Gospel of the Lord Jesus Christ is rationally explained to the hearers, they will not come to know the truth or even made a justified belief.

## Evidentialism Approach of John

The apologetic methodology adopted in John is similar to evidentialism to clarify issues on which the evidence will be either accepted or rejected. Even though John may have had presupposes the knowledge of the Old Testament possessed amongst his Jewish readers, it is by no means that his approach is presuppositionalism. John still need to provide adequate evidences and reasoned argument to convince his readers that Jesus was the one that the Old Testament prophets had prophesized. In addition, having Greek readers in mind, John embraces natural theology, similar to classical apologetics to make his primary intention to evangelize more convincingly.

Whether believing in God is a basic belief or not, unless the good news of Jesus is testified, no one will comprehend that Jesus is the Son of God. John understood this and unless he wrote of what he saw, heard and touched, concerning the Word of life, his potential readers will not experience the joy and fellowship in Jesus Christ.[306] A theist may have his burden of proof removed from his apologetic obligation, if it is true everyone is warranted in believing in God's existence with or without supporting evidences of God's existence.[307] However, the burden still rest with the

---

[306] See 1 John 1: 1-4.

[307] See Plantinga, Alvin. "Reason and Belief in God" in *Faith and Rationality*, edited by Plantinga and Wolterstorff (Notre Dame, Indiana: University of Notre Dame Press, 1983), 16-93. According to Alvin Plantinga, a belief is basic if a person holds it without basing on some other belief. A belief is properly basic if the person holding it is in some significant way warranted in doing so.

Christian apologists in proving that Christianity, amongst other available religions, is the correct religion to demonstrate God's salvation plan through Jesus Christ. Both the Apostles Paul and John understood this because "... *how will they believe in Him whom they have never heard? And how will they hear without a preacher?*"[308] Both John's potential Jewish and Greek readers may have already believed in some kind of divine being but yet they need to know and be convinced which name of the Lord to be called upon to be saved.

> For there is no distinction between Jew and Greek; for the same Lord is Lord of all, abounding in riches for all who call on Him; for WHOEVER WILL CALL ON THE NAME OF THE LORD WILL BE SAVED."[309]

Therefore, it is imperative that John's apologetic approach is to a greater extent evidentialism.

However, only to some lesser extent fideistic apologetics may be useful but by warranting Christianity's truth through legal apologetics as we can see in John's Gospel. Fideism may get its support from John 14:1 and 11:26 that faith is a demand of God; or 1:9 that only the Light will enlightens every man. In addition that man must first have faith by allowing God to enlighten them, reformed epistemologist held that belief in God, like belief in other persons, does not require the support of evidence or argument in order to be rational.[310] William Lane Craig responded with a clear refutation:

> I agree with his central thesis that "belief in God ... does not require the support of evidence or argument in order for it to be rational" ... "theistic arguments do provide some noncoercive evidence of God's existence".
>
> ... With respect to the first, I am very skeptical that any *sensus divinitatis* exists. Clark offers three reasons why we as Christians should believe that humans have a cognitive faculty that produces in us belief in God. But none of these reasons goes to show that belief in God is grounded in a natural in-

---

[308] Romans 10:14.

[309] Romans 10:12-13.

[310] This view has been defended by some of the world's most prominent philosophers, including Alvin Plantinga, leader of the recent revival in Christian philosophy. Plantinga was Reformed epistemology's first contemporary defender, and his home institution, Calvin College, supported the research of other prominent philosophers in its development, including Nicholas Wolterstorff, William Alston and George Mavrodes. See Clark, James Kelly. "*Reformed Epistemology Apologetics*" in chapter 5 of Steven Cowan (ed.) *Five Views on Apologetics* (Grand Rapids, Michigan: Zondervan Publishing House, 2000), 267-268.

stinct or inborn awareness of the human mind rather than in the witness of the Holy Spirit. I know of no scriptural warrant for such a *sensus divinitatis* (John 1:9 would be an exegetical stretch), whereas there is a wide biblical support for a *testimonium Spiritu sancti internum*. In the absence of any scriptural support for such an inner instinct, I do not know how one could justify its existence, since the witness and work of the Holy Spirit serve to explain any phenomenon of religious experience that one might think to explain by the *sensus divinitatis*.[311]

... If asked whether one's belief is warranted, one may have to confess that he doesn't know. Indeed, one could be filled with doubt and gnawing uncertainty about this belief. But this seems a far cry from the full assurance of which Paul and John speak in reference to the testimony of the Spirit. Belief in God is not the result of some secret faculty functioning silently within, but of the testimony of God himself to our soul.[312]

Let me give a less intellectual explanation. Even if there is some kind of *sensus divinitatis*, it is by no means that rational arguments and evidences cannot contribute to buttress the belief in God. In addition, if everyone has that *sensus divinitatis*, why there are so many sincere and atheists living and behaving more rationally than some theists? Does that mean that some theists do not even rationally knows that they have that *sensus divinitatis*? Why there are incidents that some theists abandon their faith and chose rationally to become an atheist? Does that mean they have lost their *sensus divinitatis* or some defeating evidences had overwhelmed them? If yes, can evidences and reasons help them to comprehend rationally the *sensus divinitatis* or any other basic belief? For example, my innate feelings (deep sense of conviction) can be my personal subjective evidence – only can convince my personal self. However, I may still doubt because there is no 100% certainty because my heart may play tricks on me. I may feel my parental love but being an overly introvert melancholic perfectionists, I may doubt my parents' love once a while. But it is the constant love they pour on me through many occasions, I begin to trust their love even more. So, their constant outpouring of love is a constant evidence confirming my innate feelings for them. In legal apologetics, evidence can help trigger that *sensus divinitatis* (if any) in us.

Reformed epistemologists' usual comparison to this innate warrant of belief is believing in other minds and beliefs in other person. But supposing there was a man who grew up in a jungle and has never met a single

---

[311] Craig's response to Kelly James Clark's Reformed Epistemology Apologetics in *Five Views*, 285-286.
[312] Ibid., 286-287.

person in his entire life, would he have that basic belief in the existence of another person or 'other minds'? Maybe he begins to suspect and gradually come to belief in other mind when he stumble unto another creature of his kind. By then, wouldn't it be right for us to say that it was the evidence of meeting the other person that causes him to believe in other mind or person? Hence, as for believing in an unseen God, the level of 'warrant of belief' (if any) is much lower than the 'warrant of belief' in other minds inside a being who is visible. Thus evidence of greater probative force is necessary. Even there is no extrinsic evidence to contribute, the fact that the experiential reality of God through the witness of the Spirit in my heart is by itself an evidence. Unlike the evangelistic driven purpose of legal apologetics, the presuppositionalist school and reformed epistemology are found wanting in its reason on the contributory and probative force of available evidences.

Craig laments Kelly James Clark's few words on apologetic per se:

> When he speaks of "good apologetic strategy" ... what he is really talking about is *evangelistic* strategy. Apologetics is that branch of Christian theology that seeks to give a rational defense of Christian truth claims. Clark's suggestions for bringing someone to belief in God have little to do with this task.[313] ... Successful evangelism involves not only harvesting, but sowing and watering, too. We must never think that because a nonbeliever remained unconvinced by our case that our apologetic has failed.[314] ... A robust natural theology and display of Christian evidences can help to foster an intellectual climate in which belief in Christ, even if not based on arguments, is a living option for thinking people.[315]

This is exactly a reflection of John's evangelistic strategy by providing clarification and evidences available to meet his primary purpose i.e. to testify as eyewitness of the signs performed by Jesus, so readers may believe that Jesus is the Son of God as in John 20: 30-31. In turn, by introducing Jesus, it is evidence for the atheist that God exist. If John took the view that belief in God is grounded in a natural instinct or inborn awareness of the human mind rather than in the witness of the Holy Spirit, he would not have wrote what were testified by the disciples and the signs performed in the presence of the disciples. If John had taken the presuppositionalist approach, there is a probability no necessity for him to have written the Gospel or had adopted the approach in writing the fourth

---

[313]  Ibid.
[314]  Ibid., 288.
[315]  Ibid., 289.

gospel. It would be unnecessary as the readers would have already pre-supposed the Christian truth, whatever the source of their presupposed conviction. If John still would want to put the story of Jesus in writing, and since the purpose is that the readers may believe, he would have had at the beginning of the Gospel or repeatedly reminded the readers that in order for them to believe, they must presuppose the truth before they start reading. But nothing of that sort instead one can notice that John meticulously wrote with theological support, philosophical reasoning and evidences similar to a lawyer attempting to convince the jury.

As we can observed in John 2:11, "This beginning of His signs Jesus did ... and manifested His glory, and His disciples believed in Him." And also in John 4:54, "This is again the second sign that Jesus performed ..." demonstrated John begin the emphasis that his gospel is developed around the signs to show that Jesus was the Son of God. John repeated elsewhere again to indicate the effect of signs performed as evidence to convince, for example in John 6:14, "Therefore when the people saw the sign which He performed, they said, 'This is truly the Prophet who is to come into the world.'"

John was so much concerned with the signs as evidence in support of Jesus' divinity that he even wish he could have written down all the signs that he had seen. John stated in 20:30, "Therefore many other signs Jesus also performed ... which are not written in this book" and before he penned off, wrote, "And there are also many other things which Jesus did which if they were written in detail, I suppose that even the world itself would not contain the books that would be written."[316]

In the next and final chapter, we shall go through the whole of Gospel of John to identify traces of legal evidential apologetic methodology. We shall scrutinize chapter by chapter of the fourth gospel to classify the types of evidence govern by the modern principles of the law of evidence. From this exercise, we may come to the conclusion that the apostle John, imitating His Lord Jesus, emphasizes the significance of reasoning and evidence as important apologetic tools of bringing forth the good news. Dr. Norman Geisler observes:

> In John's Gospel, "witness" (or "testimony") is used some thirty-three times as a verb ("bear witness") and fourteen times as a noun ("a witness"). From the very first chapter it is clear that the testimony is about the Lord Jesus Christ. John the Baptist "came for a witness, that he might bear witness of the light [Christ]" (1:7). John the Apostle wrote, "I have seen, and have

---

[316] John 21:25.

*borne witness* that this is the Son of God" (1:34). Apologetics, then, is first of all a witness to the truth about Christ.[317]

This method of relying on witness and testimony are evidences that John use to achieve his purpose for writing his gospel, tied up with demonstrating the veracity of Jesus' claim. Hence, the witness to the truth mentioned so many times in John's Gospel is first and foremost a theological, and perhaps even more accurately, a Christological concept of evidential apologetics. Thus, it shall be concluded that the Apostle John had consciously and intentionally assessed the logical flow and evidence (but may inadvertently applied the modern principles of the law of evidence) to rationally persuade his readers. If this were true, then the Apostle John is truly indeed a legal apologist and thus evidentialism is defended through Scriptures.

---

[317] Geisler. "Johannine Apologetics" *Bibliotheca Sacra*, 333-334.

# CHAPTER 5

## The Legal Principles of Evidence in the Gospel of John

Systematically surfing through chapter by chapter, we shall attempt to identify the basic judicial evidential principles as indirectly applied by the Apostle John. Apparently John's Gospel follows a lawsuit model in its defense of the claim that Jesus rose from the dead.[318] We shall see the relevant Christian evidences presented by the Apostle John which can be considered as admissible and enough to satisfy the standard of proof as embodied within the principles of the law of evidence.

### John Chapter 1: In the beginning there was the fact in issue

Like a lawyer[319], John begins his Gospel with an opening statement setting down the **ultimate fact in issue** i.e. that the jury must make a verdict that this Jesus whom he is introducing is the one from the beginning created the world (1:1-5; 10) and those who receive Jesus and believe in His name, shall become children of God (1:12). John thereon presents his argument relying on theological and philosophical concepts understood by his po-

---

[318] Broughton, W. P. "*The Historical Development of Legal Apologetics: With an Emphasis on the Resurrection*" (Xulon Press, 2009), 27.

[319] Is not relevant in this apologetic thesis to decide whether John's opening statement was of the prosecution or the defence. In either case, John presents his case similar to a trial lawyer either (as the role of the prosecution) to discharge his legal burden to prove the Christian claim or (as the role of the defence) to provide reasonable arguments with evidences to disprove or cast doubt on whatever the opposition may adduce. We can agree that John is assuming a dual role, first claiming the Gospel truth and second defending from any allegation that Jesus lack the true humanity (or divinity). Besides the evangelistic purpose (20:31), it can also be noted that John's other reason for writing the fourth gospel was to refute the false teaching of the Gnostic movement (1 John 2:18-19). Irenaeus claimed that John wrote the Gospel to refute Cerinthus – an early Gnostic teacher who held that the 'Christ spirit' descended on Jesus at his baptism and left him at the cross. If that were the purpose that triggered the motivation to write, we may confirm that John is writing in a position of a defence lawyer, giving an account to those who question his hope on the original Christian teaching. In diluting the opposition's allegation, John presented evidences that he is a credible and competent eyewitness (John 1:14; 1 John 1:1-4) and has the authority because his evidence is of admissible lay/expert opinion (John 21:24; 1 John 1:5).

tential readers, and substantiate it with eyewitnesses' testimony and 'signs' as real evidence. Andrew Lincoln is of similar opinion that the fourth gospel, 'is a narrative that asserts the truth about God, Christ, and life is to be seen in terms of the metaphor of a cosmic lawsuit, and it displays this assertion by making its discourse and plot have Jesus on trial, a trial in which the other characters (and, by extension the readers) have to come to a verdict and are invited to become witnesses'[320]

It is no coincidence that John start introducing his Christology by using *"In the beginning ... the Word was God"* having a parallel polemic nature of the creation account similar to the opening chapters of Genesis. Undeniably, John's opinion of Jesus was sufficient to equate him with God's creative work as *"in the beginning."*[321] Similar to classical apologetic, John's methodology goes straight to the point on the importance of theism before he introduces his **first witness** i.e. John the Baptist in 1:6-8; 19-34. Clearly, John embraces the importance of reasoning when he intentionally refer Jesus as the "Word". In Greek *'logos'* also can be inferred as reason or logic. Indeed, since logic is based in the very nature of God as the ultimate rational being from all rationality flows, it is appropriate to say: "In the beginning was Logic, and Logic was with God, and Logic was of the very nature of God."[322]

Taking exclusive cognizance on the connecting important side-issue (i.e. the existence of God), with the ultimate fact-in-issue (i.e. Jesus is God), John declares that both God and Jesus was there in the beginning. John wrote that this (Jesus), *"the Word was with God"* in verse 1 and reiterates *"He was in the beginning with God"* in verse 2. One may draw an inference that John's first witness is God Himself, rather than John the Baptist as mentioned in the preceding paragraph. John is aware of the significance of such usage. It is not an attempt to prove God but rather something like a *'cosmic alibi'* where Jesus was at the beginning – He was with God. God can testify to that. God do not need John to prove His existence as He already done so through general revelation. The Apostle Paul reminds us that since the creation of the world, God has revealed Himself and therefore all mankind is without excuse for not believing in Him.[323] Hence, the evidential apologetic used is to prove Jesus is the Son of God

---

[320] Lincoln, Andrew T. *"Truth on Trial: The Lawsuit Motif in the Fourth Gospel"* (Peabody, Massachusetts: Hendricksen, 2000), 169-170.

[321] Genesis 1:1.

[322] Geisler, Norman L. and Patrick Zukeran. *"The Apologetics of Jesus: A Caring Approach to Dealing with Doubters"* (Grand Rapids, Michigan, Baker Books, 2009), 68-69.

[323] See Romans 1:18-20.

who was crucified, died and resurrected; this in turn will buttress the proof of God's existence.

Note that the first 5 verses neither support presuppositionalism nor reformed epistemology. It is not about man should presuppose the existence of God in the beginning in order to understand '*the Light that shines in the darkness*'[324] or is already warranted for man to believe in God even from the beginning of creation. In fact, it is claiming that the deity of Christ and the God of whom Jesus Christ is declaring is the one true God of Abraham, Jacob, Isaac and Joseph as written in the books of Moses. Man has no problem in believing the divine as it is warranted for them to believe but it does not warrant them to comprehend the '*true Light which enlighten every man*'.[325] The world did not know Him (Jesus)[326] because the world suppresses the truth,[327] not because they were made to have depraved mind (otherwise they may be excused) but they knew God[328] and intentionally exchanged the truth of God for a lie.[329] Due to their intentional acts of moving away from God's law, "*God gave them over to a depraved mind*[330]...although they know the ordinance of God."[331] These verses implies that man know the existence and the law of God but intentionally behaved like having a depraved mind, much so God would not compel (*but gave them over*) to stop their cultivated habitual mind of a depraved lifestyle.

John's apologetic task is not to prove the existence of God but to declare that Jesus is God and similar to Moses' apologetic opening statement in Genesis, is to declare that the God of Israel is the one true God. This is a strong polemic against false religions and ideologies. To discharge this burden of polemic proof, presuppositionalism and reformed epistemology would not succeed, except to bring about evidential proof of the true identity of God. Whatever starting point of the presuppositionalist or reformed epistemologists will not help to disprove the underlying creation myth of the ancient Near East during the days of Moses. Following the argument from Professors Wayne House and Dennis Jowers:

---

[324] John 1: 5.
[325] John 1: 9.
[326] John 1:10
[327] Romans 1:18
[328] Romans 1: 21
[329] See Romans 1:22-27.
[330] Romans 1:28.
[331] Romans 1:32.

What is often missed in a reading of the creation accounts in Genesis 1 and 2 is that they were not written to establish a theory of creation as such, though certainly deductions may be made regarding the nature of creation from the text. Instead these chapters as a polemic against the pagan gods of Canaan, the land where the Israelites would soon enter. A grave danger was that the Israelites would embrace these pagan gods and abandon the true God who had delivered them from captivity in Egypt. The belief in monotheism in the ancient world was restricted to only one nation, Israel, and the pressure to conform to the surrounding nations, including the people of Canaan, would be strong.[332]

Moses' comprehension of the apologetic task in distinguishing the one true God of Israel from the false gods of the Canaan reflected in his writing through usage of historical records, signs and God's faithfulness. John similarly understood this evidential necessity to distinguish the Word who is God became flesh who were born of blood[333] from the false Ebionites doctrine that Jesus was a mere man upon whom the Spirit descended for a season but later left him.[334] Imitating the evidential apologetic style of Moses, John open his introductory emphasis with *"In the beginning ..."* commonly understood by the Jews. He also gave his Jewish reader a strong hint that there was a significant connection with the Law of Moses in verse 17. Here, John was referring to the Law of Moses as a **documentary evidence**, enlightening them that this Jesus is the Christ whom Moses and the other prophets are talking about.

## John's Use of Reason

Similar to a legal apologist who embraces other helpful relevant reasoning (either source from Scripture or other extra-biblical truths e.g. gravity or first principles logic), John may have applied other non-Jewish phil-

---

[332]  House, Wayne & Dennis Jowers. *"Reasons For Our Hope: An Introduction to Christian Apologetics"* (Nashville, Tennessee, B&H Academic, 2011), 125-126.

[333]  John 1:13-14.

[334]  This tradition is clearly stated in the second Prologue to the Gospel of John in the *Codex Toletanus* and is found also in similar language in Jerome: "John the Apostle wrote this Gospel against Cerinthus and the heretics, attacking in particular the dogma of the Ebionites, who in the perversity of their folly (that is why they are called Ebionites) asserts that Christ did not exist before He was born of Mary and was not begotten of God the Father before all ages. This is why He was compelled to mention His divine birth from the Father. [Cited from Tasker, R. V. G., *Tyndale New Testament Commentaries: John* (Grand Rapids, Michigan: IVP (1983), 34].

osophical and effective reasoning to bring about the Christian truth claim. John's methodology, hence demonstrates the necessity and permissibility of adopting **reasons** rather than base on faith as priority. The prologue in John 1 is the best evidence for this. It is said that John may have intentionally use the word *"logos"* as used by philosophers such as the Stoics and the first-century Alexandrian Jew, Philo, for the rational principle (Reason), which they thought governs the universe.[335] Against influence from this philosophical use, however, the fourth evangelist writes of divine communication, not of divine thought; and differently from all possible influences, he identifies the logos with a human being of recent history. In other words, John's methodology in the inspired Gospel applies Greek reasoning into the Christian apologetic task but not meant to authenticate Greek philosophy.

Professor of Religion Andrew Hoffecker explains:

In some instances Christian thought is simply portrayed as opposite to the ways of the "world."[336] On other occasions the authors of the New Testament specifically refer to a clash between Christian and Greek ideas. In 1 Corinthians 1:18 - 2:13, for example, Paul contrasts "the word of the cross" with the "wisdom of the world" and "wisdom of this age." By the "word of the cross" Paul means preaching Christ's death as the only atonement for man's sins. Only those who repent and trust Christ as Savior and Lord will be redeemed. How different from "the wisdom of the world," the vain attempts by Greek "wise men", "scribes," and "debaters," to find paths to salvation based on human wisdom. Explicitly Paul states that "Greeks seek wisdom, but we preach Christ crucified."[337] While Greek and Christian cultures often existed in close geographic proximity in the first century A.D., intellectual leaders from both sides viewed their controlling ideas as fundamentally irreconcilable. The apostles made little attempt to fuse elements from Christian and Greek world views into a larger synthesis. They did not believe that Christian thought should or could assimilate ideas into its basic structure. Dominating New Testament is the antithesis, the emphatic contrast, between Greek and Christian views. For example, John's use of the Greek *logos* ("word") for Jesus in the prologue of his Gospel[338] illustrates how Christian authors fundamentally altered Greek ideas if they used them at all. The apostle did not incorporate Greek concepts into

---

[335]  Gundry, Robert H. *"A Survey of the New Testament"* (Grand Rapids, Michigan: Zondervan, 2003), 266.

[336]  Cf. 1 John 2:15-17; James 4:4.

[337]  I Corinthians 1:23.

[338]  John1:1-18.

Christianity unchanged, but transformed the impersonal, abstract "word" into dynamic, personal terms as the incarnate Son of God ..."[339]

Experts in anthropology and missiology will tell us that missionary from the West during the 19th century had assimilated some of the pagan's vocabulary as a preliminary explanation on the concept of the Christian God. Back in the first century, the Apostle John has to take note of the transcultural task of evangelization. It is not just merely for John to say "Believe for the kingdom of God is at hand" but John and the other evangelists have the apologetic task to both defend from the attacks of the prevailing philosophy and to forward positively to their target audience and future readers already with a variety of religious presuppositions. Unless John bring about an objective reasoning understood by most people, it is highly unlikely for any Christian presuppositions to modify their existing pagan presuppositions. Samuel Escobar elucidates further on this:

> The faith of Jesus Christ have to be lived and interpreted in dialogue with narrow Jewish provincialism, with skeptical and sophisticated Greek philosophizing, with the Roman cult of the supreme principles of law, order and power, and with the deeply attractive spiritual experiences of the mystery religions. It was not only an intellectual task but also a resocializing experience and a spiritual struggle. The prologue to the fourth Gospel (1 John 1: 1-18) and the discourse of Paul in the Areopagus of Athens (Acts 17:22-31) are examples of the pioneer task for the first generation of transcultural missionaries of coming to terms with the intellectual challenge of the Greek thought. Evangelizing the Greek mind predominant in the Roman Empire required the missionaries be competent in the Greek language and intellectually capable of adapting Greek categories and ways of reasoning in order to express the Christian faith.[340]

Even the missionaries to China adapted the Chinese cultures and philosophies to bring about a comprehensible intellectual knowledge of the gospel. In order to express to its best intention of the Johannine Christology, it is said that when translating the word 'logos' for John 1:1, the missionaries have to take cognisance of the prevailing Chinese philosophy to attain the most suitable word closest to express the intention of the Apos-

---

[339] Hoffecker, Andrew. "*Christian Theology Emerges: The Council of Nicaea*" in Hoffecker & Smith (eds.), 'Building a Christian Worldview Vol. 1.' (Philipsburg, New Jersey: Presbyterian and Reformed Publishing Company, 1986), 73-74.

[340] Escobar, S. "*The New Global Mission: the Gospel from Everywhere to Everyone*" (Downers Grove, Illinois: InterVarsity Press, 2003), 40.

tle John. It was decided that in Chinese version of the Bible in John 1:1, 'tao' [道]³⁴¹ is chosen as the translation for "the Word". This 'tao' is often understood by the ancient Chinese as the conception of Godhead or Goodness, which also might be called 'a preface to God.'³⁴² It is also appropriately refer as 'the Way' as in the Chinese Bible version for John 14:6 when Jesus said, "*I am the Way, the Truth and the Life*". As though Jesus is saying, "I am the Tao". The wise Chinese sage, Lao Tzu admitted he could not identify or describe this 'tao'.

Lao Tzu wrote:

> I do not know His name.
> Name Him "Dao" [道] possibly.
> For lack of a better word,
> I call Him "The Almighty." [大]³⁴³

Confucius, the great compiler of all China's early writings, who was also baffled by Tao, believed it was beyond human understanding.³⁴⁴ This medieval concept of 'tao' also signifies the Godhead as righteous and of ethical characteristics. When the word 'tê' [德]³⁴⁵ is added to 'tao' it becomes 'tao tê' [道 德] as to mean the way or the ethics of good character, righteousness and of morality. It has a connotation to mean the logical way towards wisdom. Hence, reciprocally, 'logos' is the most appropriate word chosen by John as a first stepping stone to introduce Jesus as the Word of God and the only 'ethical' Way to God, easily grasped by readers either from the East or the West.

We are not saying man's reason is the measurement of truth but we are saying the John understood the predicament of man. The correct use of reasoning and appropriate relevant words are the tools God given us in our apologetic task. It is of no doubt that John recognizes that human is endowed by His Creator³⁴⁶ with the capacity to reason. Rationality and

---

³⁴¹ Literally, it means road, a path, the way by which people travel, the way of nature and philosophically is used as the way of ultimate Reality.

³⁴² Lao Tzu, "*Tao Té Ching*", translated & introduction by Blackney R.B. (New York: Signet Classic, 2007), 42-43.

³⁴³ Gia Fu Feng and Jane English. "*Translation of Lao Zi, Tao Te Ching*" (Toronto: Vintage Books, Random House, 1989), Chapter 25, p. 27.

³⁴⁴ Wang, Samuel and Ethel R. Nelson, "*God and the Ancient Chinese*" (Dunlap, TN: Sinim Bible Institute, 1998), 61.

³⁴⁵ Which mean literally, virtue, character, influence or moral force.

³⁴⁶ Genesis 1:1 & 27.

reasons is part of the "image of God" in which God made people[347] (whether from the West or the East), and even in our fallen state, we still retain His image.[348] The original sin has effaced the image of God, but it has not totally erased it. Unsaved people from every corner for the world and different languages or various religious concepts can still think rationally. We should be like the apostle John apply the right vocabulary, relevant reasoning and adequate evidence at the right time and at the right place. Throughout the fourth gospel, John demonstrated 'Jesus's mission was to teach and defend truth and to correct error (John 8:32). Through the process Jesus showed himself to be a brilliant philosopher who used the **laws of logic** to reveal truth, demolish arguments, and point out error.'[349]

## First Witness: John the Baptist

After giving his opening statement, John is prepared to introduce his **first witness**. John is forwarding a hearsay evidence because at time of writing, John the Baptist is already dead. Nevertheless, John the Baptist's testimony of Jesus is very important. We have seen in the previous chapters that **hearsay evidence** in such circumstances and if relevant is admissible. John also used the word "*confess*" in 1:20 indicating the credibility and admissibility of John the Baptist's statement. Incidentally, a confession[350] could not be given in evidence by the prosecution unless shown by them to be a voluntary statement in the sense that it was not obtained from the accused by fear or prejudice or hope of advantage exercised or held out by a person in authority[351] or by oppression.[352] A quick scrutiny of verses 19-24, we will notice that the authorities sent by the Pharisees from Jerusalem interrogated John the Baptist without inducing any fear

---

[347] Colossians 3:10.

[348] Genesis 9:6; James 3:9.

[349] Geisler & Zukeran, "*The Apologetics of Jesus: A Caring Approach to Dealing with Doubters*", 66. Chapter 4 is highly recommended as the authors demonstrate how Jesus used basic law of logic e.g. deductive syllogism; hypothetical syllogism; disjunctive syllogism, reduction ad absurdum, a fortiori argument; principles of non-contradiction, etc. in His apologetic task.

[350] Presently in England, admissibility of confession is provided in section 76 of the Police and Criminal Evidence Act 1984.

[351] *Ibrahim v R* [1914] AC 599, Privy Council as per Lord Sumner at 609 cited in Keane, 377.

[352] *Callis v Gunn* [1964] 1 QB 495 DC as per Lord Parker CJ at 495.

or favor. Hence, John the Baptist's **confession** is admissible as it was made voluntarily.

Generally, a confession is any statement wholly or partly adverse to the person making it[353] but John the Baptist's 'confession' is a kind of admission which is not an acknowledgement of guilt or in some way incriminating to him but it may be against his interests. Section 82 (1) PACE1984 covers 'mixed' statements i.e. it can be both inculpatory and exculpatory in nature. We are not saying John the Baptist was in any way guilty of a crime. John the Baptist's 'confession' may act both ways, inculpatory and exculpatory – (1) He is publicly confessing that he is not the Christ or Elijah of which John the Baptist may had all these while obliging the respect and honor he received from the crowd; and (2) Though he assumed the right to baptize,[354] it was only baptism in water and he should be exonerated because he has the authority whom was prophesized by Isaiah.[355]

By quoting from the prophet Isaiah, John in a way is tendering a **documentary evidence** from the book of Isaiah acting as a **corroborative evidence** in support of his first witness. John is building up his case by establishing the credibility and authority possessed by John the Baptist. This is significant because the next issue which is very important that goes to the root of the fact in issue is John the Baptist testifying that Jesus is the Son of God at verse 34.

If John the Baptist's hearsay confession is allowed in our imaginary court, then the content of his testimony is testifying that Jesus who is '*the Lamb of God that takes away the sin of the world*'[356] and had '*seen the Spirit descending as a dove out of heaven and remained upon*'[357] Jesus. As far as the principles of the law of evidence is concern, it is not for John the Baptist to give his opinion whether the content of his statement is true but is for the readers (acting like a trial judge or jury) to verify the truth. At this juncture, we could even, before moving on the other chapters, conclude that the apostle John acted like a lawyer presenting his evidence. His methodology does not even come close to the presuppositional apologetics.

This passage establishing the **confession** and authority of John the Baptist may also been seen as the intention of John to lay down evidences

---

[353]  Section 82(1) of the Police and Criminal Evidence Act 1984.
[354]  John 1:25-28.
[355]  John 1:23; Isaiah 40:3.
[356]  John 1:29 and 36.
[357]  John 1:32.

to combat against a Baptist cult. It is known that in Ephesus there were groups of followers of John the Baptist who were imperfectly instructed in the tenets of Christianity (cf. Acts 19:1-7). This kind of movement may well have been more widespread and it is an attractive hypothesis that this gospel may have been partially designed to counteract an allegation to John the Baptist which should have been given to Christ.[358] If presuppositionalism is the biblical authorized mode of apologetics, one may wonder why John goes to some lengths to demonstrate that Jesus was superior to John the Baptist. If evidentialism should be avoided, then John might as well have written that one need to presuppose that Jesus is more superior than anyone else including John the Baptist and stop there and then. After all isn't it warranted for man to have the basic belief that Jesus is more superior to the other baptizer? In fact, the author John, like a lawyer provides more evidence to show Jesus is superior by adding the fact that John the Baptist confessed, *"He must increase, but I must decreased."*[359]

In 1:37-40, the Apostle John also introduces witnesses who may provide their **lay opinion evidence** on the true identity of John the Baptist and Jesus since they had the opportunity to have spent time with both of them. Two of them were disciples of John the Baptist;[360] and heard him identify Jesus as the Lamb of God;[361] stayed with Jesus;[362] and amongst the two, Andrew became one of the twelve Disciples[363]

Furthermore, like a lawyer who foresee any possible **adverse inference which may be drawn from any irrelevant evidences**, John sieve away such evidences. Probably, John may have cautiously and intentionally omits the narrative of the baptism of Jesus as recorded in the three synoptic gospel. This may not give any unjustified credence to the sectarians of John the Baptist to argue that Jesus was baptized by John the Baptist and therefore was subject to him.

John end his opening speech statement and after providing **identification evidence** to distinguish the true identity between Jesus and John the Baptist, he introduces the first few disciples whom are key eyewitnesses. John also testified one of the divine attributes of Jesus i.e. omniscience as most probably from the hearsay statement of Nathanael.[364] Even with just

---

[358]  Guthrie, D., *"New Testament Introduction"* (1990), 293.
[359]  John 3:30 [NASB].
[360]  John 1:37.
[361]  John 1:36.
[362]  John 1:39.
[363]  John 1:40.
[364]  John 1:45-48.

one miracle, Nathanael believed and declared that Jesus is the Son of God.[365] But Jesus replied, 'Because I said to you that I saw you under the fig tree, do you believe? You will see greater things than these,'[366] implies that Jesus is more than willing to provide more evidences as some others may not be easily convinced by just one evidence. This also infers that John will be listing out more and convincing evidences thereon in the Gospel. This willingness to provide more signs demonstrated Jesus and John do not restrict evidentialism.

## John Chapter 2

Besides other theological information we can gather in this chapter, the epistemological point John wants to emphasize here is the importance of **signs as evidence to corroborate the true identity** of Jesus. John introduces the very first miracle performed i.e. turning water into wine at the wedding of Cana of Galilee and explains the reason for such evidences:

> This beginning of His signs ... and manifested his glory, and His disciples believed in Him.[367]

Subsequently, besides this minor sign performed to manifest His authority, as required by the Jews,[368] John is informing in advance the ultimate reason which will be proven by the ultimate evidence i.e. that Jesus will be bodily raised in three days.[369] Clearly, John stresses the importance of signs as evidence. This is what lawyers called it **demonstrative evidence**.

John is also careful to record other eyewitnesses (servants who had drawn the water) to support the headwaiter who can testify the taste of the water. This can be considered as several **circumstantial evidences** to infer the fact of a miracle performed. First circumstantial evidence may come from Mary who knew that the wine ran out.[370] Second circumstantial evidence is from the servants who heard and executed the instruction from Jesus to fill the six pots with water.[371] Third circumstantial evidence is from the headwaiter (who did not know where it came from) who can testify that the water he tasted from the pot is indeed wine.

---

[365] John 1:49.
[366] John 1:50.
[367] John 2:11 [NASB] and 23.
[368] John 2:18.
[369] John 2:19-22.
[370] John 2:3.
[371] John 2:7-8.

Combine these three circumstantial evidences, it would be strong enough
to prove that the water turned into wine had something to do with Jesus'
instruction.

As in chapter 1, John again emphasizes in this chapter the application
of eyewitnesses and miracles as important evidence. In verse 25, John
seems to impliedly clarify that evidentialism is not a mandatory methodology to prove the identity of Jesus but a necessary one due to man's situation. This is because *"Jesus, on His part, was not entrusting Himself to them,
for He knew all men, and because He did not need anyone to testify concerning
man, for He Himself knew what was in man,"*[372] and yet Jesus is willing to performed miracles so man may believe.

## John Chapter 3

This chapter introduces Nicodemus as another **witness** who had heard
the teaching of Jesus on spiritual rebirth. If John's purpose was to deliver
the 'born again'[373] message of Christ, he would have just explain this theology as a discourse. After all, the Disciples would have undergone a 'lec-
ture' by their Master on this important 'new birth' theology. Instead of
any other literary style, John conveyed this spiritual truth through a narrative as if reporting a historical fact. Again, this methodology reflects
the way a lawyer tender his evidence through witnesses, especially witnesses of caliber, **competence** and **credibility**. Nicodemus is of such person. In fact, Nicodemus assisted in the arrangement of the Jewish burial
custom for Jesus.[374] He together with other eyewitnesses can confirm that
Jesus was dead and can identify which tomb Jesus was laid (if there is an
evidential burden to be discharged against allegation that Jesus was not
dead or if the disciples credulously believe in the resurrection because
they went to the wrong tomb).

The Apostle John specifically introduces Nicodemus[375] as *"a man of the
Pharisees ... a ruler of the Jews"* in 3:1. This is appropriate as to identify a
witness' probable authority and trustworthiness before tendering the
content of the Christian truth i.e. gospel of John 3:16. John's similar legal
evidential method is to bring about a fact or teaching supported by **credible and competent witness.**

---

[372]  John 2: 24-25.
[373]  John 3:3-8.
[374]  John 19:39-42.
[375]  Also a member of the Jewish Sanhedrin.

If presuppositionalism is the apologetic method mandated by the Scripture and subscribe by the apostle John, it seems there is no necessity to introduce Nicodemus or for the matter of fact identify his qualification. John may have just chose other literary style such as poetry, prose or a collection of sayings but he did not. Instead, John recognizes the historical value and the obvious biographical purpose. No doubt John had indirectly applied the principles of the law of evidence – taking note that eyewitnesses and firsthand sources of the events were generally considered to provide a more reliable recounting of events. Greater credibility was attached to eyewitness testimony as opposed to hearsay, and the account was considered even more reliable if the source was a living eyewitness as he could verify the truth of the account.[376]

Fideism and presuppositionalism may take this passage as supporting their apologetic views that one must be first born of the Spirit in order to understand. However, on a careful reading from verse 11 to 21, nowhere Jesus infer that reason and evidence do not convince man of the truth because he is totally depraved. John records Jesus acknowledges that man testify of what they know and what they have seen.[377] This implies Jesus' acceptance of testifying with our sensory perception. The only problem is man choose not to accept the testimony. The problem is with man, not with the methodology. When Jesus said, "*If I told you earthly things and you do not believe, how will you believe if I tell you heavenly things?*"[378] This arguably seems to be *a fortiori* argument Jesus is applying. In other words, logically if ...

1) More difficult in believing spiritual things which cannot be seen.
2) Man will not even believe in earthy things of less difficulty which can be seen.
3) Therefore, it is not the level of difficulty of the object to be believed but the difficulty of the believer's willingness.

Jesus further explains the reasons for this unwillingness. It is not because they are naturally born totally depraved and has no capacity to believe but they intentionally chose to practice a lie rather than the truth. "*This is the judgment, that the Light has come into the world, and men loved the dark-*

---

[376] See Keener, Craig S. "*The Gospel of John: A Commentary*" 2 Vols. (Peabody, MA: Hendrickson, 2003), 21-22.

[377] John 3: 11.

[378] John 3:12.

*ness rather than the Light, for their deeds were evil,*"[379] and is because they "*fear that his deeds will be exposed.*"[380]

As in Chapter 1, John provide **direct statement** and **confession** of John the Baptist (though it is hearsay but admissible evidence). John also wrote that there are **other witnesses** who heard John the Baptist admission that he is not the Christ.[381] John has to write this passage[382] most probably to provide extra supporting evidence against a contemporary 'John the Baptist movement'[383] Surprisingly, John the Baptist had a following in Asia Minor decades after the ascension of Jesus. This seems to be an evidential apologetic task of the author of the fourth gospel to diminish the status of John the Baptist. Professor Andreas Köstenberger noted that this apologetic passage coheres with and support the earlier reference to John the Baptist in John 1:19-36 and explains:

> In the earlier passage, John indicated his purpose was to reveal the Messiah to Israel (1:31). Now that the Messiah had begun to work his powerful "signs", clearly the Baptist's role as a **witness** to Jesus, while abiding value (1:15), was close to become obsolete. Hence also, his imprisonment (3:24) and subsequent martyrdom were no great loss to the messianic movement, for John had fulfilled his divine assignment by the time he was called from the scene.[384]

Needlessly one should wonder why the apostle John did not encourage the Baptist devotees to *presuppose* the Messiahship of Jesus or remain silent by insisting that it is a *basic belief* that Jesus is more superior to John the Baptist. Instead the fourth evangelist took care to distinguish between John (forced to use the language of earth)[385] and Jesus (speaks God's own words)[386] from the testimony or more accurately, confession of John the Baptist. The apostle thus have to provide **evidence** and **reasoned argument** to quench whatever assumptions of the diehard followers of the Baptist in Ephesus.

---

[379] John 3:19.
[380] John 3:20.
[381] John 3:28.
[382] John 3:26-36.
[383] Bultmann, Rudolf. "*The Gospel of John*" Translated by George R. Beasley-Murray (Philadelphia: Westminster, 1971), 49.
[384] Köstenberger, "*A Theology of John's Gospel and Letters*" 201.
[385] John 3:31.
[386] John 3:34.

## John Chapter 4

In the previous chapter, John first introduces witnesses of trusted social standing or respected figure such as Nicodemus and John the Baptist. This is because their testimonies are more credible than ordinary men. However, John is also aware that witnesses from other walks of life can corroborate with each other on the identity of Jesus as different people of social standing may perceive facts according to their own prejudices. Having a variety of witnesses from different backgrounds but have the same conclusion will support each other's testimony. This raises the probative value of each individual testimony. There is little doubt why immediately after introducing John the Baptist and Nicodemus, the apostle John chose the Samaritan woman whose social standing is completely the opposite[387] from these two (whom may have more biasness towards its Jewish kin than the half-caste Samaritans). This would quench any possible criticism that a particular group of religious or social standing may interpret the identity of Jesus based on their *cemented colored glasses to his eyes which he cannot remove.*'[388]

This in turn may argue that John is mindful of the danger of presupposition. If it is true, and borrow from the vocabulary of Van Til's presuppositionalism, that there are 'no exception to' the 'jaundiced eye' of the 'sinner', there is a risk of 'reporting to himself by himself, as distorted by his own subjective conditions, which he assumes to be the facts as they really are.'[389] In other words, assuming presupposition is right, all the more John need is to provide various witnesses whilst wearing different colored glasses but conclude they perceived the same color. Like John, only evidentialists or legal apologists will find **corroborative evidences** by tendering various category of witnesses to dissipate any likelihood of wrong or contradictory conclusion due to non-supportive individual subjective prejudices.

There is no reason why John first chose the respected figure before the lower class witness and not the other way round. It is up to the discretion of John. In the UK criminal proceedings, the choice as to which witnesses are called rests primarily with the parties. Again like a careful

[387] John 4:9 –"*For Jews have no dealings with the Samaritans.*"
[388] Van Til, Cornelius. "*The Defence of the Faith*" (Philadelphia, Pennsylvania: Presbyterian and Reformed Publishing Company, 1967), 77. "*... And all is yellow to the jaundiced eye. There can be no intelligible reasoning unless those who reason together understand what they mean by their words.*"
[389] Van Til, Cornelius. *The Reformed Pastor and Modern Thought* (Philadelphia: Presbyterian and Reformed, 1971), 32 quoted in Bahnsen, Greg L. "*Van Til's Apologetics Readings and Analysis*" (Phillipsburg, New Jersey: P & R Publishing, 1998), 454.

lawyer, John ensure there are adequate witnesses to testify what Jesus taught, so that the risk of misrepresenting Jesus identity is reduced. This similar principle of judicial evidence remind us as per Lord Morris in DPP v Hester:

> Any risk of the conviction of an innocent person is lessened if conviction is based upon the testimony of more than one acceptable witness.[390]

John is aware that the disciples (maybe including himself) were not there at the time the conversation between Jesus and the Samaritan woman took place. John was honest to inform his readers in verse 8 that Jesus' *disciples had gone away into the city to buy food.*' This may not be relevant to achieve John's purpose of writing.[391] However, to ensure and testify that the disciples were reliable eyewitnesses and not merely hearsay witnesses,[392] John is wise to inform his readers that *"His disciples came, and they were amazed that He had been speaking with a woman ..."* in verse 27. There is a high possibility that Jesus told the disciples of the content of the conversation or some of the disciples had overheard while they are coming back, just before the woman left the waterpot.[393] If not, during the two-day stay, the disciples may have heard it from the city folks whom the woman had testified to them.[394] John has raises the probative value of what Jesus claim from **hearsay evidence** to **direct evidence** as he recorded:

> Many more believed because of His word; and they were saying to the woman, "It is no longer because of what you said that we believe (*hearsay evidence*), for we have heard for ourselves (*direct evidence*) and know that this One is indeed the Savior of the world."[395]

John noted that corroborating witnesses and stronger evidential value are important to persuade its readers. Furthermore the city folks didn't presuppose the truth. They heard hearsay evidence from the woman and later direct evidence from Jesus. Somebody must have told them other-

---

[390] [1973] AC 296, HL at 315.
[391] As indicated in John 20:31.
[392] As Jesus' teaching and signs were performed in the presence of the disciples, testified in John 20:30 and John 21:24.
[393] John 4:27-28.
[394] John 4:39-40.
[395] John 4:41-42 [NASB], *emphasis is mine.*

wise they will not know. It is not a basic belief 'that this One is indeed the Savior of the world." People believed because 'the woman testified.'[396]

In the subsequent passage[397] in regards to the healing a nobleman's son, Jesus mentioned, "Unless you people see signs and wonders, you simply will not believe".[398] Here, John noted that Jesus acknowledging the nature of man, constantly requiring signs as evidence. Jesus did not hold back His miracles. In fact, He performed signs and wonders (**demonstrative evidence**) so that man can be convinced through that evidence.

Presuppositionalism do not require such evidence. To them, one must first presuppose the truth even before they can seek miracles (if any). If Jesus did not withheld evidence, then we apologists should neither withhold evidence nor disregard reasoning. Again, the Apostle John demonstrated evidentialism is required, otherwise man simply will not believe. This is the second miracle Jesus performed – slightly more amazing than the first.

## John Chapter 5

With this chapter alone, it is adequate to demonstrate clearly the Johannine's apologetic methodology is of evidentialism, close to the way lawyer's tender authoritative evidences during trial. In this chapter John systematically adduced seven types of admissible and relevant evidences performed or stated by Jesus. These evidences are recognized by the modern principles of the law of evidence. Once again, we are prompted to ask if presuppositionalism is of the sole apologetic method mandated by the Scripture, one wonders why Jesus Himself emphasizes so much on evidences. In addition, the apostle John meticulously and systematically bring forward Jesus' tendered evidences as though a lawyer tender methodically his evidences in court. Could we safely say the Scripture endorses legal apologetics?

Noticeably, whilst tendering these evidences, the main **fact in issue** are constantly reminded that the evidences concerned are discharged to reach the verdict. The disputed fact in issue was of Jesus claiming equality with God, as we see in 5:17-18.

> But He answered them, "My Father is working until now, and I Myself am working." For this reason the Jews were seeking all the more to kill Him,

---

[396]   John 4:39.
[397]   John 4:46-54.
[398]   John 4:28 [NASB].

because He not only was breaking the Sabbath, but was calling God His own Father, making Himself equal with God.

As though Jesus is closing His opening statement, He reminds the hearers of the consequences of reaching the right verdict:

> Truly, truly, I say to you, he who hears My word, and believes Him who sent Me, has eternal life, and does not come into judgment, but has passed out of death into life.[399]

The first evidence is the performance of the miracle itself – **demonstrative evidence.** This is one of the best way to rebut a repudiation that a certain action necessitating the fact in issue cannot be performed. By demonstrating a miracle such as healing in front of those cynic (jury) is strong evidence to change their mind. In fact, Jesus intentionally healed the lame beggar in Bethesda on a Sabbath[400], an evidence implying He is more than a healer. This evidence has a continuous effect as the miracle is not only to be seen at the moment of healing but also every moment thereafter whenever others observed that this man is walking healthily and testifying, "He who made me well was the one who said to me, 'Pick up your pallet and walk.'"[401]

Applying the judicial principles of evidence, the term '**physical evidence**', 'real evidence,' and 'demonstrative evidence' are often used interchangeably. The '**real evidence**' is the actual object itself e.g. the gun. '**Demonstrative evidence**' is a representation of the real thing e.g. a model of the gun to illustrate the original weapon or by using the actual gun and showing the court how it was likely handled by the accused. Usually once these physical evidences have been identified by a witness, authenticated, and introduced into evidence as an exhibit, the evidence speaks for itself. This is similar with what John wrote about Jesus' healing. The healing was the 'demonstrative evidence' and the healed man walking, carrying his pallet is the 'real evidence.' In addition, the healed man **testified** that he was healed. Once his testimony is supported by his 'physical evidence,' the fact speaks for itself that Jesus must have some divine power.

However, there is still no complete assurance that successful healing equals to 100% certainty that Jesus is who He claims to be. We have discussed about probability and proving beyond reasonable doubt as a

---

[399] John 5:24 [NASB].
[400] John 5:2-10.
[401] John 5:11.

standard of proof. At this juncture, Jesus may have discharged His burden of proof but the opposite party may attempt to cast doubt to dilute the probative force of the physical evidence Jesus just performed. Similarly, a defense attorney will often do everything possible to prevent an object from being introduced as evidence or argue that the evidence is unduly prejudicial to the defendant e.g. the prosecution witness had planted the evidence; or the officer cannot positively identified the object concerned; or the object was tampered with. This is exactly what the Jews tried to do with the physical evidence of Jesus' healing. Possibly they alleged that such healing cannot be of God as it breaks the Sabbath law,[402] and Jesus had committed a blasphemy.[403] A little bit far-fetched but possible that they might cast doubts by arguing it was not Jesus but the angel of the Lord[404] that healed that man. The Jews may support their 'hypothesis' by arguing that the man cannot identify positively the healer concerned since the man did once was unsure of who healed him.[405] That is why the following verses tells us that Jesus reasoned with them and subsequently provided more **corroborating evidences** substantiating His claim.

The <u>second evidence</u> is Jesus' **personal testimony (self-attestation)** – witness for Himself[406]. The present UK law of evidence generally states that the accused is a competent but not compellable witness for the defense in all criminal proceedings.[407] Assumingly, Jesus may choose the right to remain silent[408], but to avoid the Jews to draw adverse inferences from failure to testify,[409] Jesus testify about Himself and claims that God *'gave Him authority to execute judgment, because He is the Son of God.'*[410] Vividly, John noted that this self-attestation of Jesus is one important evi-

---

[402] John 5:16.
[403] John 5:18.
[404] John 5:4.
[405] John 5:12-13.
[406] John 5:19-30.
[407] As to competence, the authority is found in section 53(1) of the Youth Justice and Criminal Evidence Act 1999. As to compellability, section 1(1) of the Criminal Evidence Act 1898 (amended) provides "A person charged in criminal proceedings shall not be called as a witness in the proceedings except upon his own application."
[408] In *Rice v Connolly* [1966] 2 QB 414, it was held that a suspect is under no obligation to assist the police with their inquiries.
[409] *R v Bathurst* [1968] 2 QB 99, CA and *R v Taylor* [1993] Crim LR 223, CA held that although in appropriate circumstances a judge may invite a jury to draw adverse inferences from failure to testify, they should be directed not to assume guilt from such a failure.
[410] John 5:27.

dence. However, John also noted that Jesus recognizes that **self-attestation** evidence do not have a strong probative force and therefore need other corroborative evidence to buttress His claim. Jesus said, *"If I alone testify about Myself, My testimony is not true."*[411]

Geisler and Zukeran take note on the procedural evidential Jewish law:

> According to the Old Testament law, a person's own testimony is not valid in a Jewish court of law. A testimony is valid only if there are two or three witnesses who testify to the truth of an individual's claims (Deut. 19:15). Jesus knows that these people need not only solid testimony to confirm his claims but also testimony that will convict them of their error regarding their understanding of him.[412]

This display a clear demonstration of the significance of evidential apologetics i.e. extra evidence is not a sign of doubt but necessarily effective and advantageous. If not, Jesus Himself would not have said, *"There is another who testifies in My favor, and I know that his testimony about Me is valid"*[413] Possibly, Jesus is referring to his co-witness, John the Baptist.[414] In evidentialism or legal apologetics, it does not mean the other witness is necessarily more convincing but collectively, they strengthened each other's probative value. Jesus seems to recognize this when he says, *"Not that I accept human testimony; but I mention it that you may be saved."*[415] In other words, Jesus is asserting that His testimony is authoritative enough but add on extra witnesses and signs as evidences required by incredulous man, so it will help to persuade them to accept the verdict, otherwise they will lose out the opportunity to be saved.

The third evidence is witness of John the Baptist. Jesus knew that many Jews accepts John the Baptist as **credible witness**. By receiving his testimony, it corroborates Jesus self-testimony. Since they *"... were willing to rejoice for a while in his light,"*[416] they should also accept whom John the Baptist has *'testified to the truth'*[417] and that he *"have seen the Spirit descending as a dove out of heaven, and He remained upon Him."*[418] Both evidences will

---

[411] John 5:31 [NASB]. NIV translated as '... is not valid'.
[412] Geisler & Zukeran, *The Apologetics of Jesus*, 17.
[413] John 5:32 [NIV].
[414] John 5:33.
[415] John 5:34 [NIV].
[416] John 5:35.
[417] John 5:33.
[418] John 1:32.

confirm what John the Baptist testified earlier that *"this is the One who baptizes in the Holy Spirit"*[419] and *"... this is the Son of God."*[420] Merely based on presuppositional apologetics, then this third witness is consider not necessary or helpful. Evidentialism is implied here as we see that John noted Jesus specifically says His testimony alone is not valid but extra witness sure make it valid (or more convincingly true). This shows the significance of extrinsic witnesses as effective evidence.

The fourth evidence tendered by Jesus has more probative force than the testimony of John the Baptist. In 5:36, Jesus affirms that '*... the testimony which I have is greater than the testimony of John; for the works which the Father has given Me to accomplish – the very works that I do – testify about Me, that the Father has sent Me."* This evidence refers to the entire ministry of Jesus, including the miracle He had just performed. This obviously an evidence that only can be consummated when Jesus fulfilled His task by dying on the cross, raised from the dead and ascended to heaven. As for Jesus' Jewish audience, it is a continuous evidence, including other miracles they just have to observe progressively. As for us who have the benefit of holding the Bible in our hands, this is the *'greater'* evidence Jesus mentioned – the death and resurrection of Jesus Christ as the ultimate evidence to testify about who Jesus really is – the One that was sent by the Father.

The fifth evidence is the testimony of God the Father Himself.[421] What better witness than the actual One who had sent Jesus? This may be said as the strongest and **direct evidence** for those who may have saw heaven opened and heard a voice came out from heaven, *"You are My beloved Son, in You I am well-pleased."*[422] Obviously, this testimonial evidence of God is greater than the testimony of men.[423] For those who were not there at Jesus' baptism and may have not heard or saw, this fifth evidence may have lesser probative value as this testimony is repeated as a **hearsay evidence** by John the Baptist,[424] or from Peter and the other disciples.[425]

The sixth evidence is the Scriptures, highly acceptable both as **authoritative** and **documentary evidence**. Jesus adduces the Scriptures as witness that testify about Him.[426] Jesus do not need to produce the origi-

---

[419] John 1:33.
[420] John 1:34.
[421] John 5:37.
[422] Luke 3:21-22; Mark 1:11.
[423] I John 5:9.
[424] John 5:32-34.
[425] 2 Peter 1:16-18.
[426] John 5:39.

nal text as a primary evidence or any manuscripts as secondary evidence as He is not proving the content in the document per se. Jesus here avers that the Scriptures (which happens to be inscribed in the manuscripts) which the Jews acknowledges as the divine source of salvation actually testify about Him. The typologies, symbols, prophecies and some ritualistic laws all points to Jesus Christ as the Messiah.[427] Jesus do not need to authenticate or prove the reliability of the Scriptures in order for it to be relevantly admissible. There is no doubt the Jewish leaders at that time presumed the Scripture as the word of God even in the absence of proof. This is the **authoritative evidence** Jesus tendered since it was already either **judicially noticed** or formally admitted. In the modern principles of the law of evidence, this evidence falls under **irrebuttable presumptions** and **judicial notice**[428].

The seventh evidence is Moses[429] as witness testifying about Jesus in his writing. Testimony of Moses as evidence arguably the most authoritative evidence acknowledged by the Jews at that time as having highly probative force. Applying modern evidential law, this is like all in one i.e. Moses as **credible witness**; admissible **hearsay evidence** of a highly respected dead person's testimony; his words written in the Pentateuch are formally admitted as **authoritative**; no doubt it is **irrebuttable presumptions** of the Jewish law; acceptable as inspired word of God by the Jewish leaders probably through **judicial notice** or **formal admission**. Apparently, Moses's writings are reduced into manuscripts scrolls constituting an admissible **documentary evidence**. Jesus argued that Moses wrote about Him and thus **corroborated** Jesus' claims. Jesus reasoned, "*For if you believed Moses, you would believe Me, for he wrote about Me. But if you do not believe his writing, how will you believe My words?*"[430] Arguably, this is like as

---

[427]  See Matthew 5:17.

[428]  'Judicial notice' are facts taken noticed by the courts for being such common knowledge acceptable by everybody beyond serious dispute and therefore they require no proof and are open to no evidence in rebuttal. For example, just like every Jews during the time of Jesus accepts the Old Testament Scriptures as word of God and Moses as an authoritative figure, similarly during the 19th century in England, it is commonly accepted that the advancement of religion and learning through the nation is one of the purposes for which University of Oxford was established, judicially noticed in *Re Oxford Poor Rate Case* [1857] 8 E&B 184; or cats are ordinarily kept for domestic purposes, judicially noticed in *Nye v Niblett* [1918] 1 KB 23; or a postcard is the sort of document which might be read by anyone as in *Huth v Huth* [1915] 3 KB 32, CA. Hence these facts are established notwithstanding the absence of proof of evidence.

[429]  John 5:45.

[430]  John 5:46-47.

though adducing an extra **circumstantial evidences** or be proven under the doctrine of *res ipsa loquitor*:

> Circumstances#1: All Moses's writings is believable.
> Circumstances#2: Moses wrote about Jesus.
> Circumstances#3: Jesus satisfied the criteria written in the Law of Moses.
>
> Therefore the fact speak for itself – that Jesus is believable.

Not surprisingly, Jesus did not say, "you should have known I am sent by My Father as it is a basic belief warranted for you to believe Me." Jesus also did not say, "if you presupposes My claims as true, you will believe Me as you also believe in Moses." Nowhere in chapter 5 encourages presuppositionalism or reformed epistemology but instead evidentialism is applied. Jesus did not blame their unbelief on their totally depraved mind due to original sin. In fact, men did not give the glory to Jesus[431] because they are *unwilling*[432] (not that they are unable to choose) to come to Jesus, so that they may have life. This is also because man do not love God[433] but rather chose to gratify one another's glory.[434] Having comprehended man's willful and self-imposed skepticism, although not necessary but yet Jesus chose to apply evidence to convince them. In fact, Jesus increases the probative force of each evidence in progression. Jesus indirectly explicates His intention and mode of persuasion, "*...greater works than these, so that you will marvel.*"[435]

The apostle John, truly like a lawyer listed systematically the evidential methodology applied by Jesus. Like in a criminal trial, the weight of the defendant's case is determined by the integrity and credibility of the witnesses who are called forth. Besides Jesus's self-testimony and His demonstrative signs, He also presents five evidences through witnesses of impeccable character. Geisler and Zukeran aptly summarizes the evidential methodology laid down in chapter 5 of John:

> ... in the Judaistic context, Jesus provides the greatest possible witnesses: the greatest prophet (John the Baptist), the greatest works (miracles), the greatest being (God), the greatest book (the Torah), and the greatest law-

---

431  John 5:41.
432  John 5:40 [NASB]; *"refuse"* in NIV and ESV similarly infer the intentional exercise of the will to reject.
433  John 5:42.
434  John 5:44.
435  John 5:20b.

giver (Moses). Any unbiased Jewish jury would have been overwhelmed by the evidence.[436]

## John Chapter 6

Immediately after the 3rd miracle healing of the lame man, John recorded Jesus saying in 5:20 that "... *greater works than these, so that you will marvel.*" It clearly states that God the Father will show Jesus grander signs so that we all will be amazed even at a greater level. The more grandeur the miracle, the more one is astounded by its difficultness. Hence the more convinced the person that such miracle is of the divine nature. Evidentialism seek for better and greater evidence to increase the probative force. Such is the love of the Father towards His Son and the methodology He chose to show Jesus, so that man will marvel at the greater works than the signs just performed. Arguably, the 4th and 5th miracles are grander than the 3rd miracle. It seems the level of difficultness and inconvenience on feeding a crowd of 5,000 with only five barley loaves and two fish[437] and Jesus walking on water in the midst of strong winds[438] are higher than the previous signs. The greater the signs, the greater the evidence. The greater the evidence, the likelihood people will believe. Just as recorded in 6:14, 'Therefore when the people saw the sign which he performed, they said, "*This is truly the Prophet who is to come into the world.*"'

Similarly, the 3rd sign is far grandeur than the 1st and 2nd signs. The difficultness of the 1st sign was merely turning the substance of a liquid to another, within the knowledge of a few servants (note that it wasn't direct evidence but **circumstantial evidence**). The 2nd sign was healing of a child but just confined to only a few people knowing about it i.e. the nobleman and maybe some of his slaves. Again this evidence is not directly observed by any witnesses but is only **circumstantial evidence**. The time when Jesus informed the royal official that his son lives coincides with the time the hour the child began to get better.[439] As for the 3rd sign, it involves a man that everyone knows he is lame for 38 years but suddenly began to walk. The probative value of this evidence is greater as it involves **direct evidence** the lame man observed himself. It also involve his **testimony evidence** to the Jews. Hence, this involves more people than the other previous two signs.

---

[436] Geisler & Zukeran, *The Apologetics of Jesus*, 23.
[437] John 6:9-13.
[438] John 6:18-19.
[439] John 4:50-52.

However, the 4$^{th}$ sign includes even more people and higher difficulty as it involves distribution to 5,000 from a few pieces of bread and fish. This may involves **direct evidence** and **demonstrative evidence.** The twelve baskets with fragments of leftovers[440] are strong **circumstantial evidence**, with greater inference. Similarly the 5$^{th}$ sign involves a large crowd of witnesses as they were amazed how Jesus can get over the other side of the sea.[441] This is **circumstantial evidence** but there was a **direct evidence** when the disciple saw Jesus defies nature by overcoming the strong wind and walking on the sea for at least four miles.[442] At this juncture, we can safely conclude, similar to any trial lawyers, John often tender the evidences progressively from lower to a stronger probative value. It has its psychological and convincing effect. Clearly, the legal evidential apologetics is applied both in the previous and present chapters.

If presuppositionalism is to be the biblical approved apologetics, there is no need for greater evidence to be tendered for man to marvel. One might as well presuppose a strong and conclusive probative value of conviction without any evidential probative force – which is illogical and lack of integrity. If presuppositionalism is true, one already completely marveled needing no extra or greater signs to have him more marvel at. If nature is enough for man to marvel and failure to marvel, is of no excuse as in Romans 1:18-20, why do the Father shows greater works (evidences) so that we will marvel (John 5:20)?

If our basic belief is warranted just based on the invisible attributes of God since the creation, why Jesus need to give other evidences as an answer to the question in 6:30, "*What then do you do for a sign, so that we may see, and believe You? What work do you perform?*" Jesus reasoned to them with evidence that their fore fathers received from God through the bread out of heaven.[443] Jesus thereon say "*I am the bread of Life that came down from heaven*"[444] Jesus is the extra and greater evidence. In fact, Jesus is the greatest evidence for the existence of God. He who see Him, see the Father. Maybe if John's readers consist purely on just lawyers, he might as well begin his gospel, "*In the beginning was the Evidence, and the Evidence was with God, and the Evidence was God.*"

---

[440] John 6:13.
[441] John 6:22-25.
[442] John 6: 18-19.
[443] John 6:32-33.
[444] John 6:35-51.

## John Chapter 7

Elsewhere we have discussed in detail the evidential methodology John applied to achieve his purpose. Similarly, this is also reflected briefly in this chapter. Evidence and reasoning are generously provided by Jesus to those seeking for an answer, athough Jesus knows the Jews presumed His identity according to their own prejudices and presupposition.[445] However many of them failed to "*first hears from him and knows what he is doing,*"[446] yet Jesus is willing to furnish some evidence and explanation. This methodology can contribute to their search for an answer. It can discharge the evidential burden of proving the fact in issue which the Jews are disputing in regards to Jesus' identity as in 7:12, 26-27, and 40-41.

In the narrative, we again observe that reasoning and referring to evidences are carefully noted by John for the purpose of proving the fact in issue. First we see that John noted the effect of **demonstrative evidence** in regards to Jesus' profound knowledge with no professional training.[447] With no education Jesus' ability to expound the Scriptures demonstrated the possibility of a special divine attributes conferred from above – a positive inference or **circumstantial evidence** verifying the truth claim of Jesus. John seems to tender in 7:16-18 a **good character evidence** as Jesus credit His teaching and authority to the divine source. **Good character evidence**, though not having strong probative value, it still have some persuasive value. Similar to what we see in precious chapters, the apostle John noted several **corroborative evidences** are furnished to strengthen the other evidence of less probative value. For example, Jesus immediately relied on Moses and His law as authority,[448] "*not to judge according to appearance*"[449] or merely based on character or knowledge to conclude the identity.

The Apostle John again noted in 7:38 and 42 that Scriptures are referred as **documentary evidence**. Finally, John infer 'uniqueness' as one sufficient condition (though not necessary) of divine characteristic. This reflected in verse 46 when the officer answered, "*Never has a man spoken the way this man speaks.*"[450] Such unique characteristics is also **circumstantial evidence**. Finally, John noted the reminder given by Nicodemus in

---

[445] John 7:12-13, 26-27, 40-43.
[446] John 7:51.
[447] John 7:15.
[448] John 7:19-23.
[449] John 7:24.
[450] John 7:46.

verse 7:50-51 that one must not presuppose and make a decision based on one sided facts. This reflects the principles of law of evidence. This chapter encourages the **doctrine of natural justice** i.e. *audi alterem partem*[451] – which means one must 'hear the other side' too. Legal apologetics, similar to the Jewish law of evidence note that one must hear the other party's explanation and assess its evidences before coming to a conclusion. Maybe is time for the presuppositionalists to heed the advice of Nicodemus.

Chapter 7 also demonstrated Jesus' use of logical reasoning such as *a fortiori* **argument**. Plainly in Latin it means *"with even stronger reason,"* which applies to a situation in which if one thing is true then it can be inferred that a second thing is even more certainly true. Thus, if Cain is too young to serve as leader, then his younger brother Abel certainly is too young. The reasoning process can be arranged in the following -

1) The truth of idea A is accepted.
2) Support for the truth of idea B (which is relevantly similar to idea A) is even stronger than that of idea A.
3) Therefore, if the truth of idea A must be accepted, then so must the truth of idea B be accepted.

Consider Jesus' argument against the Pharisees concerning the rightness of His performing a healing miracle on the Sabbath in 7:21-24:

> ... I did one miracle [on the Sabbath], and you are all astonished. Yet, because Moses gave you circumcision (though actually it did not come from Moses, but from the patriarchs), you circumcise a child on the Sabbath. Now if a child can be circumcised on the Sabbath so that the law of Moses may not be broken, why are you angry with me for healing the whole man on the Sabbath? Stop judging by mere appearances, and make a right judgment.

Jesus' *a fortiori* argument can be laid out simply:

---

[451] *Audi Alterem Partem* is a Latin legal maxim literally means 'hear the other side'. This is also one of the fundamental principles of natural justice. No person should be judged without fair hearing in which each party is given the opportunity to respond to the evidence against them. It embodies the concept in Criminal Law that no person should be condemned unheard.

1) The Pharisees endorse circumcision, even when it is done on the Sabbath, the day of rest from work.[452] This does not violate the Sabbath laws, because it is an act of goodness.

2) Healing the whole person is even more important and beneficial than circumcision, which affects only one aspect of the male.

3) Therefore, if circumcision on the Sabbath is not a violation of the Sabbath, neither is Jesus' healing of a person on the Sabbath.

Jesus' concluding comment, *"Stop judging by appearances, and make a right judgment,"*[453] was a rebuke to their illogical inconsistency while applying their own moral and religious principles.

## John Chapter 8

Another application of philosophical argument method and some principles of the law of evidence are reflected in the narratives noted by John. In this chapter, we can see Jesus uses at least two logical principles and reasoning, for example in the earlier part of John chapter 8, Jesus wisely applied the 'avoidance of the horns of a dilemma' method.

This is understood as the Socratic principles of '**Escape the horns of a dilemma'**. It teaches that when both option are not acceptable, look for the third option. Sometimes we called it as the '*Euthyphro dilemma'*. The Euthyphro dilemma is found in Plato's dialogue Euthyphro, in which Socrates asks Euthyphro: "Is the pious (τὸ ὅσιον) loved by the gods because it is pious, or is it pious because it is loved by the gods?" A third alternative answer must be wisely put forward, otherwise the two available answers will be easily refuted. Similarly, when the scribes and the Pharisees tried to trap Jesus with two unacceptable choices i.e. should the adulterous woman they caught be stoned according to the Law of Moses?[454] If Jesus gave a negative answer, He will be criticized for going against the Law of Moses. If Jesus affirmed with a positive reply, His teaching of forgiveness will be refuted. As wise as He is, Jesus escaped this horns of a dilemma by responding, *"He who is without sin among you, let him be the first to throw a stone at her."*[455]

---

[452] Circumcision was performed eight days after the birth of a male, which sometimes fell on the seventh day of the week, the Sabbath.

[453] John 7:24.

[454] John 8:3-6.

[455] John 8:7 [NASB]. Several examples on how Jesus escaped the horns of a dilemma e.g. Matthew 22:15-22 on whether it is lawful to pay taxes to Caesar; and Mat-

After releasing the adulterous woman by *'condemn her not'* and urge her to *'sin no more'*,[456] Jesus applied the principles of noncontradiction. In simple words, contradictory statements cannot both at the same time be true, e.g. the two propositions "A is B" and "A is not B" are mutually exclusive. Not necessary one of the two propositions must be true but if one statement is true, the contradicting statement is necessarily false. Longtime Professor of Philosophy at the University of Southern California, Dallas Albert Willard (1935-2013) was of the view that this is perhaps the most fundamental of all laws of thought whereby all other laws can find its source of principles to it.[457] At verse 12, Jesus implies the law of noncontradiction when He contrasts those who follow Him as the Light of the world and those who do not follow walks in darkness. Also in verses 32-34, Jesus points out those who accept the truth will be set free and those reject the truth are slave to sin. Again in verses 42-47, differentiate between those children of the devil who does not stand in the truth and those children of God who loves Jesus. Neither of them can be both. Evidential apologetics has its basis on logic, as reflected in the gospel of John. Dallas Willard expounds further:

> Not only does Jesus not concentrate on logical theory, but he also does not spell out all the details of the logical structures he employs on particular occasions. His use of logic is always enthymemic, as is common to ordinary life and conversation. His points are, with respect to logical explicitness, understated and underdeveloped. The significance of the enthymeme is that it enlists the mind of the hearer or hearers from the inside, in a way that full and explicit statement of argument cannot do. Its rhetorical force is, accordingly, quite different from that of fully explicated argumentation, which tends to distance the hearer from the force of logic by locating it outside of his own mind.
>
> Jesus' aim in utilizing logic is not to win battles, but to achieve understanding or insight in his hearers. This understanding only comes from the inside, from the understandings one already has. It seems to "well up from within" one. Thus he does not follow the logical method one often sees in Plato's dialogues, or the method that characterizes most teaching and writing today. That is, he does not try to make everything so explicit that the conclusion is forced down the throat of the hearer. Rather, he presents matters in such a way that those who wish to know can find their way to,

---

thew 22:23-33 to trap Jesus in either contradicting the Law of Moses or denying the resurrection of the dead.
[456] John 8:11.
[457] Willard, D. "Jesus the Logician," *Christian Scholars Review* (Summer, 1999), Vol. XXVIII 605-614.

can come to, the appropriate conclusion as something they have discovered--whether or not it is something they particularly care for.[458]

In the narrative John noted that the Pharisees attempted to invalidate Jesus' argument by applying the Jewish law of evidence. The Pharisees argued that self-testifying is not admissible evidence so as to diminish the evidence of authority Jesus just raised when He pronounced *"I am the light of the world.'*[459] Jesus counter-argued even if the law allows Him to be his own witness, He has more credibility because of the personal knowledge. Jesus infers that the Pharisees completely has no credibility as they have no evidence at all to invalidate Jesus' personal knowledge:

> "...Even if I testify about Myself, My testimony is true, for I know where I came from and where I am going; but you do not know where I come from or where I am going.'[460]

We had discussed in the previous chapters that a negative is more difficult to prove than a positive. The fact in issue is on the identity of Jesus and unless there is evidence to the contrary, who should be in the better position to testify about Jesus other than Jesus Himself? In the vocabulary of the judicial principles, the Pharisees cannot discharge their **burden of proof** since they do not have evidence or knowledge where Jesus came from or where He is going. Clearly, this apologetic task mirrors the legal principles of evidence. Though it is arguable[461], at verse 15, Jesus seems to imply the burden is on the Pharisees to prove as it is they who is doing the judging, and not Jesus. *"You are judging according to the flesh; I am not judging anyone"*[462] implies he who is judging must prove. The burden of proving is not on Jesus since He is not judging anyone.[463] Hence, the burden is on the Pharisees.

Jesus thereon replied, *"... even if I do judge"*[464] i.e. even the evidential burden is on Me to prove My identity, *"My judgment is true; for I am not alone in it, but I and the Father who sent Me."*[465] This is to infer that Jesus had already discharged His burden of proof because He and the Father's tes-

---

[458]  Ibid.
[459]  John 8:12-13.
[460]  John 8:14.
[461]  And I submit to the wisdom of the biblical theologians.
[462]  John 8:15 [NASB]. *"You judge by human standards; I pass judgment on no one."* [NIV].
[463]  i.e. Jesus is not here to prove the identity of anyone.
[464]  John 8:16a.
[465]  John 8:16b.

timony **corroborated** each other. In our modern law of evidence, an accused is a competent but not compellable witness for a co-accused.[466] Both may corroborate each other. When Jesus mentioned, "... *I am not alone in it, but I and the Father who sent Me*" sounds like as though Jesus is confessing that He and the Father are both co-accomplices. If the Jews demand two witnesses in order to satisfy the Jewish law of evidence, those two witnesses exists; both testifies about Jesus.[467]

From verse 26 onwards, if modern law of evidence terms are applied, Jesus is appealing either to **direct evidence** or **hearsay evidence**, depending on the purpose for tendering the facts. There is no suggestion of Jesus subscribing to presuppositionalism to convince His Jewish audience. Whatever the probative value of either direct or hearsay evidence, Jesus is tendering evidence that He has direct knowledge of what He had seen or heard from the Father. "*The things which I heard from Him ...*"; [468] "*... but I speak these things as the Father taught Me*"[469]; "*... He who sent Me is with Me...*"[470] and "*I speaks the things which I have seen with My Father ...*"[471] For Jesus to convince the jury that He knows God, He must establish His **credibility** and **competency** by demonstrating an acquaintance or relationship with God.[472]

## John Chapter 9

Theologically, the sign of healing the man born blind in this chapter is to imply that Jesus can open the eyes of the spiritually blind so that they can receive the complete sight which constitutes perfect faith.[473] In apologetics, Jesus made a blind man to see is another miracle recorded by John as important evidence. The whole chapter is devoted on this miracle and the subsequent cross-examination of the healed beggar by the Pharisees. As discussed in John Chapter 6 above, each miracles introduced becomes more intensified and in the degree of difficulty. This 6th sign i.e. healing of the blind obviously is no less difficult than the other previous five miracles. In addition, the weight of this evidence is stronger as the

---

[466]  Section 53(1) of the Youth and Criminal Evidence Act 1999 and section 1(1) of the Criminal Evidence Act 1898.

[467]  John 8:17-18.

[468]  John 8:26.

[469]  John 8:28.

[470]  John 8:29.

[471]  John 8:38.

[472]  John 8:54-56.

[473]  Tasker, *Tyndale New Testament Commentaries: John*, 122-123.

healing was a **direct evidence eye-witnessed** by the disciples and directly experienced by the person healed. The healing of the nobleman's son was not directly experienced or eye-witnessed. Furthermore, unlike the 2nd and 3rd healing, the probability of healing a blind man is zero, "*since the beginning of time it has never been heard that anyone opened the eyes of a person born blind.*"[474] This reflects the systematic arrangement of miracles by John to increase the probative value of all the evidences collectively. Typical of a lawyer arranging and prioritize every piece of evidences.

The beggar was at first asked by the neighbors[475] and later at least twice cross-examined by the Pharisees.[476] Each time the healed beggar's testimony and his **hearsay evidence** of what Jesus said, was consistent. It is also noted that the credibility of the healed beggar was challenged but established when it was **corroborated** by the parents.[477] Not only was the beggar **consistent** and **credible** but also a **competent witness** in regards to his age. The parents twice responded to the Pharisees, '*ask him; he is of age, he will speak for himself.*'[478]

Upon establishing these facts, the beggar's **lay opinion evidence** thus constitutes admissible evidence, especially when he was asked for his opinion of his benefactor, he replies, "He is a prophet."[479]

Like a prosecutor, the Pharisees was hoping to rely on the beggar's evidence and turn him into a **hostile witness** against Jesus. They tried to use his testimony to prove that Jesus broke the Sabbath law and attempted to steer his opinion against Jesus on the question, '*How can a man who is a sinner perform such signs?*'[480] Again, when the beggar was recalled, the Pharisees tried to have him declare Jesus broke the law by asking him a **leading question,**[481] "*Give glory to God; we know that this man is a sinner.*"[482] This is also to urge him to speak the truth in the presence of God and to admit that his opinion was wrong about Jesus. Subsequent verse demonstrated his opinion of Jesus is irrelevant evidence, but the facts he per-

---

[474] John 9:32 [NASB].

[475] John 9:8-11.

[476] John 9: 15 and 24.

[477] John 9: 19-20.

[478] John 9: 21 and 23.

[479] John 9:17.

[480] John 9:16.

[481] Leading questions often are simply assertions usually asked by the cross-examiner with a phrase tacked on at the beginning or at the end to convert them into a question. For example, "The car was blue, right?" or "Isn't it true that he broke the law by trespassing into the premises?"

[482] John 9:24.

ceived remains **relevant admissible evidence** – *"Whether He is a sinner, I do not know; one thing I do know, that though I was blind, now I see."*[483] Instead of trying to make him a hostile witness, the Pharisees suddenly face an impossibility in rebutting a **presumption of *res ipsa loquitor*** raised by the beggar:

> Fact #1: The beggar was blind.
> Fact #2: God does not hear sinners but only to those who are God fearing.[484]
> Fact #3: Never had anyone opened the eyes of a man born blind.[485]
> Fact #4: Jesus touched him and now he see.
>
> Conclusion: The fact speaks for itself (*res ipsa loquitor*).[486]

John's attitude in phrasing the narratives and recording the signs performed with a reason intended by Jesus, truly reflects the characteristics of evidentialism.

## John Chapter 10

Again, the logical reasoning of *a fortiori argument* is applied here. Immediately after Jesus claims, *"I and the Father are one,"*[487] the Jews understood what He meant and accused Jesus for a crime of blasphemy.[488] Jesus used *a fortiori* line of reasoning which reasonably everyone, including the Jews will have no choice but to accept a similar conclusion with even less evidence. Jesus referring to Psalms 82 and answered that if these appointed rulers and judges are called "gods"[489] (whom cannot perform miracles), how much more could Jesus be called the Son of God (whom could perform miracles). Hence, proving that if situation in Psalms 82 is true then it can be inferred that Jesus is even more certainly true because all the miracles he has performed shows that the Father is in Him.[490]

Similarly as other chapters, John noted the appeal of **evidences** by Jesus as proof of His divine claims. Alternatively Jesus based on his 'works'[491] as evidence to **discharge his evidential burden** to explain away the Jews'

---

[483]  John 9:25.
[484]  John 9:31.
[485]  John 9:32.
[486]  John 9:33.
[487]  John 10:30.
[488]  John 10:33.
[489]  John 10:34-35.
[490]  John 10:38.
[491]  John 10:25, 32, 37, 38.

allegation that He is either insane or demon-possessed.[492] William Lane Craig noted the important role of argument and evidence emphasized by Jesus:

> From the pages of the New Testament it is evident that showing the Christian faith to be true was an enterprise in which both Jesus and the apostles were engaged ... The Johannine Jesus refers to this signs as "works", and goes so far as to challenge men to believe in Him, if not on his word alone, then on the basis of the works (10:38; 14:11).[493]

**Corroborative evidence** again is pleaded as we can see that everything said by John the Baptist corroborated the facts about Jesus,[494] as this can persuade many to believe in Jesus.[495]

## John Chapter 11

As mentioned above, like a lawyer, John meticulously arranged the seven chosen miracles in climatically progression. This final sign is the evidence with the most probative force as compare with the other six signs. Amongst the other miracles, it is the impossibly expected, if not, the most difficult because this deal with raising someone who is already dead and buried for four days,[496] whose body was already in the process of dissolution. Others may accept the possibility of miracle of healing a dying man (because there is a chance of natural recovery) but will never concede the possibility of healing someone who is already dead. *"Could not this man, who opened the eyes of the blind man, have kept this man from dying?"*[497] infers that they believe Jesus can keep Lazarus from dying, but not after he died. John recorded this in a way to demonstrate the utmost impossible task, and yet Jesus is able to perform this greatest sign – thus proving Jesus' identity. This 7th sign culminates and completes John's **evidential methodology**, addressing specifically to the Jews to move them to make a verdict in believing Jesus as the Messiah.

John also noted that Jesus intentionally procrastinate in reaching to Lazarus in time. Martha lamented that if Jesus had been there earlier,

---

[492]  John 10:20-21.
[493]  Craig, 'Classical Apologetics' in *Five Views on Apologetics*, 40-41.
[494]  John 10:41.
[495]  John 10:42.
[496]  John 11:39.
[497]  John 11:37.

Lazarus would not have died[498] and that removing the stone from the tomb entrance will do no good but will cause a stench since Lazarus has been dead for four days.[499] In fact, the effect for such delay so that the crowd understands that His raising of Lazarus from the dead is strong evidence to prove the ultimate **fact-in-issue** i.e. that Jesus is *"the resurrection and the life, he who believes in Me will live even if he dies ..."*[500] This is the fact-in-issue that Jesus asked, *"Do you believe this?"*[501] A larger crowd would be present to witness the miracle. So that there will be more **witnesses.** Jesus commented His purpose, *"... because of the people standing around I said it, so that they may believe that You sent Me."*[502] Jesus also want to show His disciples of this great miracle, so that their faith will be even stronger - *"Lazarus is dead, and I am glad for your sakes that I was not there, so that you may believe ..."*[503] Clearly, the appeal to signs as evidence in fulfilling the apologetic task demonstrated in John's methodology.

## John Chapter 12

Nowhere was any emphasis by Jesus that the crowd should have presuppose His Messiahship. John 12:17 again implies the importance of evidentialism, *"So the people who were with Him when He called Lazarus out of the tomb and raised him from the dead, continued to testify about Him."*[504] If everyone (or the Jews at that time) had the basic belief of who Jesus is or had already presuppose and evidence is considered as irrelevant, then there would be no evidence to be testified. There will not be any gradual effect of **hearsay evidence,** causing information to be transferred to the Gentiles. At least to trigger their curiosity to begin searching for the truth just as the Greek seeking for Jesus mentioned in John 12:20-21. Jesus' usage of evidence can even draw more crowds who had not directly eyewitnessed the miracle[505] and this reason can cause many to believe.[506] Whatever degree the probative force is, at least the impact of the hearsay evidence has helped discharge the evidential burden of proving whatever side-issue (obstacles) each individual may have.

---

498 John 11:21.
499 John 11:39.
500 John 11:25.
501 John 11:26.
502 John 11:42.
503 John 11:14-15.
504 John 12:17 [NASB].
505 John 12:9.
506 John 12:11, 18.

In this chapter, we also note the appeal to prophecies as evidence. John refers to the book of Zechariah[507], Ezekiel, Daniel,[508] Isaiah[509] and Psalms[510] as **documentary evidence** to prove His identity. John also records Jesus' prediction of His own death[511] as evidence of His divinity.

Evidentialism acknowledges that there is no evidence that can produce 100% certainty of conviction. Not even presuppositionalism or any apologetic methodologies can produce perfect faith as it depends whether one is willing to commit total faith. Evidence and reasoning act as a tool or channel to communicate its persuasive force to someone towards belief. "*But though He had performed so many signs before them, yet they were not believing in Him*"[512] does not demonstrates the futility of evidence. Otherwise, it implies Jesus' usage of reasoning and signs as mode of proof are all in vain. In fact, John noted that, '*nevertheless, many even of the rulers believed in Him ...*'"[513] The reason for those who reject are given in 12:38-41 that their eyes are blinded and heart hardened by God. Isaiah's prophesized because he saw the vision of His glory[514] as recorded in Isaiah 6:1-3. It was a prophecy specifically for to shut the eyes of the Jews, so that Christ would then of necessity to heal them. This is to point out that the messiah is rejected by His own people, something not surprising to those familiar with the Old Testament Scriptures. Thus, this verse is not referring to all man are made blind unless they first presupposes the truth.

Nevertheless, verse 42 vividly demonstrates that there are man who believed due to the many signs performed[515] but yet they chose with their free will not to declare their faith publicly for fear and for their desire to be approved among men. If these men can choose to become secret believers, all the more there are men who can choose not to believe at all. Hence, if it is true that all man cannot willingly choose as their eyes are blinded, then they cannot even willingly presuppose anything due to their 'faculty of assumption' being inhibited. If there is no free-will because their decisions are totally controlled by God, then one do not even need (or unable) to presuppose. Having said that, shouldn't the one who was made to reject be exonerated? Then, they should be set free from any

---

507    John 12:15 - Zechariah 9:9.
508    John 12:34 – Daniel 7:14; Ezekiel 37:25.
509    John 12:38 – Isaiah 53:1; John 12:40 – Isaiah 6:10.
510    John 12:13 – Psalms 118:26.
511    John 12:27.
512    John 12:37 [NASB].
513    John 12:42.
514    John 12:41.
515    John 12:37a.

blameworthiness. If presupposition is compulsory and evidences should be disregarded, are we saying the signs performed by Jesus are merely entertainment and not as what John wrote so that you may believe?

## John Chapter 13

Chapter 12 marks the end of Jesus' public ministry to the Jews. The seven signs specially chosen by John tendered as relevant evidence to prove Jesus is the Son of God. From this chapter hereon, the Apostle John devoted more than 50% of this gospel on the last few days of Jesus, emphasizing other area of evidences so that his readers might believe. The greatest sign of the highest evidential probative value would be the resurrection of Jesus Christ.

John recorded in this chapter and noted that convincing evidence not only come from the prophecies of the Old Testament (**documentary evidence**)[516] but also from the predictions (**demonstrative evidence**) of Jesus Himself.[517] Note that Jesus predicted two betrayals, by Judas[518] and the other by Peter.[519] The reason for Jesus appealing to past and present prophecies as evidence, "*so that when it does occur, you may believe that I am He.*"[520] Tasker wrote:

"... evidence of Jesus' foreknowledge, which would be available when His prophetic words about the traitor have been proved true, will strengthen the faith of the rest of the apostles that Jesus is the Christ in whom David's prophecy in Psalms xli is fulfilled."[521]

John also took the opportunity to tender evidence that he is a **credible witness** as he is close to Jesus, hence most probably are able to give a truer version. By indicating his reclining on Jesus bosom[522] and for Peter beckoned John to ask Jesus is either implying John has privilege information or could hear better than other witnesses. Similarly in modern criminal trial, before a witness tender his lay opinion evidence, he has to first satisfy the jury that he is qualified to give such evidence of that kind. Whilst John tenders various evidences, he also has to demonstrate that

---

[516] John 13:18 – Psalms 41:9
[517] John 13:21.
[518] John 13:26.
[519] John 13:38.
[520] John 13:19.
[521] Tasker, "*Tyndale New Testament Commentaries: John*" 159.
[522] John 13:23, 25.

he is credible eye-witness to all these facts. John emphasizes again that he was there as implied in 21:24. There will be no such obligation to show the author was credible witness if the correct apologetic methodology is presuppositionalism.

## John Chapters 14 and 15

Together with chapter 13, these two chapters emphasizes that manifestation of love is an evidence of a true Christian. John's emphasis on love is reflected in 13:34, 35; 14:15, 21, 23-24, 31; 15:9-10, 12-13 &17. Jesus gave a new commandment that *"you love one another"*[523] and for the reason that it is an evidence *"that all men will know that you are My disciples."*[524] This implies that whoever really believe in Jesus will have that **good character** of love. The apostle John explained this in his first epistle:

> *"No one who is born of God practices sin, because His seed abides in him; and he cannot sin, because he is born of God."* (1 John 3:9).
>
> *"This is His commandment, that we believe in the name of His Son Jesus Christ, and love one another, just as He commanded us. The one who keeps His commandments abides in Him, and He in him. We know by this that He abides in us, by the Spirit whom He has given us."* (1 John 3:23-24).
>
> *"Beloved, let us love one another, for love is from God; and everyone who loves is born of God and knows God. The one who does not love does not know God, for God is love. By this the love of God was manifested in us, that God has sent His only begotten Son into the world so that we might live through Him"* (1 John 4:7-9).

Applying the principles of the law of evidence, it is as though John is tendering an evidence of good character to his readers. Tendering **good character evidence** is generally admissible in court. It may constitute evidence of a person's actual disposition i.e. that is his propensity to act, think, or feel in a given way, or evidence of his identity or reputation. A character or identity of a person may be proven by evidence e.g. his conduct on other occasions or the fruits of his action. God is commonly accepted as possessing a reputed disposition or propensity to love. It is doubtful anyone would deny the relevancy of God's attributes as an issue to decide the admissibility of Jesus' good character. The true God will be proven through Jesus when the evidence shows that Jesus whom God loves also love us. The love and the much fruit we bear clearly manifest that we abide in Him.

---

[523]  John 13:34.
[524]  John 13:35.

John 15:8 vividly affirms this: "My Father is glorified by this, that you bear much fruit, and so prove to be My disciples."

Alternatively, tendering good character in a way is a **circumstantial evidence** as an inference that Jesus is speaking the truth. Jesus' moral character coincides with his claims. The quality of His life was such that He was able to challenge his enemies with the question, *"Which of you convicts Me of sin?"*[525] He was met by silence, with no proof to refute his moral character. Distinctly thereon the evidential burden shifted to the Jews to prove that Jesus' character is flawed and thus draw an adverse inference Jesus might not be speaking the truth.[526] Instead of disproving His moral character with evidence, they gave bare allegation that Jesus was of demonic influence, suffering from psychological disorder[527] and contaminated blood by calling Him Samaritan.[528] But yet Jesus did not insist they must presuppose His truth claim, even though He can claim the **presumption of innocence.**

The only possible way the Jews may discharge their evidential burden is to claim the **presumption of *res ipsa loquitor*** as seen in 9:34, *"...You were born entirely in sins, and are you teaching us?"* In other words:

Circumstances#1:    All human are born entire in sins.
Circumstances#2:    Sinful man is not of God and cannot speaks the truth.
Circumstances#3:    Jesus is human.

Therefore, the fact speaks for itself.

Based on the modern judicial principles of evidence, we now have two conflicting presumptions. Who now bears the legal burden of proof? Jesus or the Jews? If the two **conflicting presumptions** are of equal strength so that each operates to place a legal or, as the case may be, evidential or tactical burden on the party against whom it operates, one obvious and equitable solution is to treat the two presumptions as having cancelled each other out and to proceed, as if no presumptions were involved, on the basis of the normal rules relating to the burden and standard of proof.[529] Whosoever bears the onus of proof, Jesus had no problem in furnishing evidence beyond any reasonable doubt. From all the verses noted by John, Jesus provided more than enough miracles and prophecy, whilst

---

[525]  John 8:46 [NASB].
[526]  John 8:45–46.
[527]  John 10:10.
[528]  John 8:48.
[529]  Keane, 705. This solution was adopted in *Monckton v Tarr* [1930] 23 BWCC 504, CA.

the Jews only rely on bare denial with not a single evidence. Adopting evidentialism, Jesus however addressed those opposition with reasoning,
arguing that if those Jews who really belongs to God will hear (or understand) the words of God declared by Jesus.[530]

The Apostle John also noted that the evidences are overwhelming for
them to be convinced of their own bare suggestion – *"These are not the
sayings of one demon possessed. A demon-possessed cannot open the eyes of the
blind, can he?"*[531] It is suffice to say that applying reason and evidence stop
the Jews from rebutting or diluting the probative value of Jesus' truth
claims. With evidentialism, it rebut the presumption relied by the Jews.

Since one cannot have a direct sensory perception of God, he can only
physically observe the evidence of love exhibited in the lives of His followers i.e. God's love perfected in us.[532] This greatest love[533] demonstrated
by Jesus was directly observed by John and the disciples. Hence, they are
testifying of this evidence that the Father has sent the Son to be the Savior of the world.[534] This is the apologetic of love – the evidential methodology by manifesting the most commonly accepted attributes of God i.e.
love, as evidence that the Father is in Jesus.[535] Continuously manifesting
love for one another can also be considered as **demonstrative evidence**.

Another evidence (seldom preached) is that a true believer will be
hated by the world because the world hated Jesus.[536] This is **character of
victim evidence**. Usually in a real homicide trial, character of the de-
ceased person is generally unimportant. The offence still remains,
whether the victim is of bad or good character. However, when the character of a victim does become an issue during trial, FRE rule 404(a) (2) allows it to be tendered when 'a pertinent trait of character of the victim of
the crime offered an accused, or by the prosecution to rebut the same, or
evidence of a character trait of peacefulness of the victim offered by the
prosecution in a homicide case to rebut the evidence that the victim was
the first aggressor.'

However, in our case, it is not to prove the victim's bad character but
character of the 'victim' as Jesus predicted that will definitely trigger hatred by the world. *"If you were of the world, the world would love its own; but
because you are not of the world, but I chose you out of the world, because of this*

---

[530]  John 8:47
[531]  John 10:21; 9:33.
[532]  1 John 4:12, 17.
[533]  Illustrated by Jesus in John 15:3.
[534]  1 John 4:14.
[535]  John 14:10-11.
[536]  John 15:18.

*the world hates you."*[537] The world's hatred towards Christ's followers is an evidence by itself indirectly proving the fulfilment of a prophecy taken from a **documentary evidence** i.e. the Old Testament Scriptures – 'But they have done this to fulfill the word that is written in their Law, "THEY HATED ME WITHOUT A CAUSE."'[538]

## John Chapter 16

The purpose of Jesus telling His disciples that they would be hated by the world is in order that not only *'you may be kept from stumbling"*[539] but when the prediction takes place, *"you may remember that I told you to them."*[540] In other words, evidentialism can strengthen one's faith when one realized that Jesus' foreknowledge is evidence of His divinity.

In the previous two chapters, Jesus introduces the Holy Spirit as the Helper[541] who *"will teach you all things and brings to your remembrance all things."*[542] Jesus said this Spirit of truth is liken to a witness who will testify about Jesus.[543] As a **credible and competent witness**, the relevancy and admissibility of His testimony is satisfied by the fact that He proceeds from the Father.[544] The Spirit of truth will testify to the disciples and in turn the disciples will testify what was learnt. The credibility and competency of the disciples as witness is satisfied due to their close acquaintance with Jesus from the beginning.[545] In chapter 16, thereon Jesus explains further on the role of this Spirit of truth. It will be another form of evidence to those who will experience the Holy Spirit's guidance into all the truth, though it may be subjective but a strong convincing evidence for each individual believer.

The presuppositionalists must answer whether the Holy Spirit provides and act as an evidence to us to be convicted of sins or we presupposed the existence of the Holy Spirit so one can be convinced of the truth? If we already presupposed the truth, isn't it unnecessary for us to be taught of the truth when we already presupposed the truth? If we presupposed the Holy Spirit convicting us, then we don't need to be convict-

---

[537] John 15:19.
[538] John 15:25 – Psalms 35:19.
[539] John 16:1.
[540] John 16:4.
[541] John 14:17.
[542] John 14:26.
[543] John 15:26.
[544] Ibid.
[545] John 15:27.

ed. Should we presuppose the truth claim of Jesus that the Holy Spirit will bring us to remembrance or the Holy Spirit will bring us to remembrance of what he said about the Holy Spirit? Should one presupposes the existence of God or the Holy Spirit will teach us the 'all truth about the existence of God'?

If the Holy Spirit is the one who teaches us about the existence of God, then is unnecessary to presuppose for it is the job of the Holy Spirit and not our presupposition. But if it is necessary to presuppose, then the starting point is also from man i.e. man must be willing to take the step to decide to presuppose. The presuppositionalists had fall into their own entrapment mistakenly created for themselves. A circular argument that goes nowhere. Indeed logic, evidence, reasons, legal principles are not an enemy of Christian apologetics. All truths and useful methodologies belongs to God, applicable for disclosing the truth, just as Jesus said, "*All things that the Father has are Mine, therefore I said that He takes of Mine and will disclose it to you.*"[546] It includes all sayings, reasoning, signs, prophecies, good character evidence belonging to Jesus, which also belongs to God, are taken by the Holy Spirit as an evidential tool to disclose it to us.

## John Chapter 17

In Jesus' high priestly prayer, Jesus repeats a similar statement as 16:15, "*...and all things that are Mine are Yours, and Yours are Mine; and I have been glorified in them.*"[547] Within the context of this priestly prayer, 'it is important for the disciples to understand the role of Jesus' vital connection to His Sender (the Father) had in His mission, for it is the same vital connection they are called to sustain with Jesus as they embark on their own mission, which in reality nothing but an extension of Jesus' mission in the power of the Holy Spirit.'[548] Applying what we discussed in 16:15 above, this vital connection infers all evidential methods Jesus uses to convince His hearers actually belongs to and endorsed by the Father; and the Holy Spirit takes this to disclose it to the disciples. With this disclosure through the apologetic method of Jesus, the disciples are sent into the world, just as the Father sent Jesus into the world.[549]

If "*all things*" in 16:15 and 17:10 literally means everything including authority, power, signs, wisdom, knowledge, methodology, etc. which be-

---

[546] John 16:15 [NASB].
[547] John 17:10 [NASB].
[548] Köstenberger. *A Theology of John's Gospel and Letters*, 248.
[549] John 17:18.

longs to the Father, this repeated emphasis in the priestly prayer has an implied intention that the disciples would also imitate Jesus in His apologetic methodology. This is for the purpose "that they may be one (*unity in faith, love, knowledge and method*); even as You, Father, are in Me, that they also may be in Us, so that the world (*see the evidence and the accomplish work of Jesus*) may believe that You sent Me."[550]

In addition, this "*perfected in unity*" is also a **demonstrative evidence** of a **good character** to persuade a verdict, "*so that the world may know that You sent Me, and loved them, even as You have loved Me.*"[551] The unity of the Christian family is a **circumstantial evidence** that God is at work.

Even from the words of this prayer, we can see an underlying intention that the disciples whom Jesus had God's name manifested to;[552] and had truly understood the word received from Jesus;[553] though not of the world;[554] will be sent out to the world,[555] to preach eternal life i.e. that the world will know the only true God and Jesus Christ whom the Father have sent.[556] With the same methodology Jesus have made God known to the disciples, they "*will continue to make You known in order that the love You for Me may be in them and that I Myself may be in them.*"[557]

Clearly, unless the world are to be preached and evidence presented to them as Jesus had manifested to the disciples, the world do not have the basic belief of the true identity of Jesus whom is sent by God the Father. Neither can the world presuppose the redemption plan for mankind nor the knowledge of the Father if what was manifested to the disciples was not evidenced to them. Jesus openly said in 17:25, "*... although the world has not known You yet .... and these* (i.e. the disciples) *have known that You sent Me,*" explicitly means the world has no basic knowledge to be justified as true belief of God yet. Christian evidentialism necessitates the preaching of the word and the preaching mode similar to Jesus way of apologetic persuasion. There is no warrant of belief of who Jesus is unless someone are to sent to preach.[558] How anyone can presuppose the true

---

550   John 17:21 (*emphasis is mine*).
551   John 17:23.
552   John 17:6.
553   John 17:8.
554   John 17:14-16.
555   John 17:18.
556   John 17:3.
557   John 17:26 [NIV].
558   Romans 10:14-15.

Christian faith in him if he had not heard the word of Christ?[559] The
priestly prayer in Chapter 17 impliedly gave us the answer.

## John Chapter 18

Apostle John appeals to several fulfilled prophecies as strong **circumstantial evidences**. First, the betrayal of Judas in 18:2-5 as predicted by Jesus[560]
Second, he specifically noted in 18:9, as predicted (or answered prayer) in
His priestly prayer that *"not one of them perished."*[561] Third, it is the prediction of Jesus that Simon Peter will deny Christ three times before the
rooster crowed,[562] which was fulfilled in 18:17, 25 & 26-27. Fourth, when
the Jews said to Pilate, *"We are not permitted to put anyone to death,"*[563] John
noted that was actually to fulfill the word of Jesus signifying the kind of
death He was about to die.[564] Tasker explains, that "it was essential for
the accomplishment of the divine plan for man's salvation that Jesus
should die, not by stoning, the penalty for blasphemy under the Jewish
law, but as He Himself had prophesied in words which the evangelist now
recalls, by being *'lifted up from the earth'*,[565] a manner of death which could
be secured only by crucifixion."[566] The fifth, John noted in 18:13-14, a
prophecy made by Jesus own enemy *'that it was expedient for one man to die
on behalf of the people'*. John explains this earlier in 11: 51 that Caiaphas
*'did not say this on his own initiative, but being high priest that year, he prophe-
sied that Jesus was going to die for the nation.'* Within chapter 18, John testified five prophecies fulfilled, though not 100% evidence but constitute a
very compelling circumstantial evidences when taken collectively can
prove beyond a reasonable doubt that Jesus has the divine authority, the
One truly Son of God sent by the Father. Fulfilled prophecies is a **demonstrative evidence** that Jesus is Who He claim He is.

John also realized that he is testifying as a **witness** and to prove that
he has knowledge of this, he indirectly noted that he was there to observe the trial of Jesus or was at the proximity of time to receive information of what did transpire. *"Simon Peter was following Peter and so was
another disciple. Now the disciple was known to the high priest, and entered with*

---

559  Romans 10:17.
560  John 13:21.
561  John 17:12.
562  John 13:38
563  John 18:31.
564  John 18:32.
565  John 12:32-33.
566  Tasker, *Tyndale New Testament Commentaries: John*, 201.

*Jesus into the court of the high priest.*"[567] This would establish him as a **credible witness** and John's presence was actually witnessed by the high priest himself. Köstenberger is of the opinion that this *"another disciple"*, who most likely is none other than *"the disciple whom Jesus loved"* in 13:23,[568] referring to the apostle John himself. This *"other disciple"* is again refer in 20:2, 3 and 8. Köstenberger gave his reason:

> Finally, Peter asks Jesus to tell him about the destiny of "the disciple whom Jesus loved" but is, in essence, told to mind his own business (21:20-23). In light of the fact that it was on Peter, by virtue of his confession of Jesus as the Messiah, that Jesus had vowed to build his church (Matt 16:18), it is remarkable that such a consistent case is mounted on the part of John for the unrivalled position on the part of "the disciple whom Jesus loved" at Jesus' side. That this is intentional is further underscored by the remarkable parallelism in language between Jesus' access to the Father and the access to Jesus enjoyed by "the disciple whom Jesus loved" at the beginning of the first and at the beginning of the second half of John's gospel:
> - 1:18: "...the one and only Son, who is himself God and is in closest relationship with the Father, has made him known" (*monogenēs theos ho ōn **eis ton kolpon tou patros** ekeinos exēgēsato*)
> - 13:23: "one of them, the disciple whom Jesus loved, was reclining next to him" (*ēn anakeimenos heis ek tōn mathētōn autou **en tō kolpō tou Iēsou** hon ēgapa ho Iēsous*; see also 20:21)[569]

In regards to Jesus' hearing before Annas in 18:19-27, we can observe that Jesus is strictly a skillful 'legal wizard' in handling cross-examination. When Jesus was cross-examined on His disciples, and about His teaching,[570] He remain silent about the good faith and character of His disciple as this was **irrelevant evidence** to the fact-in-issue. Similarly we see in Luke 23:8-9, Jesus remain silent to Herod's cross-examination most probably on the sign performed by Jesus. No answer was given by Jesus as it was completely irrelevant but until the relevant question on His identity i.e. the ultimate relevant fact-in-issue.[571]

Jesus also points out to Annas that His teaching had been given openly in unambiguous language and in the public places.[572] Jesus is appealing to them that his teaching is so common knowledge that many therefore

---

[567] John 18:15.
[568] Köstenberger, "A Theology of John's Gospel and Letters" 251.
[569] Ibid., 237.
[570] John 18:19.
[571] See Luke 22:67; 23:3; John 18:33-34, 36-37.
[572] John 18:20.

could be called as witness to testify about His teaching.[573] Jesus is aware of the evidential importance of **corroborative evidence**. He refused to answer them but states that there are many more witnesses, without the demand that He should bear unsupported witnesses to Himself in defiance of the Jewish law of evidence, which was the very thing the Jews argued that Jesus was testifying alone and therefore inadmissible (see 8:13). In addition to its irrelevancy, Jesus remain silent as not to admit that He bears the **legal burden** to prove something so obvious. It is liken to a lawyer asking Barack Obama, "Are you the president of the United States?" There is a perchance that Obama may reply, "Why do you question me? Question those people from CNN or Bloomberg." When it is of common knowledge and evidence are easily available, modern law judges would not even allow such questions to be asked to instigate the accused or the courts. For example, it is pointless to ask whether the English court is taken to know the meaning of any ordinary English expression.[574]

Truly, Jesus is an expert in the operation of legal evidential procedure. His life, teaching and methodology as written in the gospel of John emphasizes the evidential legal apologetic method.

## John Chapter 19

Together with 18:38, John also noted Pilate declared that he find no guilt in Jesus.[575] This is another **good character evidence** John wants his readers to take cognizance of the implication that Jesus has the propensity of telling the truth, hence He is who He claims to be.

In this chapter alone, John appeals to several prophecies fulfilled as **circumstantial evidence**, if taken collectively will add on more weight to the evidential value that Jesus is the Messiah foretold in the Old Testament. First, Psalms 22:18 was fulfilled in 19:24 – they divided His garment and cast lots. Second, Psalms 69:21 was fulfilled in 19:28 & 29 – Jesus was thirsty[576] and they gave Him vinegar to drink. Third, Psalms 34:21 was fulfilled in 19:33 & 36 – Not a bone of Him shall be broken.[577] Fourth, Zechariah 12:10 was fulfilled in 19:35 & 37 – will look on Him they pierced. There is also a possibility another prophecy in Psalms 45:8 fulfilled when

---

573  John 18:21.
574  *Chapman v Kirke* [1948] 2KB 450 at 454.
575   Again in John 19:4 & 6.
576  See Psalms 42:2.
577  See Exodus 12:46.

John describes the burial preparation of mixture of myrrh and aloes in 19:39 & 40.

Note that there is an introduction of **forensic evidence** in 19:34 in regards to the '*blood and water came out*' when Jesus' side was pierced with a spear. As explained in the previous chapters, this is no miraculous phenomenon but perfectly on natural medical evidence that Jesus was already dead (see under 'expert opinion evidence').

Again for the purpose of the apologetic task, John appeals to **eyewitness testimony evidence** of the whole process of how Jesus die, including the blood and water, so that his readers knows he is telling the truth. – "*And he who has seen has testified, and his testimony is true; and he knows that he is telling the truth, so that you may believe.*"[578]

No writer could have presented in such a coherent fact, so recognizable an event, unless he or someone else had actually eye-witnessed the whole process of the surrounding happenings in Jesus' crucifixion and His eventual death. The detailed facts described by the Apostle John must have happened and indeed such meticulous description reflect his emphasis on evidences with the purpose that others will believe. Truly the writer of the fourth gospel subscribes to the significance of legal apologetics.

## John Chapter 20

This chapter is the climax of Jesus' ultimate mission on earth. The resurrection is of no doubt considered as the **best evidence** to discharge the legal burden in proving that Jesus indeed is '*the way, the truth and the life,*'[579] the true Word of God who conquer death.[580] If Jesus have not resurrected, then like Paul had written, "*our preaching is vain, your faith also is vain.*"[581] Then our testimony as witnesses is false and in the modern law of criminal evidence, we commit perjury. But worst of all, "*we are even found to be false witnesses of God, because we testified against God that He raised Christ, whom He did not raise, if in fact the dead are not raised.*"[582] The risk is great when one presupposes any religion of his own fancy to be true, not taking note of any evidence. With self-imposed skepticism that man cannot be a starting point, he doesn't even realise that even common sense tells

---

[578]  John 19:35.
[579]  John 14:6.
[580]  See 1 Corinthians 15:54-56.
[581]  1 Corinthians 15:14.
[582]  1 Corinthians 15:15.

him it is impossible to have any other starting point.[583] But he should realise because his realisation starts from him. The overwhelming reliance
on evidences surrounding the resurrection is far from any notion of presuppositionalism.

As affirmed by Professor John Warwick Montgomery, "*The case for
Christ's resurrection from the dead has always been the fundamental evidential
apologetics for Christianity.*"[584] Resurrection is the ultimate historical proof
Jesus has to substantiate with vivid, unambiguous, non-mysterious evidences, able to be perceived by the man's natural sensory faculty. Otherwise, Jesus's death will be in vain if it merely culminate into some kind of
spiritual or superstition belonging to the realm of any other legends. The
resurrection must not only be done but manifestly seen and proven to be
done.

This is the purpose of why John wrote the fourth gospel, with evidence performed in the presence of the disciples, so that man might believe that Jesus is Christ, the Son of God.[585] For this purpose alone and to
reach the verdict intended, John have to arrange and furnish relevant evidences and eye-witnesses accordingly. This is the task of legal apologetics as we can see applied by the Apostle John. In this important highpoint
chapter of Jesus' resurrection, John first introduces the main **witnesses** to
testify what they saw e.g. Mary Magdalene,[586] Peter,[587] and the disciples.[588]
Though the Apostle John repeating in his writing what they say and saw
may be **hearsay evidence,** he ensure he establishes himself as the 'other
disciple'[589] who also saw, thus making him a **first-hand witness**, whom
can provide stronger probative value of **corroborative evidence**, especially when John corroborated what Peter saw in the empty tomb.[590]

---

[583] If God is the starting point (which is true in another sense), man still have to decide that God is the starting point. Presuppositionalism does not begin well even
though it begins with God because it begins with God when God requires us to
begin with ourselves. [see fantastic argument in chapter 12 of R.C. Sproul, J. G. A.
L. "*Classical Apologetics: A Rational Defense of the Christian Faith and a Critic of Presuppositional Apologetics*" (Grand Rapids, Michigan: Zondervan Publishing House,
1984), pp. 212-240].

[584] Montgomery, J. W., "*Faith Founded on Fact: Essays in Evidential Apologetics*" (Newburgh, Indiana, Trinity Press, 1978), xii.

[585] John 20:30-31.

[586] John 20:1.

[587] John 20:3.

[588] John 20:19.

[589] John 20:4.

[590] John 20:8.

John suggested the linen wrappings[591] and the face cloth[592] still lying in their original folds as **real evidence.** This is sufficient to be a strong **circumstantial evidence** to infer that in such present state, untouched by human hands yet no longer containing the crucified body is most probably a supernatural event that can only be raised by divine intervention. This is the necessary relevant evidence beyond reasonable doubt to have a verdict, enable the disciples to reach full Christian faith, which is faith in Jesus crucified-and-risen. (See also the **res ipsa loquitor** evidence discussed under the section of 'presumptions' in chapter 3).

Like in other chapters, John again appeals to the Scripture[593] (as **documentary evidence**) that Jesus must rise from the dead, which He did raise from the dead (**demonstrative evidence**) as fulfilled prophecy.[594] Another **demonstrative evidence** is the evidence of *sight* and *touch* of Jesus' wound to Thomas.[595] All these type of evidences displayed to fulfill John's purpose resemblance of the principles of the law of evidence. John truly is a legal apologist in light of his emphasis on evidentialism.

## John Chapter 21

This final chapter by no means only an epilogue but for John to again establish his identity, reliability and **credibility** of **first-hand eye-witness,** thus raises the probative value of his testimony. Elsewhere John, referring himself by way of third person as *"the other disciple"* or *"the disciple whom Jesus loved."* Many speculations of why John describes himself in an indirect way but perhaps as Tasker puts it:

> The elders of the church, probably in Ephesus, are here identifying the author of the Gospel with 'the disciple whom Jesus loved' and giving a kind of *testamur* that his witness is reliable. On this interpretation, the verse constitutes the earliest external evidence for the authorship of the Gospel.[596]

Perhaps it is John's legal methodological strategy not to refer himself at the beginning. This is to forestall any initial presupposed biasness but to

---

[591] John 20:6.
[592] John 20:7.
[593] John 20:9.
[594] Most probably from Psalms 16:10 – *"For you will not abandon my soul to Sheol; Nor will You allow Your Holy One to undergo decay."* This prophecy of the resurrection were also relied in Peter's sermon on the day of Pentecost in Acts 2:27 and Paul's first missionary journey sermon in Acts 13:35.
[595] John 20:25-29.
[596] Tasker, *John*, 235.

first lay down the apparent evidences. Gradually and at a later stage, the facts and the evidences may establish his credibility. In other words, instead of satisfying his qualification of a credible lay witness to admit any hearsay evidences or opinions, John have all the relevant evidences admitted in advance and later from the facts admitted, reminds the 'jury' of his close acquaintance and opportunities for direct first-hand evidences. For example, he reminded the readers in 21:20 of the 'disciple whom Jesus loved following them' and the 'one who also had leaned on His bosom at the supper,' most probably receiving insider information of who will betray Jesus. This makes his testimony of credible value.

In addition, Jesus defended John by rebuking Peter when he shows himself idly curious about the future of John.[597] Furthermore, John testify that this beloved disciple is the first to identify Jesus[598] even in the dark grey morning[599] midst, thus infer his ability in making a right **identification evidence.** Having a perfect memory for even able to remember that Simon Peter was half naked[600] at that time and the exact number of fish caught was a hundred and fifty-three,[601] gives support to John's **credibility** and **competency** to his testimony and as an eyewitness. How natural that the recognition should be made by this sensitive brooding disciple, who had so readily deduced from the evidence of the grave-clothes that Jesus was raised from among the dead! He who had leaned on his Master's breast at supper has the quickest and surest perception of Him as the risen Lord.[602] And this credible witness is none other than the one "testifying to these things and wrote these things" so for the verdict that "we know that his testimony is true."[603]

It is also noted that Jesus wants to bring the disciples into remembrance and able to identify Him by providing several **similar fact evidences.** For example, the same miracle He can performed[604] and the divine attribute of omniscient, knowing where to cast the nets to find a catch.[605] Jesus also wants to bring them to mind by similarly taking the

[597] John 21:21.
[598] John 21:7a.
[599] John 21:4.
[600] John 21:7b.
[601] John 21:11.
[602] Tasker, John, 229.
[603] John 21:24.
[604] Luke 5:1-11 (though at that incident a few months before, the nets was broken and the boat began to sink).
[605] John 21:5-6.

bread and distribute to them as an answer to his identity.[606] His similar appearances are recurring evidences to strengthen their faith that He was raised from the dead.[607]

In the principles of the law of evidence, similar fact evidence is usually evidence pertaining to similar conduct on other occasions or of the commission by the accused of similar offences. It is to some extent circumstantial evidence to demonstrate propensity. Generally, it is presumptively inadmissible if it is to infer similar bad character. However, its admissibility will depend upon probative effect of the evidence balanced against the prejudice caused to the accused by its admission, whatever the purpose of its admission. But in our case, Jesus is tendering similar fact evidences not of bad character but of His similar good characteristics that can indicate His identity to the disciples. Though it may sound so simple and obvious a thing to do to trigger the memory of the disciples, yet such similar fact evidences were used by Jesus instead of relying the disciples' presupposition or warrant of belief (if any) that the person talking to the disciples is or should be Jesus Himself.

John also noted Jesus' prophecy on the kind of death Peter would glorify God as **demonstrative evidence** of Jesus' divinity. Most probably the readers already knew Peter was killed and realized the prophecy came true. It may sound like a broken gramophone, but it should be appropriate to repeat that John's emphasis in the various types of evidences, compel us to conclude the inspired fourth Gospel subscribes to legal evidential apologetics. Indeed, the author of the fourth Gospel has more evidences to testify but due to the natural restriction, he wrote:

> "And there are also many other things which Jesus did,
> which if they were written in detail,
> I suppose that even the world itself would not contain the books
> that would be written."
> John 21:25 [NASB].

---

[606] John 21:12-13.
[607] John 21:14.

# CONCLUSION

Without doubt, the evidentialists agrees with the presuppositionalists that God is sovereign and the Scripture is the ultimate authority. However, one of the presuppositionalists' main swaggering denouncement is that the Christian evidentialists put their reliance on probabilistic argumentation. They deprecates the evidentialists' approach as philosophically misguided, apologetically unworkable, and unbiblical. The evidentialists cannot stomach this overweening notion which is usually nothing but often windup in circular argument.

Fortunately, there are 'apologetic mediators'[608] attempting to reconcile these ever-wrangling apologetic distant cousins. Nevertheless, all diplomatic attempts are merely saying "let's agree to disagree" and yet forgetting the philosophical doctrine of non-contradiction and the excluded middle. How can certainty be probability and probability be certainty? How can we say the starting point is man and also starting point is from God? Isn't it either/or and cannot be both? Either we follow this philosophical logical rule of non-contradiction or we don't. We cannot have both ways, unless like the lawyers usually will say, "in every general rule, there are always exceptions." But even the specific exceptions cannot fall under both extremes. Anyway, Professor Ronald B. Mayers[609] humbly explains both presuppositionalism and evidentialism are correct. Whilst supporting presuppositionalism:

> This written witness of the life of Christ is the extension of his spoken word. One cannot therefore today accept the authority of Christ's spoken

---

[608] Such as Mayers, Ronald B. *"Balanced Apologetics: Using Evidences and Presuppositions in Defence of the Faith"* (Grand Rapids: Kregel, 1996). Reprint of *"Both/And: A Balanced Apologetics"* (Chicago: Moody, 1984). To some great extent, probably Boa, Kenneth and Robert Bowman Jr. *"Faith Has Its Reason: An Integrative Approach to Defending Christianity"* (Paternoster, 2005); Clark, David K. *"Dialogical Apologetics: A Person-Centered Approach to Christian Defence"* (Grand Rapids: Baker, 1993); Evans, Stephens C. *"The Historical Christ and the Jesus of Faith: The Incarnational Narrative as History"* (Oxford: Oxford University Press, 1996); Schaeffer, Francis A. *"The Complete Works of Francis A. Schaeffer"* 5 Vols. (Westchester, Ill.: Crossway Books, 1982); Carnell, Edward John. *"An Introduction to Christian Apologetics: A Philosophic Defence of the Trinitarian Theistic Faith"* (Grand Rapids: Eerdsman, 1948; 4th ed., 1953); etc.

[609] Retired Emeritus Professor of Religion at Cornerstone University.

word or understand his message without understanding and accepting the authority of the NT.[610]

Ronald Mayer sincerely encourages both apologetics school to reconcile:

> It seems to me, however, that the debate between the evidentialists and presuppositionalists ... must end in a both/and framework that does not inhabit one or the other polar region of truth. This attempt to maintain both poles simultaneously is uncomfortable because it will not be driven to either pole by promoters of logical consistency at the expense of actual reality. It is not, however, inherently contradictory but reflects the actuality of both man and God, both body and spirit, both fact and mind, both event and interpretation.[611]

And yet he realises the reality of fallen man's predicament and restricted in their epistemological capability. Hence, it necessitates man to start from themselves:

> For some, man can know nothing aright until he knows God, and thus God must be the epistemological starting point. But autonomous, fallen man cannot, because he will not, start with God. Thus the unbeliever and the believer are not simply morally exclusive of one another but intellectually disparate as all must be theistically presupposed. The other apologetic track believes fallen man can arrive at God from the non-god, that is, *a posteriori* argument from the world as it is to the perfect Creator, an hypothesis that Hume rightly believed dubious.[612]
> ... that in regard to personal identity and historical reality we of necessity must begin actually with ourselves, but in regard to ultimate meaning and eternal verities we must begin logically with God.[613]

However, Professor Mayers warned about the risk of evidence and the benefits of relying on the mind of God through the revealed Scripture:

> Evidence is never open to just any interpretation if it is claiming to be true. Interpretation must correspond to reality, which is ultimately the mind of God. Man's mind must simply follow God's mind.[614]

---

[610] Mayers, Ronald B. "Both/And: The Uncomfortable Apologetics", *Journal of Evangelical Theological Society* 23/3 (September 1980) 231-241 at 234.

[611] Ibid., 234.

[612] Ibid., 234.

[613] Ibid., 234.

[614] Ibid., 235.

Paul never drifts from a Scriptural understanding (or presupposition). While there are these common ground facets due to the ontological structure of created and thus conditioned being, Paul never forgets that fallen man does not have adequate epistemological tools without the meaning given to created reality by unconditioned Being, the revelation of the very mind of God himself. His exposition of their experience therefore is thoroughly Biblical and congruent with his subsequent statement on the meaning and significance of general revelation in Romans.[615]

... there are common facts between believer and unbeliever because they are both God's creatures living in God's universe, but the unbeliever will not rightly interpret these facts because he lives without God and therefore lacks his definitive interpretation.[616]

And yet diplomatically and as uncomfortably as Professor Mayers writhes, he appropriately explains the parallel effect of both objective and subjective faith:

While objective belief can only be probable, subjective affirmation is sealed in the certitude of the Holy Spirit. Both apologetic traditions are correct. Belief based on historical evidence is only probable. But faith is not exhausted by belief, though it is a prerequisite of the existential dimension of trust. Faith as belief is rational (propositional word) but insufficient, given the experience of the demons (James 2:19). One must both comprehend the message and "throw one's entire being out upon the Lord" (personal). The latter is not possible without the work of the Holy Spirit in creating a new will and love by means of the new word provided in the gracious gift and work of Christ.[617]

Biblical faith is thus both belief and trust, both objective and subjective, both rationally propositional and existentially personal.[618]

Whilst strongly concurring with Professor Mayers' balanced apologetics, the raucous sound of the curiosity bell still rings in the head, asking on which starting point Mayers (including any other potential believers) relied on just before making the decision in accepting Christ as Lord and Savior. Unless he is already a Christian and whatever existing presuppositions instilled by his family since birth, it is of no doubt he and other similar human beings are exposed by some reasoning and evidence to be assessed by themselves and thereon from themselves as a starting point

---

[615] Ibid., 235.
[616] Ibid., 236.
[617] Ibid., 237.
[618] Ibid., 237.

while making a decision of faith. As far as the author of this book is concerned, evidentialism and any other apologetic methodologies are never perfect. They are balanced imperfect apologetic methodologies. Only the Holy Spirit is perfect and all His endorsed apologetics tools are perfect, if use under His control and for the glory of God.[619] However, the supercilious criticism against the Christian evidentialism is uncalled for. If the presuppositionalists argues that everyone has the tendency to be prejudicial, bias, and ordinary preferences affect our interpretations in all areas, there is no way for them to argue that their methodology is correct as they like others are also stained with prejudice and biasness. Consequently, they too are affected by their own preconceived notion in their interpretations of apologetics.

If the presuppositionalists say that the starting point is from God, that statement itself is circular or self-referential argument since that statement itself must start from themselves. If the Christian presuppositionalism strongly maintain Scripture is ultimate authority, that means all teachings and methods espoused in the Bible should be adhered to.

Hence, if in the Gospel of John[620] and especially Jesus Himself uses reasoning and evidences, isn't it correct to say we presupposes that evidentialism is the biblical apologetic method set out by Jesus and the other apostles? Shouldn't we follow Jesus' examples? Concisely, evidentialism embraces presuppositionalism but it would be almost impossible for evidentialism to be subsumed into presuppositionalism because presuppositionalism is as rigid as any other dogmatically religious skeptics or agnostics. It is possible and easier for evidentialism to be balanced with presuppositionalism than presuppositionalism to be balanced with evidentialism.

Evidentialism believes that once a person has evaluated the reasons and evidences and made a commitment to the Christian faith with the help of the Holy Spirit, he can thereon 'presuppose' the truth of the Scriptures to further teach him or her to higher level of knowledge. It can work both ways even to those who credulously wants to believe before further receiving more evidences or reasonings. This would be an ideal situation but cannot be the only method. Presuppositionalism on the other hand is a non-negotiable epistemology – believe first and ask later. To them, requesting evidence is a sign of depraved minded person and is unbiblical. Is better to quote John Warwick Montgomery as he appositely

---

[619] As John Frame as put it for his title book, "*Apologetics to the Glory of God*" (Phillipsburg, New Jersey: Presbyterian and Reformed Publishing Company, 1994).
[620] And elsewhere in the Old and New Testaments.

put it when he criticises Carl F.H. Henry's *God, Revelation and Authority*[621] together with other presuppositionalists:[622]

> Though uncomfortable with the most consistent form of "revelational pre-suppositionalism," which holds that even laws of logic have no justification apart from special revelation (Vol. 1., p. 236), he follows the main presuppositionalist line in rejecting empirical verifiability and falsifiability (Vol. 1 pp. 96-111). He rejects any and all use of "an experiential criterion for validating theology ...[623]
>
> The presuppositionalists finds it impossible for non-Christian and Christians to experience common ground in the matter of revelational fact and interpretation. But consider that in the realm of secular fact (e.g. the chemical composition of water or the historical crossing of the Rubicon by Caesar), both Christian and non-Christian are capable of discovering truth and interpreting it. All university life is predicated on this assumption, and advances in human knowledge are indisputable evidence that even unregenerate man can understand the factual nature of the world and rationally interpret the data of his experience. Now if we say that the events of Christ's life (or for the biblical events in general) are not subject to comparable treatment, then whether we like it or not we are actually divorcing "Christian facts" from secular, nonreligious facts.[624]

Professor John Warwick Montgomery pulls no punches when he fervently affirms that the Bible identifies truth with the person of Jesus Christ, the God-man who came to earth to die for the sins of the world. Thus knowing the truth ultimately depends on one's personal relationship to Christ:[625]

> If you continue in My word, then you are indeed my disciples, and you shall know the truth, and the truth shall make you free.[626]

Hence, Professor Montgomery concludes:

> Evidently, what is necessary for effective Christian witness in a pluralistic world is an objective apologetic – "a reason for the hope that is in you" – that will give the non-Christian clear ground for experientially trying the

---

[621] (Waco, Texas: Word Books, 1976).
[622] Such as Cornelius Van Til, Gordon Clark and Herman Dooyeweerd.
[623] Montgomery, John Warwick. "*Faith Founded on Fact: Essays in Evidential Apologetics*" (Newburgh, Indiana, Trinity Press, 1978), xviii.
[624] Ibid., 33-34.
[625] Ibid., 35.
[626] John 8: 31-32.

Christian faith before all other options. Absolute proof of the truth of Christ's claims is available only in personal relationship with Him; but contemporary man has every right to expect us to offer solid reasons for making such a total commitment. The apologetic task is justified not as a rational substitute for faith but a ground for faith; not as a replacement for the Spirit's working, but as a means by which the objective truth of God's Word can be made clear so that men will heed it as vehicle of the Spirit who convicts the world through its message.[627]

This is exactly what this book purports by identifying the apologetic methodology of the apostle John. Whilst relying on the Spirit of truth, various types of evidences as commonly comprehend by the legal fraternity are tendered as means by which the objective truth of God's Word can be made clear so that men will believe. In the previous chapters, we discuss the practicality of the principles of the law of evidence in searching for the truth. Although it is not perfect, there is no other method more humanly understood and better than the ones judicially applied in the courts of law. All sciences and philosophical rules in seeking any truth claims are embrace by the courts as long it is relevant and admissible.

There is a great advantage in applying the principles of the law of evidence in our apologetic task. It is practicable and applicable in our daily task in almost every area of our lives. In searching for an answer whether through existing modern document or ancient documents, the evidential law has propounded several basic principles. Professor Montgomery illustrates, *'law is necessitarian, coloring all aspects of societal life; so its solutions to fundamental problems carry powerful weight. On the interpretation of contracts, wills, statutes and constitutions hang the lives and property of us all'.*[628] Hence, it is utmost appropriate to apply these legal principles in our evidential apologetic task. Dr Ross Clifford vividly asserts:

> A legal apologetic is appropriate to a fact based religion. It is an apologetic that by its nature is accustomed to sifting evidence to find the principle items, that can clearly discriminate between issues and sources, and that can weigh the significance of subordinate facts; such as a relationship that would tend to make a witness biased, and the competency of a witness. It

---

[627] Montgomery, *Faith Founded on Fact*, 40.
[628] Montgomery, John Warwick. *'Legal Hermeneutics and the Interpretation of Scripture'* in Evangelical Hermeneutics edited by Michael Bauman and David Hall (Camp Hill, Pennsylvania: Christian Publications, 1995), 18.

also offers criteria to evaluate oral testimony, hearsay and circumstantial evidence in determining the facts.[629]

Having say that, it is not only an appropriate apologetic methodology but is also being set as an example by Jesus as we seen on the writings of John. As we scrutinise chapter by chapter, we see the signs, miracles, reasoning and the appeal to prophecies and scriptures as relevant admissible evidences. We also see that John noted several testimonies from eyewitnesses of credibility and competency to testify. Just in chapter 5, we can see seven evidences forwarded by Jesus. All the various types of evidences tendered within the narratives of the fourth gospel, similar to the types we understood from the modern judicial principles of evidence. We also observe the reasoning and philosophical rules of logic applied by Jesus in His argument with the Pharisees. In every chapters of the fourth gospel, there is both express and implied indication of the use of various principles of the law of evidence – which is tabulated in Table A (see Table A at page 223).

There are benefits of the evidential principles of philosophical reasoning applied by Jesus in His argument with the Jewish leaders, which we apologists can learn from our Lord. Dr. Norman Geisler vehemently affirms the Johannine Christological methodology is liken to a courtroom procedure:

> Like the rest of the New Testament, the dominant apologetic model in John is legal rather than military. That is, the background motif is a courtroom where evidence is presented for the purpose of persuading the reader. The apologetic task is not performed on a battlefield where an enemy is to be fought and defeated. In this sense John's apologetic motif fits well the locus classicus of 1 Peter 3:15, which urges the believer to present an ἀπολογία or defense such as one would give in court.[630]

If presupposition of the existence of God is necessarily as a mandatory presumption enabling one to believe in Jesus, one wonders why those Jews who already presupposed (or strongly believed) in the God of Israel and the authority of the Law of Moses could not believe in Jesus, the Son whom God has sent? John tells us that "*though Jesus had performed so many*

[629]  Clifford, Ross. "*John Warwick Montgomery's Legal Apologetic: An Apologetic for all Seasons*" (Bond, Germany: Verlag für Kultur und Wissenschaft Culture and Science Publ., 2004), 239.

[630]  Geisler, Norman L. "Johannine Apologetics" *Bibliotheca Sacra* 136, 544 (October–December, 1979): 333-343, at p. 333.

*signs before them, yet they were not believing in Him."* (John 12:37). Despite already having the knowledge of the Scriptures in advance, the Jews do not believe. Presupposition is not a prerequisite to belief. Neither is evidence nor reasons. When one's eyes are blinded and has his hearts hardened, they can neither presuppose nor even make a right decision. However, we do no justice if we discard the evidential tools and the intellect that God has endowed on us as a mode of persuading one to believe.

Unlike the rigidity of presuppositionalism, evidentialism is not subject to rules but on flexible principles. Rigidity has a connotation that man is deprived of freedom. Jesus and the writer of the fourth gospel are fully aware of the condition of man. Evidentialists agrees with John Calvin that the minds of man are depraved due to original sin but not absolutely depraved as in the sense it becomes a vegetative state of a mindless glob. We need to comprehend the necessary structure of God's dealing with features of His creation. Creation itself may be contingent, but once God has created, then whatever world God makes is always limited in relation to God. If God is to interact, or deal with features of that world, he has to operate within the limits of the things he has made.[631] It does not mean God is not sovereign and hence is limited by His own making. If God intentionally goes against His created order by giving no freewill to man to decide and evaluate upon available evidence and rationalise, there would be no interaction.

The perfect image of God once conferred on man was partially corrupted due to original sin and the consequence is human limitation which is now an obstacle for God to interact with us. Therefore, the more man intentionally suppresses the truth, the more evidences of higher probative value are needed to be furnished to persuade man to believe. Even Jesus understood the human limitation but by no means is an excuse for them, *"for they loved the approval of men rather than the approval of God."*[632] But yet in His great mercy, Jesus produces seven signs (as we observed in the fourth gospel) as each signs are progressively demonstrated, its probative value becomes higher in its effectiveness. Some believed whilst some absolutely refuses to believe. Some feared due to the authorities whilst some may believe depending on their individual temperaments and how probable the evidences are according to their level of

---

[631]  King, Rolfe. *"Obstacles to Divine Revelation: God and the Reorientation of Human Reason"* (London: Continuum, 2008) 13.

[632]  John 12:43 [NASB].

faith. Rolfe King[633] observes the necessity of probability and evidences in past events of divine activities:

> The problem is that evaluating what is and is not probable, as regards God acting in history, is difficult to determine, unless one already knows something about God. But that, it seems, could not be through revelation as history, without begging the question. Normal canons of historical reasoning are just that: they are based on assessments of normal human life. Admittedly, this may be very difficult to codify, but in terms of practical judgment it is quite clear that there are vast areas on which historians agrees that there is sufficient evidence to establish many matters, with at least a very high degree of confidence. This is done through assessments of the norms of probability, and how evidence accumulates in inferring, evaluating and arriving at the best explanation for that evidence.[634]

In His grace, our Lord Jesus leave us not only with strong evidences of His resurrection but has set a methodological example for us to follow. With this legal evidential apologetic sample for us to adhere with, comes along a special power both to strengthen our faith but also our intellect to understand the truth. As noted by the apostle John, Jesus promises, "*But when He, the Spirit of truth, comes, He will guide you into all the truth; for He will not spoke on His own initiative, but whatever He hears, He will speak; and He will disclose to you what is to come.*"[635] The Apostle John is aware of the evidential value under the supervision of the Spirit of truth. If it is presuppose that evidences and reasons are not required in our apologetic task but leaving all the work to be done by the Holy Spirit alone, there is no need for the apostle John to write the fourth Gospel. John would not need to write about the signs Jesus performed as evidence to convince his readers. Due to the awareness of the value of apologetic evidentialism (as guided by the Holy Spirit), John wrote with evidence "*so that you may believe that Jesus is the Christ, the Son of God; and that believing you may have life in His name.*" (John 20:31).

In conclusion, this book demonstrates that the scripture do accentuate the use of evidence and rationality over blind faith. It is avers that Christian evidentialism is defended once again through the precedents set out in the fourth gospel. Throughout almost every passages propounding the Johannine Christology, we see every trace of the basic prin-

---

[633]  Honorary lecturer in the School of Philosophy, Theology and Religion at the University of Birmingham, UK.

[634]  King, R. "*Obstacles to Divine Revelation*", 34.

[635]  John 16:13.

ciples of the law of evidence. The author of the fourth gospel had consciously and intentionally assessed the logical flow and evidence (but may unconsciously applied the modern principles of the law of evidence) to rationally convince his readers. If this were true, then the author of John's Gospel is truly indeed an evidential apologist and one who loves God with all his mind. Indeed, we see no strong emphasis of presuppositionalism by the apostle John. Through the writings and his evangelistic driven purpose, John is an evidentialist. To be more precise, the Apostle John is a strong supporter of legal apologetics.

# APPENDICES

## Table A

TABLE A: VARIOUS TYPES OF JUDICIAL EVIDENCE AND RULES OF LOGIC IN EACH CHAPTER OF JOHN'S GOSPEL

| | Natural Justice | Character Evidence | Direct Evidence | Real Evidence | Circumstantial Evidence | Demonstrative Evidence | Testimony | Presumption | Authority | Lay Opinion | Corroboration | Confession | Hearsay | Documentary Evidence | Identification Evidence | Reason/Logic | Witnesses | Facts in Issue |
|---|---|---|---|---|---|---|---|---|---|---|---|---|---|---|---|---|---|---|
| John 1 | | | | | | | | | | √ | | | √ | √ | √ | √ | C+C | √ |
| John 2 | | | | | √ | | | | | | | | √ | | √ | | √ C+C | |
| John 3 | | | | | | √ | | | | | √ | √ | √ | | | a fortiori | √ C+C | |
| John 4 | | √ | √ | | | | | | | | √ | √ | √ | √ | | | √ | √ |
| John 5 | | | √ | | √ + res ipsa | √ | √ + Self | √ + JuNo | √ | | √ | | √ | | | | √ C+C | √ |
| John 6 | | | √ | | | √ | | | | | | | | | | √ | | |
| John 7 | √ | | | | √ | √ | Self | | | | | | | √ | | √+ a fortiori | | |
| John 8 | | | √ | | | √ | | res ipsa | | | √ | | √ | | | √+HD+NC | √ C+C | BOP |
| John 9 | | | √ | | | √ | | √ | | | √ | | √ | | | | √ C+C | |
| John 10 | | | | | | | | | √ | √ | √ | | | | | a fortiori | | |
| John 11 | | | | | | √ | | | | | | | | | | √ | √ | √ |
| John 12 | | | | | | | | | | | | | √ | √ | | √ | √ | |
| John 13 | | | | | | | | | | | | | | √ | | | C+C | |
| John 14 | | | | | | | | | | | | | | | | | | |
| John 15 | | | | | | √ | | | | | | | | √ | | | | |
| John 16 | | | | | √ | √ | √ | | | | | | | | | | √ C+C | |
| John 17 | | √ | | | √ | √ | | | | | √ | | | | | | | |
| John 18 | | √ + victim | | | | √ | | Silence | | | | | | | | | √ C+C | √ |
| John 19 | | √ | | Forensic | √ | √ | | | | | √ | | √ | √ | | | √ | |
| John 20 | | √ | | √ | √ SFE | √ | | res ipsa | | | | | | | | | | Best Ev |
| John 21 | | | | | SFE | √ | | | | | | | | | √ | | √ C+C | |

**KEYS:**

BOP - Burden of Proof   HD - Horns of dilemma   res ipsa - res ipsa loquitor   Silence - Presumption of Innocence   Victim - Victim's character

Best Ev - Best Evidence   NC - Non Contradiction   C+C - Credibility & Competency   SFE - Similar Fact Evidence   JuNo - Judicial Notice

## List of Cases

Bishop of Meath v Marquis of Winchester [1836] 4 Cl. & F. 445; 3 Bing. N.C. 183.

Bratty v A-G for Northern Ireland [1963] AC 386.

Byrne v Boadle [1863] 2 H&C 722.

Callis v Gunn [1964] 1 QB 495 DC.

Chapman v Kirke [1948] 2KB 450.

Chapronière v Mason [1905] 21 TLR 633, CA.

Chard v Chard [1956] P 259.

Crawford v. Washington, 541 U.S. 36 (2004).

Davie v Edinburgh Magistrates [1953] SC 34. Court of Sessions.

Doe d Gilbert v Ross [1840] 7 M&W 102.

DPP v Boardman [1975] AC 421.

DPP v Hester [1973] AC 296, HL.

DPP v Kilbourne [1973] AC 729, HL.

DPP v P [1991] 2 AC 447.

Ellor v Selfridge & Co Ltd [1930] 46 TLR 236.

Folkes v Chadd [1782] 3 Doug. K.B. 157.

H v Schering Chemicals Ltd [1983] 1 All ER 849.

Heath v Deane [1905] 2 Ch 86 (manorial rolls).

Holland v Zollner, 102 Cal. 633, 638-39 (1894).

Huth v Huth [1915] 3 KB 32, CA.

Ibrahim v R [1914] AC 599, Privy Council.

Lafone v Griffin [1909] 25 TLR 308.

Mahon v Osborne [1939] 2 KB 14, CA.

Miller v Cawley [2002] The Times 6 Sept 2002, CA.

Miller v Minister of Pensions [1947] 2 All ER 372.

Monckton v Tarr [1930] 23 BWCC 504, CA.

Nye v Niblett [1918] 1 KB 23; 26 Cox CC 113; [1916-17] All ER Rep 520.

R v Barsoum [1994] Crim LR 194, CA.

R v Bathurst [1968] 2 QB 99, CA.

R v Blastland [1985] 2 All ER 1095, HL.

R v Byrne [1960] 2 QB 396.

R v Collins [1960] 44 CR App R 170.

R v Daye [1908] 2 KB 333.

R v Dehar [1969] NZLR 763, New Zealand Court of Appeal.

R v Dix [1981] 74 Cr App R 306, CA.

R v Exall [1866] 4 F & F 922.

R v Goodway [1993] 4 All ER 894, CA.

R v Hall [1987] The Times, 15 July, CA.

R v Kearley [1992] 2 All ER 345.

R v Masih [1986] Crim LR 395, CA.

R v McIlkenny [1992] 2 All ER 417, CA.

R v Nethercott [2002] 2 Cr App R 117, CA.

R v Randall [2004] 1 ALL ER 467.

R v Sharp [1988] 1 WLR 7.

R v Strudwick [1993] 99 Cr App R 326, CA.

R v Taylor [1993] Crim LR 223, CA.

R v Turner [1975] 1 QB 834; [1975] 1 All ER 70; [1975] 2 WLR 56, 60 Cr App Rep 80.

R v Ward [1993] 2 All ER 577.

R v Wood [1990] Crim LR 264, CA.

Re Oxford Poor Rate Case [1857] 8 E&B 184.

Re S (a child) (adoption: psychological evidence) [2004] EWCA Civ 1029; [2004] All ER (D) 593 (Jul).

Read v Bishop of Lincoln [1892] AC 644.

Rice v Connolly [1966] 2 QB 414.

Scott v London & St Katherine Docks Co. [1865] 3 H&C 596.

Seyfang v GD Searle & Co. [1973] QB 148 at 151.

Springsteen v Flute International Ltd. [2001] EMLR 654, CA.

Sturla v Freccia [1880] 5 App Cas 623.

Subramaniam v Public Prosecutor [1965] 1 WLR 965.

Teper v R [1952] AC 480 at 489, Privy Council.

Ward v Tesco Stores Ltd [1976] 1 WLR 810, CA.

Woolminton v DPP [1935] AC 462.

Wright v Doe d Thantam [1838] 4 Bing NC 489.

Wynne v Trywhitt [1821] 4 B. & Ald. 376.

## List of Statutes

Children and Young Persons Act 1933.

Children and Young Persons Act 1969.

Civil Evidence Act 1972.

Civil Evidence Act 1995.

Criminal Evidence Act 1898.

Criminal Evidence Act 1898 (amended).

Criminal Justice Act 2003.

Criminal Justice and Public Order Act 1994.

Criminal Procedure (Insanity and Unfitness to Plead) Act 1991.

Criminal Procedure (Insanity) Act 1964.

Evidence Act 1938.

Homicide Act 1957.

Human Rights Act 1988.

Indian Evidence Act 1872.

Magistrates' Act 1980.

Malayan Emergency Regulations.

Malaysian Dangerous Drugs Act 1952.

Malaysian Penal Code.

Police and Criminal Evidence Act 1984.

United States Federal Rules of Evidence.

Youth Justice and Criminal Evidence Act 1999.

## Bibliography

Albright, William F. *"Archaeology and the Religion of Israel"* (Baltimore: John Hopkins Press, 1942).

Allen, Christopher. *"Basic Concepts"* Chapter 1 of Allen, C., Sourcebook on Evidence (London: Routledge Cavendish, 1996).

Anonymous in California, "Not My Weak Will But A Greater Power," *The Grapevine* (February 1968).

Appleton, John. *"The Rules of Evidence: Stated and Discussed"* (Philadelphia: T. & J. W. Johnson & Co., 1860).

Aquinas, St. Thomas. *'Posterior Analytics"*, 1.8 quoted in McDowell, Josh. The New Evidence That Demands A Verdict (Here's Life Publishers, 1999), 599.

Aquinas, St. Thomas. *"Summa Theologiae"*.

Archer, Gleason L. Jr. *"A Survey of Old Testament Introduction"* (Chicago: Moody Press, 1974).

Aristotle, *"De Arte Poetica"* (Oxford Classical Texts) edited by Rudolf Kassel (Clarendon Press, 1964).

Ashworth, Andrew. "Four Threats to the Presumption of Innocence", *International Journal of Evidence & Proof* (2006) Vol. 10(4), 241-279.

Bahnsen, Greg L. *"Van Til's Apologetics Readings and Analysis"* (Phillipsburg, New Jersey: P & R Publishing, 1998).

Bentham, Jeremy. *"Rationale of Judicial Evidence: Specially Applied to English Practice: From the Manuscripts of Jeremy Bentham"* (London: Hunt and Clarke, 1827), [reprinted 1978].

Bergman, Paul. *"Trial Advocacy in a Nutshell"* (Thompson West, 2003).

Best, William Mawdesley. *"The Principles of the Law of Evidence: With Elementary Rules for Conducting the Examination and Cross-Examination of Witnesses"* (London: Sweet & Maxwell, 1902).

Blanshard, B., *"Reason and Belief"* (London: Allen and Unwin, 1977).

Boa, Kenneth. D. and Robert M. Bowman Jr., *"Faith Has Its Reason: An Integrative Approach to Defending Christianity"* (Paternoster, 2005).

Brody, Baruch A. (ed.), *"Readings in the Philosophy of Religion"* (Englewood Cliffs, N.J.: Prentice-Hall, 1974).

Broughton, P. William. *"The Historical Development of Legal Apologetics: With An Emphasis on the Resurrection"* (Xulon Press, 2009).

Bruce F.F. *"The New Testament Documents: Are They Reliable?"* (Downer Grove; Illinois: InterVarsity Press, 1964).

Bruce, F.F. *"Archaeological Confirmation of the New Testament"* in 'Revelation and the Bible' edited by Carl Henry (Grand Rapids: Baker Book House, 1969).

Bruce, F.F. *"The Books and the Parchments: How We Got Our English Bible"* (Old Tappan, New Jersey: Fleming H. Revell Co., 1950, reprint 1984).

Bruce, F.F. *"The Gospel of John"* (Basingstoke: Pickering & Inglis, 1983).

Bultmann, Rudolf. *"The Gospel of John"* Translated by George R. Beasley-Murray (Philadelphia: Westminster, 1971).

Carnell, Edward J. *"Christian Commitment: An Apologetic"* (New York: MacMillan, 1957).

Carnell, Edward John. *"An Introduction to Christian Apologetics: A Philosophic Defence of the Trinitarian Theistic Faith"* (Grand Rapids: Eerdsman, 1948; 4th ed., 1953).

Carson, D.A. & Douglas J. Moo. "An Introduction to the New Testament" (Grand Rapids, Michigan: Zondervan, 2005).

Clark, David K. *"Dialogical Apologetics: A Person-Centered Approach to Christian Defence"* (Grand Rapids: Baker, 1993).

Clark, David K. and Norman L. Geisler. *"Apologetics in the New Age: A Christian Critique of Pantheism"* (Grand Rapids: Baker, 1990).

Clark, James Kelly. *"Reformed Epistemology Apologetics"* in chapter 5 of Steven B. Cowan (ed.) Five Views on Apologetics (Grand Rapids, Michigan: Zondervan Publishing House, 2000), 267-268.

Clark, Kelly James. *"Reformed Epistemology Apologetics"* in 'Five Views on Apologetics,' edited by Steven Cowan (Grand Rapids, Michigan: Zondervan Publishing House, 2000)

Clifford, Ross. *"John Warwick 's Legal Apologetic: An Apologetic for all Seasons"* (Bond, Germany: Verlag für Kultur und Wissenschaft Culture and Science Publ., 2004).

Clifford, Ross. *"Leading Lawyers Look at the Resurrection"* (Albatross, 1991).

Clifford, Ross. "Justification of the Legal Apologetic of John Warwick Montgomery: An Apologetic For All Seasons" *Global Journal of Classical Theology.* Vol. 3 No. 1, (2002).

Clifford, William Kingdon. *"The Ethics of Belief"* in Lectures and Essays (New York: Macmillan, 1901).

Cook, Frederick Charles, (ed.) *"Commentary on the Holy Bible"* (London: John Murray, 1878).

Cowan, Steven (ed.), *"Five Views on Apologetics"* (Grand Rapids, Michigan: Zondervan Publishing House, 2000)

Craig, William Lane. *"Classical Apologetics"* in Five Views on Apologetics edited by Steven B. Cowan (Michigan, Grand Rapids: Zondervan, 2000).

Craig, William Lane's response to Kelly James Clark's Reformed Epistemology in Cowan, S. B., *"Five Views on Apologetics"* (Grand Rapids, Michigan: Zondervan Publishing House, 2000).

Dworkin, Ronald M. "*A Matter of Principle*" (New York: Oxford University Press, 1986).

Dworkin, Ronald. M. "*Is Law a System of Rules?*" in 'The Philosophy of Law' edited by Ronald Dworkin, [Oxford Readings in Philosophy] (New York: Oxford University Press, 1977).

Edwards, William D., M.D., et al. "On the Physical Death of Jesus Christ" *Journal of the American Medical Association* [255:11, March 21, 1986], 1463.

Escobar, S. "*The New Global Mission: the Gospel from Everywhere to Everyone*" (Downers Grove, Illinois: InterVarsity Press, 2003).

Evans, Stephen C. "*Pocket Dictionary of Apologetics & Philosophy of Religion*" (Leicester: IVP, 2002).

Evans, Stephens C. "*The Historical Christ and the Jesus of Faith: The Incarnational Narrative as History*" (Oxford: Oxford University Press, 1996).

Ewen, Pamela Binnings. "*Faith On Trial: An Attorney Analyzes the Evidence for the Death and Resurrection of Jesus*" (Nashville, Tennessee: Broadman & Holman Publishers, 1999).

Feinberg, Paul D. "*Cumulative Case Apologetics*" in chapter 3 of Steven B. Cowan. 'Five Views on Apologetics' (Grand Rapids, Michigan: Zondervan Publishing House, 2000).

Fisher, J.T. and L.S. Hawley. "*A Few Buttons Missing*" (Philadelphia: J.B. Lippincott, 1951).

Flew, Anthony. "The Presumption of Atheism", *The Canadian Journal of Philosophy* (2/1972) 29-46.

Frame, John M. "*Apologetics to the Glory of God*" (Phillipsburg, New Jersey: Presbyterian and Reformed Publishing Company, 1994).

France, R.T. "*The Authenticity of the Sayings of Jesus*" in 'History, Criticism, and Faith' edited by Colin Brown (Downers Grove: Inter-Varsity, 1976), 101-143.

Garland, Norman and Gilbert Stuckey. "*Criminal Evidence for the Law Enforcement Officer*" (Woodland Hills, California: Glencoe/McGraw-Hill, 1998).

Geisler, Norman and Frank Turek. "*I Don't Have Enough Faith to Be an Atheist*" (Wheaton, Ill.: Crossway Books, 2004).

Geisler, Norman L. "*Baker Encyclopedia of Christian Apologetics*" (Grand Rapids: Baker Book, 1999).

Geisler, Norman L. "*Christian Apologetics*" (Grand Rapids: Baker, 1976).

Geisler, Norman L. "Johannine Apologetics" *Bibliotheca Sacra* 136, 544 (October–December, 1979): 333-343.

Geisler, Norman L. *"Thomas Aquinas: An Evangelical Appraisal"* (Grand Rapids: Baker, 1991).

Geisler, Norman L. and Patrick Zukeran. *"The Apologetics of Jesus: A Caring Approach to Dealing with Doubters"* (Grand Rapids, Michigan, Baker Books, 2009).

Geisler, Norman, L. and William E. Nix. *"A General Introduction to the Bible"* (Chicago: Moody Press, 1968).

Gerhardsson, Birger, *"Memory and Manuscript: Oral Tradition and Written Transmission in Rabbinic Judaism and Early"* (Uppsala: Gleerup, 1961).

Gia Fu Feng and Jane English. *"Translation of Lao Zi, Tao Te Ching"* (Toronto: Vintage Books, Random House, 1989).

Glueck, Nelson. *"Rivers in the Dessert: History of Negev"* (New York: Farrar, Straus, and Cadahy, 1959).

Goetz and Blomberg. "The Burden of Proof", *Journal for the Study of the New Testament* Vol. 11 (1981).

Greenleaf, Simon. *"Testimony of the Evangelists, Examined by the Rules of Evidence Administered in Courts of Justice"* (1846) republished in the appendix in Montgomery, John Warwick. 'The Law Above the Law' (Minneapolis, Minnesota: Bethany House Publisher, 1975), 91-140

Greenleaf, Simon. *"The Testimony of the Evangelists: The Gospel Examined by the Rules of Evidence"* (Grand Rapids: Kregel Classics, 1995).

Grigor, Francis. *"Sir John Fortesque's Commendations of the Laws of England: The Translation into English of 'De Laudibus Legum Angliae"* (Sweet & Maxwell, 1917).

Groothuis, Douglas. *"Truth Decay: Defending Christianity Against the Challenges of Postmodernism"* (Leicester: Inter-Varsity Press, 2000).

Gundry, Robert H. *"A Survey of the New Testament"* (Grand Rapids, Michigan: Zondervan, 2003).

Guthrie, Donald. *"New Testament Introduction"* (Leicester, England: Apollos/IVP, 1990).

Hale, Sir Matthew. *"The Testimony of the Pleas of the Crown"* (published posthumously by Sollom Emlyn, 1736) (Vol. 2) (reprinted 1971).

Hamer, David. "The Presumptions of Innocence and Reverse Burdens: A Balancing Act", *Cambridge Law Journal* 66(1), March 2007, 142-171.

Henry, Carl F.H. *"God, Revelation and Authority"* (Waco, Texas: Word Books, 1976).

Hoffecker, Andrew. *"Christian Theology Emerges: The Council of Nicaea"* in Hoffecker & Smith (eds.), 'Building a Christian Worldview Vol. 1.' (Philipsburg, New Jersey: Presbyterian and Reformed Publishing Company, 1986).

Hooker, Morna D. "Christology and Methodology", *NTS* 17 (1970-71):485.

Hooker, Morna D. "On Using the Wrong Tool", *Theology* 75 (1972): 580.

Hort, Fenton John Anthony. *"Way, Truth and the Life"* (New York: MacMillan, 1894).

House, Wayne H. and Dennis W. Jowers. *"Reasons for Our Hope: An Introduction to Christian Apologetics"* (Nashville, Tennessee: B&H Academic, 2011).

Huxley, Aldous L. *"Ends and Means"* (New York: Harper, 1937).

Inwagen, Peter Van. *"It is Wrong, Everywhere, Always, and for Anyone, to Believe Anything upon Insufficient Evidence"* in Faith, Freedom, and Rationality: Philosophy of Religion Today edited by Jeff Jordan & Daniel Howard-Synder (London: Rowman & Littlefield, 1996).

Johnson, Philip. "Juridical Apologetics 1600-2000 AD: A Bio-Bibliographical Essay" *Global Journal of Classical Theology* Vol.3 No. 1, (March, 2002).

Josephus, Flavius, *"Flavius Josephus Against Apion"* in William Whiston (trans.), Josephus Complete Works (Grand Rapids: Kregel Publications, 1960), 179-180.

Keane, Adrian. *"The Modern Law of Evidence"* (Oxford University Press, 6th ed., 2006).

Keener, Craig S. *"The Gospel of John: A Commentary"* 2 Vols. (Peabody, MA: Hendrickson, 2003).

Kenyon, Frederic *"The Bible and Modern Scholarship"* (London: John Murray, 1948).

Kenyon, Frederic, *"The Bible and Archaeology"* (New York: Harper & Row, 1940).

Kenyon, Frederic. *"Our Bible and the Ancient Manuscript"* (London: Eyre and Spottiswoode, 1939).

Kertzmann, Norman. *"Evidence Against Anti-Evidentialism"* in Our Knowledge of God; Essays on Natural and Philosophical Theology edited by K. Clark (Dordrecht: Kluwer Academic Press, 1992).

King, M. "Understanding the Legal System: A Job for Psychologists", *Bulletin of the British Psychological Society*, Vol. 35, December 1982, A92-A108.

King, Rolfe. *"Obstacles to Divine Revelation: God and the Reorientation of Human Reason"* (London: Continuum, 2008).

Köstenberger, Andreas. J. *"A Theology of John's Gospel and Letters"* (Grand Rapids, Michigan: Zondervan, 2009).

Köstenberger, Andreas. J. *"Encountering John: The Gospel in Historical, Literary, and Theological Perspective"* (EBS; Grand Rapids: Baker, 1999).

Lao Tzu, *"Tao Té Ching"*, translated & introduction by Blackney R.B. (New York: Signet Classic, 2007).

Latourette, Kenneth Scott. *"A History of Christianity"* (New York: Harper & Row, 1953).

Lewis, C. S. *"Dogma and the Universe"*, in, God in the Dock edited by Walter Hooper (Grand Rapids: Eerdmans, 1970).

Lewis, C.S. *"The Chronicles of Narnia: The Lion, the Witch and the Wardrobe"* (HarperCollins, 2003).

Lewis, C.S., *"Mere Christianity"* (New York: MacMillan, 1952).

Lincoln, Andrew T. *"Truth on Trial: The Lawsuit Motif in the Fourth Gospel"* (Peabody, Massachusetts: Hendricksen, 2000).

Lindbeck, G., *"The Nature of Doctrine: Religion and Theology in a Postliberal Age"* (Kentucky: Westminster John Knox Press, 1984).

Locke, John. *"An Essay Concerning Human Understanding"*. Edited by Alexander Campbell Fraser (New York: Dover, 1959).

Loftus, Elizabeth F. *"Eyewitness Testimony"* (Harvard University Press, 1979)

Mackie, J., *"The Miracles of Theism"* (New York: Oxford University Press, 1982).

Malcolm, N. *"The Groundlessness of Belief"* in Contemporary Perspectives on Religious Epistemology edited by Geivett, R. D. & B. Sweetman (Oxford: Oxford University Press, 1992).

Mayers, Ronald B. *"Balanced Apologetics: Using Evidences and Presuppositions in Defence of the Faith"* (Grand Rapids: Kregel, 1996). Reprint of *"Both/And: A Balanced Apologetics"* (Chicago: Moody, 1984).

Mayers, Ronald B. "Both/And: The Uncomfortable Apologetics", *Journal of Evangelical Theological Society* 23/3 (September 1980) 231-241.

McDowell, Josh. *"New Evidence That Demands a Verdict"* (Here's Life Publishers, 1999).

McGrath, Alister E. 'Evangelical Apologetics', *Bibliotheca Sacra* 155 (January-March 1998), 3-10.

Metzger, Bruce M. *"The Text of the New Testament: Its Transmission, Corruption and Restoration"* (New York: Oxford University Press, 1992).

Mills, B. QC. "Justice For All – All For Justice" (1994) 144 *New Law Journal*, 1670 & 1672.

Mitchell, Basil. *"The Justification of Religious Belief"* (New York: Seabury, 1973).

Montgomery, John Warwick, "*Is Man His Own God*" in Montgomery, J. W. (ed.) Christianity for the Tough Minded (Edmonton, Canadian Institute for Law, Theology, and Public Policy Inc., 2001).

Montgomery, John Warwick. '*Legal Hermeneutics and the Interpretation of Scripture*' in Evangelical Hermeneutics edited by Michael Bauman and David Hall (Camp Hill, Pennsylvania: Christian Publications, 1995), 15-29.

Montgomery, John Warwick. "*Faith Founded on Fact: Essays in Evidential Apologetics*" (Newburgh, Indiana: Trinity Press, 1978).

Montgomery, John Warwick. "*History and Christianity*" (Minneapolis, Minnesota: Bethany House Publishers, 1965).

Montgomery, John Warwick. "*How Muslims Do Apologetics: The Apologetic Approach of Muhammad Ali and Its Implications for Christian Apologetics*" in Faith Founded on Fact, (Newburgh, Indiana, Trinity Press, 1978).

Montgomery, John Warwick. "*Human Rights and Human Dignity*" (Grand Rapids: Zondervan, 1986).

Montgomery, John Warwick. "*Law & Gospel: A Study Integrating Faith and Practice*" (Edmunton, 1994).

Montgomery, John Warwick. "*Neglected Apologetics Styles: The Juridical and the Literary*" in Evangelical Apologetics, edited by Bauman, M., D. Hall & R. Newman, R., (Camp Hill, PA: Christian Publications, 1996).

Montgomery, John Warwick. "*The Death of the 'Death of God*,'" in Suicide of Christian Theology edited by J.W. Montgomery (Minneapolis: Bethany Fellowship, 1970).

Montgomery, John Warwick. "*The Jury Returns: A Juridical Defense of Christianity*" in Christian in the Public Square, ed. C.E.B. Cranfield, David Kilgour & J. W. Montgomery (Edmonton, AB: Canadian Institute for Law, Theology and Public Policy, 1996), 223-250.

Montgomery, John Warwick. "*The Law Above the Law: Why the Law Needs Biblical Foundations / How Legal Thought Support Christian Truth*" (Minneapolis: Bethany House, 1975).

Montgomery, John Warwick. "*Tractatus Logico-Theologicus*" (Bonn, Germany: Verlag fur Kultur und Wissenschaft, 2002).

Moreland, J.P. "The Rationality of Belief in Inerrancy" Trinity Journal 7 (Spring 1986), 75-86

Muravchik, Stephanie. "*American Protestantism in the Age of Psychology*" (New York: Cambridge University Press, 2011).

Nash, R. H. "*Faith & Reason: Searching for Rational Faith*" (Grand Rapids, Michigan: Zondervan, 1988).

Noyes & Kolb. "*Modern Clinical Psychiatry*" (Philadelphia and London: Saunders, 1958).

O'Hear, A., "*Experience, Explanation and Faith: An Introduction to the Philosophy of Religion*" (London: Routledge & Kegan Paul, 1984).

Phillips, D.Z. "*Faith After Foundationalism*", (London; New York: Routledge, 1988).

Phillips, D.Z. "*Faith, Skepticism and Religious Understanding*" in Contemporary Perspectives on Religious Epistemology edited by Geivett, R. D. & B. Sweetman (Oxford: Oxford University Press, 1992).

Phillips, D.Z. "*The Concept of Prayer*" (London: Routledge & Kegan Paul, 1966).

Phillmore, J.G. "*History and Principles of the Law of Evidence*", 357 (1850).

Plantinga, Alvin and Nicholas Wolterstorff. "*Faith and Rationality: Reason and Belief in God*" (Notre Dame, Indiana: University of Notre Dame Press, 1983).

Plantinga, Alvin. "*Reason and Belief in God*" in Faith and Rationality, edited by Plantinga and Nicholas Wolterstorff (Notre Dame, Indiana: University of Notre Dame Press, 1983).

Powell, Edmund. "*The Practice of the Law of Evidence*" (London: John Crockford, 1856).

Redmayne, M. "*The Admissibility of Expert Evidence: (2) the Rule in R v Turner*", Chapter 6 of Expert Evidence and Criminal Justice (Oxford: Oxford University Press, 2001).

Roberts, Paul and Adrian Zuckerman. "*Relevance, Admissibility and Fact-Finding*" Chapter 3 of Criminal Evidence (Oxford: Oxford University Press, 2004).

Rowe, W.L. "*Philosophy of Religion: An Introduction*" (Belmont, CA: Wadsworth, 2001).

Sabath, Robert A. "*LSD and Religious Truth*" in Christianity for the Tough-Minded edited by John Warwick Montgomery, J.W. (Edmonton: Canadian Institute for Law, Theology and Public Policy Inc., 2001).

Schaeffer, Francis A. "*The Complete Works of Francis A. Schaeffer*" 5 Vols. (Westchester, Ill.: Crossway Books, 1982).

Schaff, Phillip. "*The Person of Christ*" (New York: American Tract Society, 1913).

Schweitzer, Albert. "*The Psychiatric Study of Jesus*" Trans. By Charles R. Joy (Boston: Beacon Press, 1948).

Skilton, John. "*The Transmission of the Scriptures*" in Ned B. Stonehouse & Paul Wooley (eds.), Infallible Word (Philadelphia: Presbyterian and Reformed, 1946)

Smith, J.C. "The Presumption of Innocence", *Northern Ireland Legal Quarterly* (1987) Vol. 38, No. 3, 223.

Smith, Wilbur M. *"A Great Certainty in This Hour of World Crises"* (Wheaton Ill: Van Kampen Press, 1951).

Sproul R.C., J. Gerstner & A. Lindsley. *"Classical Apologetics: A Rational Defense of the Christian Faith and a Critic of Presuppositional Apologetics"* (Grand Rapids, Michigan: Zondervan, 1984).

Sproul, R.C. *"The Case for Inerrancy: A Methodological Analysis"* in 'God's Inerrant Word: An International Symposium on the Trustworthiness of Scripture' edited by John Warwick Montgomery (Minneapolis: Bethany Fellowship, 1974), 242-261.

Stark on Evidence (4th edn.).

Stephen, James Fitzjames, *"A Digest of the Law of Evidence"* (Stevens, 12th edn., 1948).

Stephen, James Fitzjames. *Indian Evidence Act 1872.*

Stone, Marcus. *"Proof of Fact in Criminal Trials"* (Edinburgh, W, Green & Sons Ltd., 1984).

Strobel, Lee. *"The Case for Christ: A Journalist's Personal Investigation of the Evidence for Jesus"* (Grand Rapids, Michigan: Zondervan, 1998).

Studenroth, John C. *"Archaeology and the Higher Criticism of Genesis 14"* in 'Evidence For Faith: Deciding the God Question' edited by John Warwick Montgomery (Dallas: Probe Books, 1991) 155.

Stump, Eleanor & Michael Murray (Eds.). *"Philosophy of Religion: The Big Questions"* (Oxford: Blackwell, 2003).

Sunstein, Cass. R. *"Legal Reasoning and Political Conflict"* (New York: Oxford University Press, 1996).

Tasker, R. V. G. *"Tyndale New Testament Commentaries: John"* (Grand Rapids, Michigan: Inter-Varsity Press, 1983).

Teh, Henry Hock Guan. "Legal Apologetics: Principles of Legal Evidence as Applied to the Quest for Religious Truth", *Global Journal of Classical Theology*: 5(1) (July 2005).

Turner, H.E.W. *"Historicity and the Gospels"* (London: A. R. Mowbray and Co., 1963).

Van Til, Cornelius. *"The Defence of the Faith"* (Philadelphia, Pennsylvania: Presbyterian and Reformed Publishing Company, 1967).

Van Til, Cornelius. *"The Reformed Pastor and Modern Thought"* (Philadelphia: Presbyterian and Reformed, 1971).

Waltz, John R. and Roger C. Park, "*Evidence, Cases and Materials*" 82 (8th ed. 1995).

Wang, Samuel and Ethel R. Nelson, "*God and the Ancient Chinese*" (Dunlap, TN: Sinim Bible Institute, 1998).

Whitcomb Jr., J.C. "Contemporary Apologetics and the Christian Faith, Part IV: The Limitations and Values of Christian Evidences" *Bibliotheca Sacra* 135 (1978), 25 – 33.

Wigmore, J.H. "*The Judicial Principles of Judicial Proof*" (1931, 2nd edn.) cited in Christopher Allen, 'Basic Concepts' Chapter 1 of Allen, C., Sourcebook on Evidence (London: Routledge Cavendish, 1996).

Willard, Dallas. "Jesus the Logician," *Christian Scholars Review* (Summer, 1999), Vol. XXVIII 605-614.

Wilson, Ian. "*Jesus: The Evidence*" (HarperSanFrancisco, 1996).

Wilson, Robert Dick, "*A Scientific Investigation of the Old Testament*" (Chicago: Moody Press, 1959).

Wittgenstein, L. "*Lectures and Conversations on Aesthetics, Psychology and Religion*" edited by C. Barrett, (Oxford: Blackwell, 1966).

Wittgenstein, L. "*On Certainty*", D. Paul & G.E.M. Anscombe (tr.), (Oxford: Blackwell, 1979).

Wittgenstein, L. "*Philosophical Investigations*", G.E.M. Anscombe (tr.), (Oxford: Blackwell, 1953).

Wolterstorff, Nicholas. "*John Locke and the Ethics of Belief*" (Cambridge: Cambridge University Press, 1996).

Wolterstorff, Nicholas. "*Once Again, Evidentialism—This Time Social*" in Practices of Belief edited by Terence Cuneo (Oxford: Oxford University Press, 2010).

Yamauchi, Edwin M. "*Archaeology and the New Testament*" in Introductory Articles, in Frank E. Gaebelein (ed.), Expositor's Bible Commentary, Volume 1 (Grand Rapids: Zondervan, 1979), 645-669.

www.ingramcontent.com/pod-product-compliance
Lightning Source LLC
Chambersburg PA
CBHW060335100426
42812CB00003B/1000